EAVESDROPPING ON THE

MOST SEGREGATED HOUR

Andrew Manis must have been 'eavesdropping' on my prayers! He must have heard me say, 'Lord, how do I preach on racism in a way my White congregation can hear it? Why is there so much resistance to this subject among "good Christian people"?' In this book Manis gives clear answers to those questions, and Sandy Martin's excellent observations about Black congregations makes me believe that in my own city we could begin a conversation about race that would break down the barriers and integrate the nation's 'most segregated hour.'

—Jim Somerville, pastor of First Baptist Church, Richmond, Virginia

What a gift to those of us who are called to lead the contemporary church at this hour! A group of Macon's pastors get together and courageously, candidly, biblically do what the American church has found difficult—confront the history and the present apostasy of our complicity in America's original sin. The fruit of these pastor's conversations give us theological background, sociological analysis, and practical, congregational exemplification for how we White American Christians can be more faithful in regard to repentance and reparation of the sin of racism.

—Will Willimon, professor of the Practice of
Christian Ministry, Duke Divinity School

It may be no coincidence that just when America was exploding over the deadly legacy of systemic racism and police brutality, Andrew Manis and Sandy Martin were bringing forth this remarkable testimony to how little has changed since MLK Jr. first called out the most segregated hour. What awaits the reader here is not only powerful and prophetic, it also serves as a kind of mea culpa for the shameful silence of so many cowardly preachers—then and now.

—Robin R. Meyers, retired senior minister of Mayflower
UCC Church, Oklahoma City, Oklahoma,
distinguished professor of Social Justice
emeritus at Oklahoma City University

In 2006, Al Gore produced a documentary entitled *An Inconvenient Truth*. Surely this could have been the subtitle for this most timely book by Andrew Manis and Sandy Martin. For even though it has been more than 157 years since the Emancipation Proclamation was put into full force, the ugly aftermath of slavery is still a major driving force in the church and in American society. The authors have enlightened us with our bitter history, challenged us with our twisted theology, and lifted us in poetic and musical verse that we might live up to the faith(s) we profess. *Eavesdropping on the Most Segregated Hour* is a must-read for anyone who doesn't mind being confronted with a glaring truth that can help to set the Church in America free.

—Ronald L. Bobo, Sr., pastor emeritus of West Side
Missionary Baptist Church, St. Louis, Missouri

EAVESDROPPING ON THE

MOST SEGREGATED HOUR

A City's Clergy Reflect on Racial Reconciliation

Edited by
Andrew M. Manis

with
Sandy Dwayne Martin

MERCER UNIVERSITY PRESS
Macon, Georgia
2021

MUP/ P626

© 2021 by Mercer University Press
Published by Mercer University Press
1501 Mercer University Drive
Macon, Georgia 31207
All rights reserved

25 24 23 22 21   5 4 3 2 1

Books published by Mercer University Press are printed on acid-free paper
that meets the requirements of the American National Standard for
Information Sciences—Permanence of Paper for Printed Library Materials.

Printed and bound in the United States.

This book is set in Adobe Caslon Pro.

Cover/jacket design by Burt&Burt.

ISBN   978-0-88146-791-8
Cataloging-in-Publication Data is available from the Library of Congress

Dedicated to my colleagues in the
Department of History of
Middle Georgia State University at Macon

Robert Burnham
Stephen Taylor
Carol Melton
Buck Melton
Matt Zimmerman
Matt Jennings
Charlotte Miller
Larry Israel

With appreciation for your friendship and support
through good times and bad, in times of elation and loss.

And to our gracious helpers
Debra Slagle and Michelle Klingaman, may she rest in peace.

May we all rest in grace.

MERCER UNIVERSITY PRESS

Endowed by

TOM WATSON BROWN
and
THE WATSON-BROWN FOUNDATION, INC.

Contents

Preface

This book was conceived in 1983, not long after the United States for the first time celebrated the birthday of Martin Luther King Jr. as a national holiday. Sometime after that, I began to notice that African American churches devoted entire services to celebrating the King holiday. Predominantly White churches, at least the conservative to moderate Southern or Cooperative Baptist churches I preached in or otherwise knew about, proceeded through the third Sunday in January rarely if ever mentioning King's name or speaking of racial matters at all. As the African American poet Phyllis Wheatley once wrote to a minister friend named Samson Occam, "It doth not take the Penetration of a Philosopher" to figure out why.

Having studied how Southern Baptists responded to King's efforts as part of my seminary studies and dissertation research, I had fairly accurate ideas as to why Black and White Baptists differed so widely about King, the Civil Rights Movement, and race more generally. Gradually, the more I understood about those differences, the less I liked them. After growing up in Birmingham, Alabama, during the Civil Rights Movement, being converted from Greek Orthodoxy to the Southern Baptist ministry in the wake of the Jesus Movement of the early 1970s, I left Birmingham for seminary in Louisville, Kentucky, to prepare for the pastorate. But when it came to race matters, I naively believed that the White Southerners either were of the same mind that I was regarding race or would be fairly easy to persuade. Who, after all, could resist convincing preaching eloquence such as mine? By the end of my first year of Master of Divinity studies, my optimism about Southern Protestants continued unabated, while my eagerness to be one of their pastors lessened.

My educational goal shifted away from a professionally oriented Doctor of Ministry to the research and teaching PhD, and my vocational goal shifted toward the classroom rather than pastoral ministry. My naïve optimism, however, remained more or less intact, and I believed, like my professors in college and seminary, that I would be invited into pulpits fairly regularly as a guest or interim minister. I also thought that pastors would nonetheless come to view me as a "designated" go-to guy to preach on racial reconciliation when they found themselves reluctant to do so themselves.

Somewhere along this odyssey, I encountered the well-worn dictum that "eleven o'clock to twelve o'clock on Sunday morning is the most segregated hour of the week." At first, my prophetic zeal determined to demolish such moral heresy, but my historical research in African American church history convinced me that African American clergy and laypeople are much less enthusiastic about multicultural or multiracial churches than many White liberal Christians are. They are rightly concerned with whether leadership in such churches will be equally distributed between White and Black. Other than being a handy slogan in some local efforts at racial reconciliation, like Mercer's annual Building the Beloved Community Symposium and its sister institution, the Paired Clergy Breakfasts and twice-annual Unity Services, desegregating Sunday's eleven o'clock hour any time soon will be as likely as Donald Trump becoming a monk when he (Please God, soon) leaves the White House.

Rather than chasing the unlikely multiracial church as the omega point of all efforts toward racial reconciliation, I began to wonder if perhaps there was a more reasonable, more feasible goal that concerned Christians might seek. Instead of taking the King dictum as a goal or as an "impossible dream," maybe leaning in to eavesdrop across the racial divide could help White and Black Christians discern what Black and White pastors say to their respective congregations about race. This volume seeks to display the efforts of fifteen members of the clergy preaching on racial reconciliation to various congregations in Macon, Georgia.

Macon is Georgia's fifth largest city some eighty-five miles south of Atlanta. According to 2019 US Census records, Macon-Bibb County has a combined population of 153,159, of which the White minority represents 40.9 percent of the total population. An African American majority represents 54.1 percent. Latinx make up 3.2 percent, while Asians represent 2 percent of Macon's population. By contrast, the total population of the United States is divided by race in the following percentages: White (76.3 percent); Black (13.4 percent); Hispanic/Latinx (18.5 percent); and Asian (5.9 percent). Thus, as a small city in the middle of a Deep South state, Macon has a racial distribution that makes conditions ripe for a White population that is unaccustomed to being outnumbered by the city's African American majority. These unusual demographics also make the racial and cultural diversity of this collection of preachers all the more remarkable.

So I want to express my deep gratitude to the fifteen clergypersons who agreed to contribute one of their sermons and allow me and the readers of this book to "eavesdrop" on their reflections on the crucial issues pertaining to racial reconciliation. I name and introduce each of them in the "Contributors" section of this book, so I won't do it here. But if ever an author/editor owed a group of collaborators the words, "without whom this work would not have been possible," I am that author/editor. Thank you, my dear friends, for your insights, for your hard work reflected in your sermons, and for the seriousness with which you came to this project.

Sandy Dwayne Martin, a cherished friend of thirty-five years, agreed to enter into the conversation represented in these pages. He braved the unusual, perhaps even unique format of the book and plowed into what I rather opaquely called a "reflection on the sermons, but not a critique." My further attempts to explain what I wanted in these reflections probably added to his confusion and made his assignment even more difficult. Sandy, however, enthusiastically embraced the challenge. I am grateful to him for his long friendship, for his perceptive chapters looking at these issues from his perspective as both a minister and a scholar of African American religion, and for the privilege of having him as part of this project.

A couple of other friends in the ministerial profession agreed to read the manuscript in early and late stages. Craig McMahan, Minister to the University at Mercer University, read some of the early sections of the book and gave his encouragement. Doug Dortch, pastor of the Mountain Brook Baptist Church in Birmingham, Alabama, read the entire manuscript and made some helpful suggestions. My sister, Kathy Manis Findley, enthusiastically read a chapter or two and gave me some excellent suggestions for promoting the book around Macon. The somewhat unusually long period from conception to the birth of this project has given me many opportunities to answer *the* question, What are you working on now? Of course, I can't remember everyone who has asked me that question. I distinctly and gratefully remember, however, that nearly every one of these impromptu conversations gave evidence of legitimate interest and no small degree of enthusiasm about my project. I am grateful to them all for patiently listening while I blathered on (and on) about the book. As I trudged through the occasionally dreary days when a sermon was late arriving or I thought that the incessant chasing after fifteen individual sermons would put me in an early grave, I still remembered these friendly critics cheering me on. At that moment, their comments helped me keep putting one foot in front of the other; at this moment, they cause me to "give thanks for every remembrance" of them (Philippians 1:3).

One of those just remembered, Marc Jolley, must now be remembered again, in his role as the Director of Mercer University Press. He naturally was interested in receiving a sequel to my previous book published by Mercer, *Macon Black and White.* Even when I described for him the unusual format of this rather quirky sort of sequel, he continued to encourage me and showed an eagerness to get this manuscript, which, at long last, will be finished in the next few minutes. He has always been more complimentary of my writing than I deserve. Others on the Mercer staff have been of great assistance in this process: Marsha Luttrell, Publishing Assistant, and Jenny Toole, master of the Business Office, have been unfailingly cheerful and helpful in ways too numerous to count. Marketing Director Mary Beth Kosowski and Customer Service Associate Heather Comer have been the essence of professionalism all along the way.

I write these acknowledgments one month before my official retirement from full-time teaching after thirty-eight years in the historical profession. At one of the final rites of passage in my life, and since life is so fleeting and short—especially as I write this in the middle of the horrific coronavirus pandemic of 2020—I want to express my appreciation for professors who have inspired me, fellow students who have been in the trenches with me, and family who have loved and nurtured me.

Wayne Flynt, my advisor in history during undergraduate days at Samford University, has continued to encourage me and praise my work more than it deserves. At the beginning of virtually every book or article I have ever produced, I have always invoked the abbreviation WWWD—"What would Wayne do?" I also thank James Brown, whose Western Civilization course inspired me to major in history along with my religion major. Karen R. Joines is my last religion professor standing, and I am grateful that his courses and friendship always showed me what critical thinking looked like. Of course, I honor the memory of those teachers who made us better human beings as well as better students: Arthur L. Walker Jr., W. T. "Dub" Edwards, Mabry Lunceford, R. Lee Gallman, and Vernon G. Davison.

Professors at the Southern Baptist Theological Seminary in Louisville, Kentucky, built on the foundation laid at Samford: New

Testament scholars Frank Stagg and Alan Culpepper as well as the late E. Frank Tupper, who taught me systematic theology and whose dictum, "There is a difference between something being biblical and being Christian," I have quoted in every semester since I began teaching in 1983. Church historians par excellence, E. Glenn Hinson and Timothy George, each made their mark on a young wannabe history professor in important ways, while Walter B. Shurden's friendship has been a surprising gift as I found myself turning from young Turk historian into a gray-beard professor with occasional senior moments. Bill Leonard was the one whose Church History class converted me from the life of a pastor to that of a professor. One of the honors of my life has been to say I was Leonard's first PhD student. For forty-three years he has been my teacher, mentor, cheerleader, and friend. If he ever wants to be listed in The Guinness Book of World Records, he can almost certainly earn that honor for having written more letters of recommendation for me than any professor in the history of American education.

In an effort to keep the length of this list of acknowledgments from being longer than some of the sermons in the book, my deepest thanks goes to the following friends of the sort I could call during an emergency at 3:00 in the morning: Bruce E. Wilson, Ron Wilson, Doug Weaver, David W. Downs, Wayne Hager, Candace Burch Wilson, Dick Wilson, Michael Willett Newheart, Debi Lastinger, Chris Conver, and Doug Dortch. These are deep, abiding friendships without which I would not have made it through my doctoral work. The same may be said about colleagues who taught with me at three universities. At Xavier University of Louisiana, my thanks goes to Gordon Wilson, Kathleen Gaffney, and William Lindsey; at Averett University, I thank Richard B. Vinson, John Laughlin, and William Trimyer. I will withhold my sentiments for my most recent colleagues at Middle Georgia State University. Since I am dedicating this book to them, they have a page of their own elsewhere in this volume.

Finally, I owe some words of thanks to my family. My sister Kathy Manis Findley and her husband Fred H. Findley have been sources of love and support and good humor for fifty years. I have made a few choices in my life that I have regretted; my decision to become a follower of Jesus is not one of them. But that is a decision I may never have made apart from the encouragement of my sister. I owe her an eternal debt of gratitude for that if for nothing else.

My other sister, Anastasia Katros, and I had parted ways for fifteen or twenty years, until life simultaneously brought us to live in Georgia. Actually my cousin, she and I both grew up enough to reconcile. Since then I have come to cherish her and her partner, Donna McGahee, as relationships without which my life would not be as happy, beautiful, or meaningful.

Another reconciled relationship that I must acknowledge here—I believe for the first time in print—is that with my brother, Peter Chronis Manis. Pete and I spent some eighteen years in bitter discord, not even speaking to each other during that time. Life and age and wisdom finally brought us back together, and again we became brothers. Within four years, cancer brought him down and ended his forty-four-year allotment in 2000. So in this short tribute, I honor the brother I loved and lost twice.

I have not been a perfect father to my daughter, Meigan Manis Brennaman, but she and I have spent her lifetime saying "I'm proud of you" to each other—and meaning it. I am thankful beyond measure for her smile, her intelligence, her gracious concern for others, her beauty, and her wisdom. One sign of that wisdom was her decision to marry Chris Brennaman. For Chris and Meigan and the beautiful granddaughter they brought into the world, I cannot thank God enough. I write this book in hopes that Lucy Kalliope Brennaman will grow into a world infinitely more loving and nurturing than the world as it is in the pandemic year 2020.

I also acknowledge the love and support of my stepson, Ryan Bennett, and his wife Brandie, who are the parents of my other granddaughters, Hannah and Ansley Bennett.

Linda Manis, my wife, has filled my life with more love and laughter and beauty and compassion than I ever could have imagined, much less being incarnated right in front of me every day of our life together. I am proud of and grateful to her more than words can ever say.

I also wish to express my gratitude to the men and women with whom I have labored in the Department of History at Middle Georgia State University for the past twenty years. Together we built a strong department, even as we helped a local junior college change into a state university. To these friends and coworkers I gratefully dedicate this book.

Finally, I write these acknowledgments a little more than a month after the death of George Floyd at the hands of a white police officer in Minneapolis, Minnesota, and the protests that followed. As the protests spread across all fifty states, millions of Americans who yearn for racial justice and reconciliation (preferably in that order) are finding hope that the long list of African American men and women killed by White police officers will come to an end. We also hope that the protests, absent any attendant riots and other forms of violence, will be the tipping point that will result in real reform and not just empty rhetoric. As it happens, the last few lines of this book are being written on Independence Day. These lines include author's hope that anticipates the day when July 4 will celebrate not only independence but also "liberty and justice for ALL."

—Andrew Manis
July 4, 2020

Introduction
Eavesdropping and Reflecting on Race

Andrew M. Manis

Early in the twentieth century, the German existentialist philosopher Martin Heidegger described human existence as the experience of "thrownness." To be human is to experience a sense of having been thrown into the world.[1] Having been thrown leads us rationally and ineluctably to a pair of other ultimate questions: When did we land, and where did we land? I was thrown into the world in 1954, just three months before the US Supreme Court's *Brown v. Board of Education* ruling that ended racial segregation in American public schools. The landing took place in Birmingham, Alabama, the Deep South city most likely to explode in angry rejection of and resistance to the high court's momentous decree.

By the time of *Brown*, a series of nicknames had been hung on my birthplace. Two were commercial in nature—"The Magic City," to describe its rapid growth after the Civil War, and "The Pittsburgh of the South" to cite its most important industry, steel. The latter two nicknames were existential and ironic: The White folk proudly called Birmingham the "City of Churches." In dramatic contrast, African American citizens were said to live and possibly die in "Bombingham," where some twenty-nine bombings of African Americans' homes, businesses, or churches between the end of World War II and 1963 had gone unsolved.

Growing up in Birmingham during the civil rights years meant that race and religion were never far from my consciousness. My sister remembers being in the Divine Liturgy of the Holy

Trinity-Holy Cross Greek Orthodox Church on September 15, 1963, and hearing Father Soterios Gouvellis announce the bombing of the Sixteenth Street Baptist Church. Against the wishes of much of the congregation's lay leadership and betraying his sympathies for the movement, Gouvellis described the bombing as an attack on the Body of Christ by the forces of evil. Seven years later when the Jesus Movement followed the Civil Rights Movement through Birmingham, I experienced a teenage conversion, and, had our courageous priest not been run off by more conservative segments of the congregation, I might now be a Greek Orthodox priest. Instead, I began a pilgrimage that led to the Baptist ministry. Within a couple of days after my initial conversion experience, a local radio news broadcast informed me that controversy had arisen when a Black woman and her young daughter sought to become members of Birmingham's First Baptist Church. Instinctively I wondered out loud with a not-quite-converted vocabulary, "What the hell is wrong with these people? How can they turn away someone from church just because of their skin color?"

While the racial controversy at FBC gave me a moment's pause about casting my lot with the Baptists, ultimately it slowed me down but did not stop me from enrolling at the local Baptist-affiliated Samford University to prepare for the ministry. One of the selling points of attending Samford was the Religion Department's H-Day Program, an arrangement whereby ministerial students were invited to preach in Alabama Baptist churches at various times during the school year. Established before the university had changed its name to Samford, "H-Day" signified "Howard College Day" for participating churches in most Baptist associations across Alabama. As new as I was to the ways of Baptists in the Deep South, the learning curve was steep.

Sometime in my junior year, an H-Day appearance in a Tuscaloosa church taught me a never-to-be-forgotten lesson. Preaching in a congregation where my brother-in-law was minister of

2

music, I was excited to have the chance to preach in front of part of my family. I had been reading about the early twentieth century Social Gospel Movement and decided to hold forth on the Kingdom of God. I finished the sermon with a celebratory flourish borrowing from the stirring peroration from Martin Luther King's "I Have a Dream" speech. I waxed emotional, expressing my dream that the Kingdom of God might soon become a reality. Caught up in the moment, I was only able to notice an angry parishioner slamming the door as he exited the rear of the sanctuary. The mere mention of King's name in a sermon was enough to infuriate him and others as well.

When my brother-in-law greeted me after the service, he had a serious tone in his voice when he asked, "What was that hubbub all about?" Immediately I felt the chilling fear that he was rebuking me for having crossed some line of propriety in my sermon. Not to worry. He was just inquiring into what I had observed from the pulpit, disturbed and a bit embarrassed that a member of his church had reacted so angrily to a simple reference to King. Relieved that his disappointment was not in me or my sermon, I did not miss the lesson of the day: in a White church, a preacher addresses racial themes at his or her own peril.

Over the years since that pulpit appearance, additional such experiences reinforced the lesson of Tuscaloosa. As I progressed through my theological education, studying American religious history, I eventually earned my PhD with a dissertation on Black and White Baptist expressions of civil religion during the Civil Rights Movement. With some revisions, the dissertation became my first book.[2] I had long since noticed that hearing a Southern Baptist minister preach on racism or racial reconciliation in a local church was as unlikely as winning the lottery. Now it was dawning on me that when I preached in local churches, the ministers or laypeople who introduced me never mentioned the publication of my book. The singular occasion when the book *was* mentioned was at a church in small-town Alabama, where a deacon hosting me for lunch commented that the pastor's introduction "didn't win you any brownie points."

Only in the last ten years or so have some White pastors begun to feel free or prophetic enough to mention Martin Luther King Jr. in their sermons, but most still make no effort to preach about race on the Sunday before America's Martin Luther King national holiday. So I was pleasantly surprised some thirty years later, in 2005, when my pastor in Macon asked me to preach in our church. My book on race relations in Macon, Georgia, had recently been released, and he wanted me to preach on some of the findings mentioned in my book.[3] At first I was glad to be congratulated by my pastor in this manner. But then I detected a bit of shrewdness in his invitation. I was pleased that he intended to give attention to the King holiday but realized he did not commit to preaching on the subject himself. Still, he was in a position to take some flak over the matter, both for addressing this volatile subject in a worship service at all and, possibly, over the specifics of what I might say. My wife and I had only recently joined this congregation, however, and I had some concerns about preaching about race in what I hoped might be the first of many opportunities to fill the pulpit there.

I preached a heartfelt sermon, and for the most part the congregation received it well. A large number of members thanked me for the sermon, and a few were effusive in their praise, but I noticed one man hanging back. When he approached, he smiled, shook my hand, and said, "I'm glad I don't have to agree with you to be a Christian." He said nothing else, but he had much more to say in his Sunday school class later that morning. This experience once again reinforced and vividly drove home the message I had received as a college "preacher boy": preaching about race in a White church will not win you any popularity contests.

My experience at Samford University taught me a lesson or two about African American churches as well. Sometime in my four years there, I entered Reid Chapel for a convocation. While many students objected to being required to attend nine such events per semester, I was glad for the opportunity. On this occasion, the speaker was the Reverend John T. Porter, pastor of the Sixth Avenue Baptist Church, one of the most prominent African American congregations in Birmingham. Porter had been an associate pastor under Dr. Martin Luther King Jr. at Dexter Avenue Baptist Church in Montgomery, Alabama. He became pastor of Sixth Avenue Church in 1962, when the Civil Rights Movement began percolating in Birmingham. Later, he was one of four ministers who were arrested for leading a prayer demonstration during the 1963 Birmingham protests. I and two of my friends were so impressed with his chapel address that we decided to worship at Sixth Avenue the following Sunday.

My first impression of Sixth Avenue Baptist Church was the obvious fact that my friends and I were the only White faces in the congregation. It occurred to me that I had never seen a Black face in any of the Baptist churches I had attended since I left the Greek Orthodox Church in 1971. Moreover, I recalled that the one Black ministerial student studying at Samford, John Harris, never participated in H-Day because sending a young Black minister to a White Baptist church in Alabama was much more controversial than the university was willing to risk. This state of affairs was regrettable and a denial of the Christian gospel, but growing up in the segregated South, I had grown accustomed to all the White faces. Now, though, the shoe was on the other foot. Now *my face* and those of my friends were the odd ones in the crowd. And instead of receiving nonverbal invitations to get out of their church—as they were likely to receive if they attempted to visit a White church—we three White college students were welcomed as if we were long-lost sons.

So in addition to the education I received in White churches, what racial lessons did my friends and I learn at Sixth Avenue Baptist Church? We learned a truth that has now become a cliché, an embarrassing truth that Martin Luther King Jr. first communicated to his home congregation at Atlanta's Ebenezer Baptist Church in 1953: "I am ashamed and appalled...that Eleven O'clock on Sunday morning is the most segregated hour in Christian America."[4] On one level, one might justifiably make the argument that if it was indeed appalling and shameful in 1953, how much more of an abomination that it is *still true*, even as we now stand more than half a century since the 1964 Civil Rights Act and the Voting Rights Act of 1965—the high-water marks of the historic struggle for racial equality in America.

The trouble with making that rather simple argument is that the reasons for the continuing segregation of not only the *Christian* churches but also the varieties of religious institutional life in America cannot be reduced to racism. Cultural worship patterns, leadership issues, and a host of other concerns play a role in keeping the eleventh hour segregated. Although the contributors to this volume may fervently hope and pray that the "middle wall of partition" (Eph 2:14) may someday "come a-tumbling down," that day will not soon arrive. We seek to address the reality as it is and has been.

The second reality that my friends and I learned at Sixth Avenue Baptist Church on that Sunday in the mid-1970s was that as much as typical White congregations normally but not always want their preachers to leave racial matters out of their sermons, African American congregations expect and in many instances demand that their pastors address the challenges and struggles that a still-racist society inflicts upon them. Today, race is rarely discussed from White pulpits for a number of reasons that will discussed in this volume. The extent to which race is the topic of White and Black preaching in contemporary America can certainly be debated. What is fairly certain is that neither religious Whites nor African Americans are typically on hand to hear what preachers of the other race have to say to their congregations on the subject of racial reconciliation. Indeed, this volume's title assumes that because most White and most African American Christians are still segregated when they worship, for Whites to hear what Black preachers say about race and for African Americans to hear what White preachers say about race will both require some deliberate eavesdropping.

This volume is conceived as a "sequel" to my book, *Macon Black and White*. It seemed obvious that any historian who wrote about a century of Black-White relations in his or her city of residence would naturally be asked by readers, "What do you believe contemporary Maconites should do to improve race relations in our city?" Anticipating the question as I finished my earlier book, I decided to include my answer in a practical epilogue called "Prescriptions for Racial Healing." *Eavesdropping on the Most Segregated Hour* merely makes public the "prescriptions" of a *team* of "doctors" who are responsible for the "cure of souls." The team works together in fervent hope and commitment to helping heal the "soul of America," beginning in Macon and Middle Georgia.

We have recruited an impressively diverse array of clergy, all of whom have ministered or still minister to congregations in Macon, Georgia. The servant leaders who agreed to contribute to this project were asked simply to develop a sermon on racial reconciliation, deliver it to their respective congregations, and then to deliver it to us for wider dissemination.

The team numbers fifteen "physicians of the soul." Eight are White; seven are African American. Among these are three women, two White and one African American. The White clergy consist of two Baptists, accompanied by one each from the Methodist, Presbyterian, Assembly of God, Catholic, Unitarian, and Conservative Jewish traditions. Among the African Americans on the team are four Baptists, one African Methodist Episcopal (AME), one Non-Denominational, and one Muslim.[5]

Part I of this volume is titled "Breaking the Sound of Silence." It will provide historical and theological background for the sermons by addressing the challenge of preaching on racial reconciliation from both the European and African American perspectives. The central purpose of the section is to ask why the American pulpit has so often been rendered mute on the subject of race. The section concludes with a bit of cheerleading, encouraging ministers to stand up and speak out on these concerns.

Part II, titled "Prophetic Utterances on Race: Ministries of Racial Reconciliation," will present the sermons, lightly edited for publication, with special care to leave their content intact. They are presented in no particular order other than alphabetical and to alternate between White and African American pulpiteers.

Part III, titled "Historical Reflections," will put both editors to work analyzing and reflecting on the sermons in this collection. Editors Andrew Manis and Sandy Dwayne Martin are longtime friends whose scholarship threw them together at Princeton University over thirty years ago at a National Endowment for the Humanities Summer Seminar on African American Religion. Both are ordained Baptist ministers, one White and one African American. Both are scholars of American religion, one with a PhD from Columbia University/Union Theological Seminary in New York City and the other with a PhD from the Southern Baptist Theological Seminary in Louisville, Kentucky. Each of them will meditate on these sermons and eventually weave together the sermon themes with historical, theological, ethical, and racial perspectives of their own.

Part IV, titled "A Covenant of Racial Reconciliation: Narrative, Liturgy and Proclamation," will conclude this volume with a liturgical expression of a covenant of reconciliation between the two First Baptist churches in Macon, one White and one African

American. In 2015, the friendship between the Reverend Scott Dickison, pastor of the White First Baptist Church of Christ, and the Reverend James Goolsby Jr., pastor of the African American First Baptist Church on New Street, blossomed into a committed covenant relationship between two churches that before the Civil War were one congregation. These two pastors and their congregations have provided a powerful model for mutual ministry across racial lines. In May 2015, with the assistance of the New Baptist Covenant,[6] they held a joint service of commitment to their Covenant of Action. This section will reflect the order of worship for that deeply moving service, including the abbreviated sermons by both pastors.

PART I—

BREAKING THE SOUND OF SILENCE

1

Bringing Race into the American Pulpit: A White Christian Perspective

Andrew M. Manis

Nobody seems to know who first made the observation or the exact moment when it went from new insight to old cliché, but two things we do know with some certainty: first, Martin Luther King Jr. often quoted it, and second, it is still true. Eleven o'clock on Sunday morning remains the most racially segregated hour of the week. This persistent truism set me to wondering what White and Black ministers are saying these days to their congregations about race matters, utterances that are never heard on the other side of the color line. To try to find out, I contacted homiletics professors at forty-one Protestant seminaries across America, soliciting their and their students' sermons on racial reconciliation. I collected a paltry twenty-four sermons. It was not an auspicious beginning, but the exercise did generate the idea of this book. Next, I asked some of the most prominent clergy around town to contribute a sermon on the subject of racial reconciliation in Macon, Georgia. Some of these I had to pester, but eventually—after a much longer time than I am inclined to admit in print—I received the ministers' best thinking on the subject. Suffice it to say that racial reconciliation appears not to be a favorite topic for sermons in the contemporary American pulpit.

As of this writing, America has just passed the fifty-fifth anniversary of the Birmingham civil rights demonstrations and Martin Luther King Jr.'s "I Have a Dream" speech at the March on Washington. Yes, our nation has seen progress. The combination of the Civil Rights Movement and the activism of the Kennedy-Johnson administrations and a liberal Congress yielded the two most important civil rights advances in our history. Thus we finally rid our American souls of Jim Crow, and Congress forced the South to protect Black voting rights. But none of this happened without a White backlash, both South and North, that has left a residue of bitterness on both sides of the color line. That bitterness not only remained but deepened and coarsened during the two terms of our nation's first African American president.

Then arose a presidential candidate whose uniquely divisive campaign repackaged the message of the morally and factually bankrupt Birther movement. Immediately out of the starting blocks, he ran a race that fanned the flickering flames of racism into another roaring fire. Like no candidate in our national political history ever had, Donald Trump ridiculed "low IQ" citizens who seemed always to be people of color who came here from "shithole countries," and he denounced Mexicans and other Latinos as "rapists and murderers." Some, he supposed, "were good people."

Some regional politicians in the civil rights era, like Alabama's segregationist governor, George C. Wallace, played his race card with abandon in gubernatorial contests. But he toned down his rhetoric to "dog-whistle" code words when he ran for president. By the end of his life, he managed to repent and confess his sins to congregations of Black Christians, admitting to a friend that back in his political heyday, he had "said things that killed people."[7] Anyone waiting for similar remorse from President Trump, who rode into the White House to the cheers of Tea Partiers, Klansmen, neo-Nazis, White Nationalists, and an assortment of other Obama haters, had better not hold his or her breath.

If the heightened racial tensions of the Barack Obama years were not tragic enough in themselves, they almost certainly led to greater tensions in the Trump era. On the eve of the 2016 election, *Miami Herald* and syndicated columnist Leonard Pitts perceptively and provocatively summed up the mood of the electorate: "America elected a black man to the presidency and white people went crazy!"[8]

No wonder African Americans still lag behind Whites in every significant economic index. Why does Black life expectancy still average five to six years less than that of White Americans? Why is Black unemployment still double that of Whites? Why does the average Black college graduate earn only 78 percent of her White counterpart? Why is Jennifer still 50 percent more likely to be called for a job interview than LaKeisha? Why is it still so easy, despite all the evidence of modern science, for some to attribute these deficiencies to Blackness? As Oklahoma City pastor and Yale University Beecher Lecturer Robin R. Meyers might ask, Why can "yet another white man shoot dead yet another unarmed black teenager and get away with murder?"[9]

And why is it still so difficult to hear from our pulpits a clear "Thus says the Lord!" on matters of race? Well, from White pulpits anyway. Generally, African American ministers deal with race issues of some kind virtually every Sunday. This is why very few African Americans are surprised by pointed prophetic utterances from their pastors. Naturally, the difficult realities that still exist among Blacks regularly elicit prophetic words from their preachers regarding their continuing lot in America. I am certain that many African American ministers have developed strong cases of "race fatigue" and have stopped even addressing the matter with White people. They echo an exasperated Thurgood Marshall who once complained, "Sometimes I get so tired of trying to save the white man's soul."[10]

Unlike Sisyphus, however, they have simply stopped trying to push that particular boulder up that particular hill. So our progress lags because many White Americans and their ministers are eager to convince themselves that we have already reached the Promised Land of a post-racial America. Seriously? Many of these otherwise caring Christian citizens surely want it to be true. Others are, as the late political scientist Ronald Walters suggested, frustrated by conditions they feel they've tried to fix but will not go away.[11]

Homiletics scholar Richard Lischer has perceptively described the challenge of bringing race into the pulpit of a predominantly White congregation. He notes, "The problem of race relations in America is not one topic among many to be addressed in the pulpit, but the dilemma that has haunted American life from the beginning."[12] The brutal fact is that any minister who has delivered a frank sermon on racial reconciliation to a dubious White congregation can personally attest to the distinct chill in the air or the heated comments that almost always accompany sermons on this topic. Baptist Old Testament scholar Gerald L. Keown, who grew up in Alabama during the Civil Rights Movement, vividly remembers a church leadership that failed in deed as well as word:

> I am familiar with some of the amazing stories of courageous ministers, and some courageous churches, who challenged the racist patterns of the communities where they were located, often at great cost. The reality was that such were notable because they represented rare exceptions to the normative attitudes and actions of the churches in the South.[13]

As I say elsewhere in this book, no one who understands the word "Christian" and who has paid the slightest attention to the ways White Americans have treated the sons and daughters of Africa could ever characterize the United States as a "Christian nation." Ida B. Wells-Barnett, one of the late nineteenth and early twentieth centuries' most eloquent Black opinion makers, would concur. She complained that a recent lynching in her home state of Mississippi had excited no public outcry: "American Christianity heard of this awful affair and read of its details and neither press nor pulpit gave the matter more than a passing comment."[14]

The entire Christian community in America, and especially its preachers, would do well to train in the school of Ida B. Wells-Barnett. Fighting lynching and other forms of oppression, she asserted, "Civilization cannot burn human beings alive or justify others who do so....The nation cannot profess Christianity, which makes the golden rule its foundation stone, and continue to deny equal opportunity for life, liberty and the pursuit of happiness to the black race." She implored her readers for an answer: "Why is mob murder permitted by a Christian nation?"[15]

Her editorials and speeches also impugned the integrity of two of the most influential White Christians in nineteenth century America. She excoriated evangelist Dwight L. Moody for acquiescing to Southern racial mores and preaching to Black audiences on separate days and in separate churches. A delegate to the African Methodist Episcopal Church's annual conference blasted Moody: "His conduct toward the Negroes during his southern tour has been shameless, and I would not have him preach in a bar room, let alone a church."[16] An aging Frederick Douglass compared him with America's most famous nineteenth century atheist, Robert G. Ingersoll:

> Infidel though Mr. Ingersoll may be called, he never turned his back upon his colored brothers, as did the evangelical Christians of this city [Philadelphia] on the occasion of the light visit of Mr. Moody. Of all the forms of Negro hate in this world, save me from that one which clothes itself with the name of the loving Jesus.[17]

Wells-Barnett saved her most potent verbal barrage, however, for Frances Willard, president of the Women's Christian Temperance Union:

> Miss Willard has gone even further [than Moody] in that she has put herself on record as approving the Southerners method of defining the constitution and suppressing the Negro vote;...She has unhesitatingly broadcast a slander against the entire Negro race in order to gain favor with those who are hanging, shooting, and burning Negroes alive.[18]

"Where," she asked, were the legal or civil authorities, "to say nothing of the Christian churches when such barbaric practices were permitted in a supposedly civilized society?" Everyone in authority, from the president down, had declared themselves impotent to address the issue. In perhaps her most pointed barb, she asserted:

> [O]ur American Christians are too busy saving the souls of white Christians from burning in hell-fire to save the lives of black ones from present burning in fires kindled by white Christians. The feelings of the people who commit these acts must not be hurt by protesting against this sort of thing, and so the bodies of the victims of mob hate must be sacrificed, and the country disgraced because of that fear to speak out.[19]

She might well have asked, as has the like-minded contemporary president of Colgate-Rochester Divinity School, Marvin A. McMickle, "Where have all the prophets gone?"[20] Their whereabouts remain a mystery. But why are preachers—especially conservative or fundamentalist ones who so fervently preach about pastoral authority—still so silent on matters of race? In spite of their willingness so often to pontificate on matters of sexual ethics, why are they muzzled on "America's Original Sin"?

For what it's worth, here's my theory: Some ideological stars in the American constellation burn so brightly that they blind most of us from seeing clearly the situation on the ground right before us, hidden in plain sight. How many such bright stars are casting their blinding light over us? Who can tell? But for starters, I can name five.

AMERICAN INDIVIDUALISM

The first is American individualism, which dominates both our political and our religious language. Under its virtually sacred influence we praise or blame individuals for their good or bad behavior. It almost infallibly holds that the individual choices we make and actions we take really do matter. But the light of individualism seems too bright to allow us to see that the collective, social situations around us matter just as much.

Public opinion polls consistently find that most Americans blame poverty on the failure of the poor to take individual responsibility for their livelihoods. A 2002 poll showed that 48 percent of respondents held that people are poor because they are not doing enough to avoid it. By contrast, 45 percent attributed poverty to circumstances beyond the control of the poor.[21] More recently, a 2016 poll found that 45 percent of respondents believed poverty among African Americans was increasing, compared to 35 percent who thought it was staying about the same.[22] A third poll found that 46 percent of Christians (50 percent of Catholics, 51 percent of Protestants, and 53 percent of White evangelicals) blame poverty on a person's lack of effort, compared to 29 percent of all non-Christians.[23] A survey conducted in 2000 by the University of Akron showed that 73 percent of evangelical laypeople agreed with the statement, "If enough people are brought to Christ, social ills will take care of themselves." Along the same lines, another White evangelical told researchers, "If everybody was a Christian, there wouldn't be a race problem. We'd all be the same."[24]

Individualism is certainly one of, if not the central defining characteristic of, American culture. As a belief system, individualism "privileges the individual over the group, private life over public life, and personal expression over social expression." As a worldview, it is thought to be the state of nature, with self-reliance and self-determination as its chief values. A longtime sociology professor tells the story of a student who approached him asking if sociologists believe that society controls individual behavior. Relieved when his professor answered "No," the student replied, "So individuals control their own future." Again, the professor answered "No." The perplexed student demanded a straight answer, insisting, "It has to be one or the other; it can't be both!"[25]

Real life is more complex than the student's reductionist either/or. Sadly, much of the dominant American religious tradition makes the same philosophical mistake. Millions of American Christians, especially those steeped in the Southern Evangelical tradition, have grown up convinced that the evangelism of individuals constitutes the totality of the Christian gospel. That conviction embraces this corollary: social or political concerns have no proper place in the pulpit. As a result, observes Leonora Tubbs Tisdale, the prophetic texts of the Bible have been relegated to the periphery of American preaching.[26]

In the Southern Evangelical-revivalist tradition, this has particularly been true of texts inclining toward a prophetic denunciation of racial bigotry. Where Christianity was narrowly, even exclusively conceived as the conversion of individual sinners, the ethical fruit of that conversion was individualistic moral change. In this context, even if racial concerns did rise from revivalist pulpits, they were much more likely to address Black and White individuals' need to love one another than to be aimed at addressing White advantage embedded in American society and culture. Southern churches, as many Southern historians have agreed, "make all of individual Christianity and regard the conversion of men as virtually the whole task of the church."[27]

This hyper-individualism leads to a brand of preaching that is allergic to politics. To conceive of the ministry of preaching in such a narrow, individualistic way is to misunderstand so much that it would take another entire book to explain. For starters, however, preaching that focuses only on converting the individual soul misconceives human nature itself or, if you will, the nature of the human soul, which is both individual and social. A baby born without human contact with others cannot become truly human.

Such preaching also misunderstands the message of Jesus. The individualistic Johannine language of eternal life is overbalanced by the Synoptic Gospels' depiction of a Jesus who came preaching the rule or reign of God, also known as the Kingdom of God. Such preaching has no grasp of the separation of church and state, which limits our government's involvement with religion and religious institutions but does not imply that Christian ministers should steer clear of political subjects.

In my sophomore year of college, planning to pursue my theological education after graduating, I headed across campus one morning to hear the new president of one of the Southern Baptist seminaries preach in the university chapel. In one of the president's applause lines, he announced, "If everyone in the world would come to Jesus, all the social problems in the world would come to an end." I left the experience with two certainties in mind. One was that this was the dumbest thing I had ever heard a supposedly educated minister say. The other was that I would not be attending his seminary. Anyone who had ever been a member of a church should have been able to detect how questionable such a claim was. Just getting a collection of individual souls to give their hearts to Jesus will never solve their every potential problem—much less solve the problem of race and racism in our families, our churches, our cities, our states, our nation, or the world.

Related to this is the conception of Christian worship as a refuge or a "shelter in the time of storm." Many people attend public worship as a way of escaping the political battles of contemporary life in America. "People come to church," argued one pastor, "because they hunger for a place of belonging that is not as divided as our nation is. They hunger for a sense of unity and purpose. And the last thing they want is a church that is as divided as the rest of society."[28]

How ironic then that the African American churches, whose theme song celebrates God as a "rock in a weary land, a shelter in the time of storm," has always been the most political and prophetic segment of American Christianity. As one of the princes of the African American pulpit and an eloquent voice of the Civil Rights Movement, Otis Moss Jr. has warned that "The world does not like prophets and the church often refuses to celebrate them." But he notes that Jesus' first public sermon in Luke 4 certainly did not try to avoid political controversy. Moss added:

> "The spirit of the Lord is upon me…God has anointed me"— that has to be theological. "To proclaim good news to the poor"—I believe that's economics…. ["R]elease to the captives"?—that must be political. To "recover the sight of the blind"—that's educational and sociological. "To let the oppressed go free"—that's liberation theology. And then, "to proclaim the year of Jubilee, to proclaim the acceptable year of the Lord"—that's theological. So at the top of the text is theology. And in between is economics, politics, and sociology. In between it's all of the social public policy….So, if you are preaching a gospel that has nothing about politics, nothing about economics, nothing about sociology, it's an empty gospel.[29]

As a pastor of an African American church, Moss's Sitz im Leben, or his situation in life, has been to serve as his people's "rock in a weary land." To the extent that his congregation has been "wearied" by social and political conditions in which they live, Pastor Moss cannot afford to narrow the scope of his sermons to the individual spiritual life. But for most of American history, White ministers have had to do their work in ecclesial contexts, such as those described by Lenora Tubbs Tisdale, that separate spirituality (prayer, devotional reading of scriptures, and meditation) from social activism and social justice.[30] George Mason, pastor of the Wilshire Baptist Church in Dallas, Texas, has learned this lesson the hard way. After leading his congregation to grant full membership, including weddings, to members of the LGBT community, he saw his church expelled from the Baptist General Convention of Texas. Undeterred from bringing race and other social or political concerns into his pulpit, Mason remains committed:

> Today, these political and economic conservatives would like political and economic issues to be separated from their church lives. I hear it all the time from those in the pew who feel that my preaching has gotten too political. White preachers like me, however, are increasingly feeling what black preachers have always known—namely, that it is untenable to proclaim a gospel of the heart that is disconnected from public life.[31]

Moreover, White evangelicals lean heavily on what sociologists Michael O. Emerson and Christian Smith call a "Ku Klux Klan model of racism." This involves deliberate, hostile prejudice against individual Blacks by other individuals. Building on this research, another study suggested that "Individualism not only blinds white evangelicals to structural inequalities involving race, but it also assigns blame to those who are disadvantaged by race and normalize...cultural practices, beliefs, and norms that privilege white Americans over others."[32] Is it then any wonder that individualism reads the New Testament and only sees the missionary Paul converting individuals all along his journeys? Individualism, however, blinds us to the Paul who tried to aid Jewish Christians by gathering money from every Gentile church he visited all the way to Rome and perhaps to Spain. He even put off some of his missionary activity until he had taken the offering back to Jerusalem. We see his evangelism, but we seem oblivious to his social vision at work in virtually every one of his letters, which contain material designed to break down the "middle wall of partition" between Gentiles and Jews.

Retraining our eyes and refocusing our vision, we can learn to see ourselves as truly human beings when we acknowledge our corporate nature as well as our individuality. As my beloved New Testament professor Frank Stagg argued every chance he got, a truly biblical anthropology must paradoxically hold these two aspects of human existence in creative tension.[33] True humanity is a balance of individualism and communalism. It is never an either/or. It must be both/and.

Such a dual focus widens our field of vision, which in turn enables human beings to see beyond our blind spot and helps us grasp that just as human nature has both individual and collective dimensions, so do Christianity and racism. It would help us see that even a miracle that changed our individual racial attitudes overnight would still leave us as part of a society with deep inequalities that require collective action commensurate with our changed attitudes toward individual people of color. When our understandings of human nature, the Christian faith, and of racism improve, prophetic preaching on race will find its way into American pulpits as never before.

AMERICAN CONSUMERISM

Another blinding star in our sky is the tradition of voluntarism created by our freedom of religion. As Americans protected by the religious clauses of the First Amendment, we are religiously free, and no government can force us to be religious or join a congregation. Our churches, as Sidney Mead told us long ago, must convince "prospects" to become voluntary members. This in turn creates a marketplace of religion where religious organizations must compete with other religious organizations to convince "customers" voluntarily to become members.[34]

Now judging from the typical customer service I see in the American marketplace today, our churches may be the last institutions in America where the old slogan still holds true: "The customer is always right." They are right even if they are actively racist or passive bystanders who allow the inequality of the racial status quo to remain intact. In either case, they want to hear something spiritually uplifting from the pulpit. Preachers get the message rather clearly: risk too many homiletical references—never mind entire sermons—on race, and you may soon be looking for a new gig somewhere else.

Thus it was in early America for ministers who avoided criticizing and then eventually advocated slavery for the sake of the wealthy Christians who owned both slaves to build their plantations and hireling ministers to build their churches. Clearly, any and all messages and methods calculated to attract new members superseded the urgency of prophetic witness. For example, as early as the Revolutionary era, Baptists in Kentucky vigorously opposed the introduction of slavery into their state. By the 1830s, however, virtually all antislavery sentiment in their churches had dwindled to a flicker as the influence of slaveholding members increased.[35]

Historians have long since established that rather than moral suasion or church discipline, it was war and government coercion that ended slavery. John R. McKivigan has shown that before the Civil War, no major denomination, South or North, endorsed immediate emancipation of the slaves. Many church leaders rejected any position that might drive away supporters of slavery. One early abolitionist, Albany Stewart, denounced "moral cowardice" among preachers, warning that "silence soon becomes acquiescence, which is soon defense, which is soon vindication." He and other firebrand abolitionists inveighed against church practices that even appeared to justify slavery, particularly "the acceptance of financial contributions from slave owners."[36]

Of course, most American churches not only accepted the tithes and offerings of wealthy slaveholders, but also wrestled over whether to put them in leadership roles in the churches. By the mid-1840s, these latter debates had torn asunder both the Methodist and the Baptist denominations. Yet even after the Southern members had departed to begin the Methodist Episcopal Church, South (MECS), and the Southern Baptist Convention (SBC), their erstwhile coreligionists, as McKivigan has shown, still neither declared slaveholding to be sinful nor subjected slaveholders to church discipline.

Meanwhile the MECS and the SBC, in large measure because their ministers were even less inclined to speak prophetically against slavery, enjoyed an unprecedented period of growth, both in numerical measures and in cultural prominence. Within two years of the birth of their denominations, MECS and SBC pastors had begun preaching sermons or publishing books, pamphlets, or journal or newspaper articles defending "the Christian character of slavery."[37] These same pastors oversaw impressive growth in denominational bureaucracy, local churches, and financial contributions. "Through appeals to wealthy patrons and church members alike," observes Beth Barton Schweiger, "denominational coffers swelled several fold in the decade and a half before the Civil War." Examining religious life in Virginia, she notes that Methodist membership grew by 27 percent, more than doubling the state's 12 percent population growth. The number of Methodist churches increased by more than one third, while Baptist churches grew by one fifth. Methodist church property more than doubled in value, while Baptist property values increased by 80 percent. Together the property of both denominations—worth some $2.9 million—was worth more than twice the property of Presbyterians and Episcopalians combined.[38]

Members of the Southern planter class who wielded intellectual, political, economic, and social power in the Antebellum

South were almost universally men of the church. In that context, can anyone doubt that they also exercised religious power? Their ministers gave them ample reason to do so. First, the Methodist and Baptist clergy defended the honor of the slaveholding Christian leaders against the aspersions cast by antislavery coreligionists. Second, they enthusiastically embraced a spiritual or, better, a "denominational" secession. Third, they wrote and published a large percentage of some 275 very persuasive biblical and theological defenses of slavery. Fourth, they built "planter-friendly" congregations, often with large and full sanctuaries. Fifth, they inspired large financial offerings, no doubt with planters as their most generous donors.

In a reciprocal relationship this successful, it is difficult to imagine these pastors delivering sermons that did not meet the approval of their most important, most influential consumers. From their beginnings in the Great Awakenings to the present day, the American ecclesiological context and evangelical theological emphases have conspired to create a ministerial class that specializes in "soul-winning" and "church-building." But are the churches they built also monuments to expedience, where keeping one's pulpit meant keeping the customers satisfied and keeping their churches and denominations growing? What was the nature or message or spiritual legitimacy of such churches when they became vocal advocates of slavery or when they became zones of silence about the untold millions of sons and daughters of Africa whose lives were ended or damaged for generations to come by slavery and segregation? As Frederick Douglass told a London audience in 1846:

> ...the pulpit and the auctioneer's block stand in the same neighborhood; while the blood-stained gold goes to support the pulpit, the pulpit covers the infernal business with the garb of Christianity. We have men sold to build churches, women sold to support missionaries, and babies sold to buy Bibles and

communion services for the churches.[39]

Nor was the customer right only in the Antebellum era. More recent scholarship has argued that White evangelicalism today is even more inclined toward consumerism. One study seeking to create "a homiletic for racial reconciliation" warns that consumerism can reduce both human beings and the spiritual life to commodities, while criticizing "church shopping." Another important study charges that the evangelical church tends to cater to individual needs and spiritual preferences. Often spoiled congregants insist that their ministers "please worshippers in order to keep them coming back to church," or they change churches when another better suits them. This in turn can diminish a pastor's resolve to address topics like race.[40]

AMERICAN PATRIOTISM

Bible scholars will recall that most of the Hebrew prophets received particularly cool receptions from their audiences. Amaziah, the priest of Bethel, complained to King Jeroboam that the land of North Israel "was not able to bear" all of the prophet Amos's words and then invited him to run along back to Judah "and prophesy there" (Amos 7:10–12). In fact, so many of the prophets were seen as so unpatriotically judgmental that one of Jesus' most famous sayings was that "A prophet is not without honor, except in his own country" (Matt 13:57).

Even in (post) modern nations like the United States, whose citizens are trained to view their country as God's Country, the prophetic voice is often silenced. What else would one expect in a country where, according to a 2010 Gallup poll, 80 percent of respondents agreed with the statement that the unique character of the United States made it "the greatest country in the world"?[41] Americans love to mix God and country. American males often show up for church services sitting closed-mouthed during the congregational hymns—unless the Sunday is the one nearest the

Fourth of July and the hymn is "God Bless America." In such a context, however, both the mouth and the tear ducts open up, deep emotions are tapped, and tears wet patriotic cheeks. Americans want their patriotism positive.

The moment when the strains of "America the Beautiful" reverberate in American hearts is no time to be reminded of "America the Racist." The Office of the NFL Commissioner and President Trump have left no doubt that they believe the public performance of the National Anthem is not a proper context for exercising one's First Amendment right of protest. That seems particularly true if one happens to be a Black player who thinks the USA allows White police officers to shoot Black suspects with impunity. To protest by, for example, kneeling during the National Anthem the way NFL player Colin Kaepernick did is to run the risk that the President of the United States will call you a son of a bitch and wonder if you "should even be here."[42]

Patriotism and prophetic critique tend not to go together in America. In the 1960s, to protest US presence in the Vietnam War was almost invariably to be invited to "Love It or Leave It." Any politician willing to acknowledge that our nation has had its share of moral failings is almost certain to have an opponent induct her or him into the "Blame America First" Club. "If you don't like it here," one will always offer, "then just move to North Korea." Indeed, the Vietnam era was the perfect backdrop to illustrate the "See No Evil, Hear No Evil, Speak No Evil" nature of patriotism in the United States. A national Gallup poll was taken in May 1970 a week or two after the shootings at Kent State University. It revealed that 58 percent of the respondents believed the responsibility for the deaths lay with the demonstrators; only 11 percent blamed the National Guard. Later, an author of a book about the shootings would write, "These were the most popular murders ever committed in the United States."[43]

More recently, on the Fourth of July 2018 the *Washington Post* printed an article based on interviews with seven Americans regarding their understandings of patriotism, protest, and President Trump. Agreeing with the president's attacks on the NFL's kneeling protests, a restaurant owner from Denham Springs, Louisiana, asserted, "When they kneel for the anthem, they are disrespecting the people who have fought for the right for them to do so."[44] This brand of patriotism appears to exclude any criticism of the nation, whether it comes from a God-anointed prophet or a run-of-the-mill protester. This sort of "my country, right or wrong" patriotism is perilously close to saying, "In America you have the right to protest—but you are wrong to exercise that right." To a good historian, this widely held view misunderstands both the nature of patriotism and the Constitution's protections. To a faithful prophet, this view misunderstands the nature of Christianity itself.

Patriotism does not imply or require the absence of criticism. It means loving, honoring, and defending the nation's core values; it does not mean accepting uncritically or without question any and all actions of a particular governing administration. Even an often jingoistic president like Teddy Roosevelt could articulate a critical patriotism: "Patriotism means to stand by the country. It does not mean to stand by the president or any other public official.... To announce that there must be no criticism of the President, or that we are to stand by the President, right or wrong, is not only unpatriotic and servile, but is morally treasonable to the American public."[45] More recently, author and activist James Baldwin has written in a similar vein, "I love America more than any other country in the world and, exactly for this reason, I insist on the right to criticize her perpetually."[46]

Of course, Baldwin could bring a perpetual and searing critique to his country because, like most African Americans, he viewed the United States as mired in racial quicksand from our beginnings to the current generation. No wonder he wrote that "people are trapped in history and history is trapped in them."[47] At least twice the stranglehold of racism in our history was loosened by titanic events on American ground. The Civil War broke the chains of slavery, and the Civil Rights Movement released African Americans from the prison of segregation. In both instances the nation had some success pulling itself out of the quicksand. In both cases, however, America wearied of the struggle against the forces of reaction, and the nation sank back into the mire. So now we find ourselves flailing furiously in our post-Obama/Trumpian efforts to escape. And one powerful reason Trump has been able to attract an almost unchallengeable base of support is that his followers have become so fatigued by criticism of America and especially by accusations of racism that they have learned to turn the tables: now they accuse the anti-racists of being racist themselves when they bring up the subject of race. Even to mention racism in public discourse is to be unpatriotic.

Yet beyond the opinions of prominent Americans—albeit of different races and generations—are America's founding documents, purportedly venerated by conservatives. The First Amendment establishes the absolute right of American citizens to criticize their nation and its government. In fact, four of the five fundamental freedoms granted as a right by the First Amendment—(1) freedom of religion, (2) freedom of speech, (3) freedom of the press, (4) freedom of assembly, (5) freedom to petition the government for redress of grievances—pertain specifically to the absolute and unassailable right to protest. Moreover, our Declaration of Independence implies that the very idea of a United States of America was conceived and born in the context of protest.

More important still for Christians and their prophets, an uncritical patriotism violates the First Commandment, "You shall have no other gods before me" (Exodus 20:4; Deuteronomy 5:6), and misunderstands the nature of the Christian religion. Within the Jewish and Christian religions, both understood as covenant

31

relationships with God, to love one's country absolutely is to raise a human, national allegiance to the level of God, which violates the commandment against idolatry. The primary temptation of the first century Christian movement [was] to participate in the ritual of the emperor cult and declare "Kyrios Kaisaros" ("Caesar is Lord"). In that context, Christian pastors and prophets insisted that their followers reject idolatry and declare, "Kyrios Christos" ("Christ is Lord"). Loyalty to and love for one's earthly kingdom was always to be subordinate to Christians' loyalty to and love for the Kingdom of God and of his Christ. In other words, loyalties to one's local or national identity were superseded by one's allegiance to an international identity known as the Kingdom or Rule of God.

Thus patriotism is acceptable for the Christian as long as one's love and loyalty to country do not supersede his or her loyalty to Christ and his Kingdom. Donald W. Shriver Jr., emeritus president of Union Theological Seminary in New York City, suggests the perfect description of the proper form of patriotism. Christian patriots must be "honest patriots" who "love a country enough to remember its misdeeds." The most egregious of America's misdeeds, I would argue, is White America's history of mistreatment of Black Americans. Apart from Shriver's mode of expression, American patriotism can shine too brightly, blinding us to our obligation to preach prophetically on racial reconciliation.

AMERICAN NOSTALGIA

Over the course of the twentieth century, America's two political parties gradually swapped places on the political-ideological spectrum. Since the nature of conservatism is to conserve and preserve the past, the Republican Party has almost always looked to establish its policies in the "old times" that "were not forgotten." This nostalgia for days gone by has taken several forms in America since the 1920s. When Teddy Roosevelt came out of retirement in the election of 1912 to lead the Progressive or "Bull Moose" Party, the Progressive wing of the Republicans squared off against the Republicans not-quite so progressive wing. This intra-party split allowed Woodrow Wilson, a progressive *Democrat,* to move into the White House.. From *his* bully pulpit Wilson applied modestly progressive principles to both domestic policy and to a foreign policy mission to "make the world safe for Democracy." Two terms of Wilsonianism created a Republican party yearning for a "return to Normalcy," as Warren Harding's campaign slogan advised the voters in 1920.

"Normalcy" meant back to the "good ol' days" before TR opened the Pandora's Box of progressivism. Specifically, it meant returning to the days when the federal government was small and inactive, depending solely on an unregulated business cycle governed solely by market forces—a policy that eventually led to the Great Depression. Later, a *Democratic* Roosevelt fought the Depression with a New Deal, gaining more than a little, albeit imperfect, success. Republicans during and since the New Deal once again looked backward, hoping for just the right spokesman who could re-apply the pre-FDR "old deal." Later, in the civil rights years, Nixonian Republicans became the "Silent Majority" who created nicknames for civil rights and anti-Vietnam War activists: first, they advised "un-Americans" to "Love America or Leave It," or simply mocked them as the "Blame America First crowd." Once again, they counseled a return to the past policies of states' rights and Free Market Capitalism that prevailed in the days before JFK and LBJ embraced the agenda of the Civil Rights movement.

In his award-winning book, *The End of White Christian America,* Robert P. Jones, Director of the Public Religion Research Institute, has re-named this impulse, calling it the "politics of nostalgia." Jones astutely analyzes a conservatism that did not need to wait for Donald Trump's promise to "make America Great again." Ever since the Democratic Party of Kennedy and Johnson came to be identified with what the crassest of White Supremacists might have called a "party of 'N-word' lovers." almost every Republican presidential nominee has campaigned with some version of the "Southern Strategy." Begun in 1964 by Barry Goldwater, named by the Richard Nixon campaign, perfected by more authentic ("sho' 'nuff") Southerners like George Wallace, Strom Thurmond, and Jesse Helms, the strategy was crafted to appeal to whites' still angry over the civil rights movement's success. By the time Ronald Reagan was finished, the "solid South" remained solid, even if it did change its color to Republican red.

Jones offers perhaps the clearest explanation in print of how the Southern Strategy of the 1960s and 70s was transformed into the White Christian Strategy that undermined the efforts of new, post-civil rights southern presidents Jimmy Carter and Bill Clinton. "In an ironic twist," he argued, "it was disappointment with Carter's moderate politics that transposed the Southern Strategy into an overtly religious key."[48] Primarily because Carter rejected a hardline anti-abortion stance, Southern Evangelicals, who had helped elect Carter in 1976, had become part of the Reverend Jerry Falwell's "Moral Majority" and spurned Carter for Ronald Reagan in 1980.

But Jones shows how the White Christian Strategy burned most brightly in the White Christian reaction to Barack Obama. Ultimately, neither Carter nor Clinton prevailed against their respective opponents, possibly because they were both steeped in the Baptist doctrine of church-state separation and came to be vilified by fellow religionists when they stepped into voting booths. The election of Obama, however, set up new battles in the Culture Wars.

One can find in this group of Americans a Great White Christian preference for the good old days before the Civil Rights Movement when African Americans remained rather quietly in their "place," and when white Christians dominated American culture and politics. In this connection, Jones buttressed the previous argument by analyzing surveys that polled a wide diversity of Americans regarding the changes in American culture since the 1950s. Strong majorities of 67 percent of Republicans and 72 percent of White Evangelicals believed that changes since the 1950s had been changes for the worse.[49]

Jones describes the Obama Era clashes of between nostalgic Evangelicals and Obama's multiculturalists. Just after Obama's re-election, Pat Robertson's Christian Coalition sent its supporters an email with an image depicting a white, patriarchal (the Father at the head of the table), middle-class (no servants), Christian family praying before their Thanksgiving meal in 1942. Jones correctly interprets this mailing as pointing recipients back to the halcyon days when America embodied a (White) Christian nation. But Jones detected a stark contrast in the vision of America represented by Obama's Second Inaugural Address:

> We, the people, declare today that the most evident of truths—that all of us are created equal—is the star that guides us still; just as it guided our forebears through Seneca Falls, and Selma, and Stonewall....
>
> It is now our generation's task to carry on what those pioneers began. For our journey is not complete until our wives, our mothers and daughters can earn a living equal to their efforts. Our journey is not complete until our gay brothers and sisters are treated like anyone else under the law—for if we are truly equal, then surely the love we commit to one another must be equal as well....Our journey is not complete until we find a better way to welcome the striving, hopeful immigrants who still see America as a land of opportunity. That is our generation's task—to make these words, these rights, these values of life and liberty and the pursuit of happiness real for every American.

Into such a polarized America came a Strongman riding an escalator, promising to build a wall at the nation's Southern border and to "Make America Great again." From his escapades on network television to his status as a "birther" convinced that Obama was not born in the United States and therefore constitutionally ineligible to be president, Donald Trump discovered that he had an immediate fan club primed to follow him into an old Promised Land where their fear and loathing of black and brown Americans would launch a thousand conspiracy theories but also win the presidency in 2016.

Just before that election a Pulitzer-prize winning journalist named Isabel Wilkinson attended a social gathering in Washington DC. As she mingled her way across the room, she soon fell into conversation with the late Gwen Ifill, then the moderator of the *PBS Newshour*. After they talked about Wilkinson's current writing project—which would go on to become another critically-acclaimed book, *Caste: The Origins of Our Discontents*—the two African American journalists compared notes on the political events of the day. Ifill asked Wilkinson's opinion on the secret of Trump's success. Wilkinson mused momentarily and then speculated: "I think the White People are thinking about 2040—the year that sociologists predict that Whites will no longer constitute a majority in the United States. They hope Trump can save them from being reduced to minority status.

Nostalgia for past glories when White Christian America was dominated by Whites and Blacks were submissively "in their place" thus animates the followers of Donald Trump. To the converse, this cohort of American voters despises the segment of citizens who have made peace with the changes in America since 1950. Thus these Americans yearn for "old times not forgotten," for times when Christian men dominated American life and culture. Thus when they speak of race at all, they fall back into the language of individualism and claim that they "haven't a racist bone in their bodies—just as things were in the old days when their cultural norms were dominated by White Protestant Americans.

These followers of Trump are bereft of the cultural, political, religious, and racial hegemony they enjoyed back in the days when Black and Brown Americans posed no threat to their status. This posture makes sense in the America they envision. They are among the angriest of all Americans. For when one has been King all one's life, equality feels like a demotion. For most of American history, Evangelical Christians have dominated life in America. Since the Civil Rights Movement, however, events and political decisions have "demoted' them to the necessity of sharing equal status with African Americans and other minorities groups. The anger and fear they express thus comes from having been "demoted by equality," and it is no wonder they are mad about it. Their vision of America inspires not an effort to embody Martin Luther King's multicultural Beloved Community, but instead they deliver a pulpit message to "take back our country."

AMERICAN EXCEPTIONALISM

Uncritical super-patriotism as it appears in the United States is organically related to citizens' firm and unwavering belief in American exceptionalism. In 1620 and 1630, two English ships named, respectively, the *Mayflower* and the *Arbella*, cut through Atlantic waters brimming with Puritans who had the confidence that God had chosen them for an "errand into the wilderness."[50] As God's "chosen people," these planters of the English colonies of Plymouth and Massachusetts Bay saw themselves as called and commissioned by God to create Christian commonwealths in a "new England" to serve as examples to a religiously corrupt Old England. While these Puritans could not imagine that their actions would lead to a new country, their idea of being a "new Israel" has persisted into contemporary America.

This concept of being specially chosen by God, however, has not continued over time without a few important changes. The First Great Awakening (1740s–1750s) saw spiritual declension reversed as revivals swept the colonies, especially in New England. Large numbers of conversions renewed the idea of the covenant between the Puritan colonies and God. Puritan language was supplemented by Enlightenment ideas during the Revolutionary era, when the idea of chosenness again was renewed but also refocused on the newly independent United States. So powerful was this idea that even a religious skeptic like Thomas Paine still held to an America with a special mission. In one of his final appeals in his pamphlet *Common Sense*, published in January 1776, Paine personified freedom as a fugitive and implored his readers to "Welcome the fugitive, and prepare in time an asylum for mankind."

Creating a new government structure in a Constitution that made no specific reference to God, Americans nevertheless saw God as watching over the American enterprise, as evidenced by the affirmations "Annuit Coeptis" ("He has watched over our doings") and "Novus Ordo Seclorem" ("A New Order for the Ages")—both of which appear on the back side of the Great Seal of the United States. Americans also interpreted the July 4, 1826, deaths of John Adams and Thomas Jefferson on the fiftieth anniversary of the Declaration of Independence as a miraculous sign of the Almighty's special relationship with America. Before long, Alexis de Tocqueville would become the first commentator to refer to America as exceptional in his classic analysis *Democracy in America*.

One could trace the ideas of chosenness or exceptionalism through every period of American history down to the 2012 presidential primaries when all the Republican candidates hammered the incumbent President Barack Obama (and each other) on the question of whether or how fervently they believed in American exceptionalism. Suffice it to say that in our current political atmosphere (during the 2020 election season), no one—regardless of party, gender, race, or ideology—could possibly be elected president without intoning that the USA is the "greatest country in the world" and ending every speech with "God bless the United States of America."

The problem with American exceptionalism is its temptation to raise the nation to a divine status. In his 1967 article "Civil Religion in America," Robert N. Bellah called it "national self-idolatry." This seminal article launched a thousand or so books on the concept of civil religion. Most interpreters of the subject accept not only its existence but also the existence of a variety of civil religions.

Similarly, there are varieties of American exceptionalism. In a recent study, John D. Wilsey argues for exceptionalism as an aspect of civil religion. Understanding the true relationship of these two controversial concepts remains unclear despite Wilsey's provocative analysis.[51] It may very well be that the clearer explanation is simply to view exceptionalism as a more secular, more political name for the concept of American civil religion. What many historians and sociologists have called a prophetic or an inclusive civil religion, Wilsey calls an open exceptionalism, which avoids absolutizing America into an object of worship. Rather, open exceptionalism functions to unite the American people by calling the nation to embody its own deepest core values of inclusion, freedom, and "liberty and justice for all." By contrast, closed exceptionalism "calls for a God-ordained empire" and corresponds to what scholars often call a priestly or exclusive civil religion.[52]

Thus, when American exceptionalism is closed and functioning as a component of a priestly civil religion, the nation and its characteristics are deified to a transcendent status and its believers are guilty of idolatry. In such a condition, Americans become blind and deaf to modern prophets calling them to humbly "live out the true meaning of their creed." No surprises here.

From the American Puritans to the super-patriots of today, believing that America is God's chosen nation has typically led the people of the covenant to a boastful self-image that brooks no criticism. When living in what purports to be God's chosen nation, when pledging allegiance to the flag is as sacred a ritual as being baptized into Christ and his church, the prophetic word regarding racism—America's Original Sin—will fall on deaf ears. At least among most White Americans.

At this point, White Americans can take a lesson from African American believers. From the moment when enslaved Africans first warmed to the Christian gospel in the Southern camp meeting phase of the Second Great Awakening, they have correctly interpreted the Christian gospel and its scriptures as hostile to human oppression. In the post-Reconstruction era, African Methodist Episcopal (AME) ministers denounced Jim Crow and excoriated the silence of their White Protestant counterparts on the scandal of lynching. For them, America could be considered a Christian nation only when racism ended. Edward J. Blum tells of their defiance of White claims of American Christian nationhood and argues that for people of color, religion was as much a sword as it was a shield.[53]

Cornel West, perhaps the foremost Black public intellectual in contemporary America, rejects the concept of American civil religion insofar as it is a religious version of American exceptionalism. He condemns both civil religion and American exceptionalism as "one of the most self-deceiving concepts in the history of the nation." Acknowledging a distinctive American democratic experiment, he insists, "America is in no way a nation as chosen, in no way a nation that God smiles at and winks at and shuns others." Martin Luther King Jr., West believes, did employ a form of American exceptionalism, calling on America to "live out the true meaning of its creed, that all men are created equal." Yet he argues that late in his life King came to view American exceptionalism as a "major impediment for the struggle for justice in America and around the world."[54]

No longer blinded by these bright stars in their homiletical sky, it is time for White ministers to join the counterclockwise dance of the ring shout, with a cavalcade of African American prophets who have marched to a different drummer against time as their masters defined it. They moved in rhythm against the grain of a racist culture, always singing songs of freedom with their prophetic voices. There were the Antebellum voices of Frederick Douglass, Nat Turner, David Walker, Jarena Lee, and Sojourner Truth. There were the Jim Crow era voices of Henry McNeal Turner, John Jasper, Reverdy Ransom, Harriet Cole Baker, Emily Christmas Kinch, and Mary Lena Lewis Tate. There were the civil rights era voices of Vernon Johns, Martin King, Howard Thurman, C. L. Franklin, Gardner Taylor, Jeremiah Wright, Thea Bowman, Katie Cannon, Vashti Murphy McKenzie, and Prathia Hall. All of them were voices of Christian liberation.

Throughout Christian history in America, too few White ministers have been a part of this chorus. The time has long since come for White ministers en masse to join in the dance. The Reverend Fred Shuttlesworth was one of bravest ministers ever to set foot in this ring shout of liberation. He singlehandedly carried the Civil Rights Movement in Birmingham, Alabama, on his shoulders until, after five years of his cajoling, Martin Luther King Jr. joined forces with him for protest demonstrations that rocked America in 1963. When White ministers told him they would lose their pulpits if they spoke up in the movement's behalf, he replied, "I would do it at least once and see if God didn't find you another pulpit." He always added this tagline: "When God says 'Jump!' it's my job to jump; it's his job to fix a place for me to land."[55]

Simplistic as it sounds, when we ministers look at the world through a faith perspective like this, our eyes can be shaded from the brightness of individualism, religious consumerism, patriotism, and American exceptionalism and actually see the continuing devastation caused by racism and our cowardly silence about it.

"The lion has roared," the prophet Amos once said. "Who can but prophesy?" Who indeed? The preachers in Part II—Christian, Jewish, Muslim, male and female, liberal and conservative, Black and White—have dared to join the dance of liberation. They have sung songs of freedom and boldly brought race into the American pulpit.

2

Bringing Race into the Pulpit:
An African American Christian Perspective

Sandy Dwayne Martin

Professor Manis is absolutely correct as he argues in the preceding chapter that religious leaders, especially those who occupy pulpits in local congregations, have a great and urgent moral obligation to deal with the pressing issue of race. Accordingly, this chapter strives to complement the preceding one rather than to dissent from it. It intends to call our attention to some of the same issues already raised, but to do so from a different perspective. One objective of this chapter is to speak more from *an* (not *the*) African American perspective. As my colleague has challenged the White church community to the risky task of racial justice and reconciliation by some critiques he has made of those churches, I hope to invite the Black church community to do likewise with critical observations of our churches, so that the two fellowships and any mixed communities might work more intentionally to bring race into the pulpit and the wider religious ministry.

RACISM:
A DEFINITION AND SOME RELATED TERMS

It is helpful to provide some definitions and reflections on certain key terms that Blacks, Whites, and others often use when we talk about race and race relations in the United States. This is helpful because quite often two or more people might use the same term but in radically different ways, leading to misunderstanding and unnecessary conflict. Let us discuss my definitions and descriptions of a select number of terms relating to race: race, racism, ethnocentrism, White dominance, White supremacy, religious prejudice and bigotry, and White privilege. The definitions and descriptions provided below are my own and not necessarily shared by others. Hence, in these next few pages I will seek to make very clear exactly what I mean by the terms. I also recommend that readers adopt a similar method whenever they discuss race with others.[56]

First, let us consider the terms *race* and *racism*. Some would contend that there is no objective, biological, or genetic basis for assigning humanity into various racial groupings. This chapter will not discuss the accuracy of that contention. One thing is clear, however: the economic, political, social, and sometimes religious reality is that people do in fact claim racial identification and do relate to people based on differences or similarities in skin color, hair texture, or geographical origins, etc. Therefore, I will use the term "race" because it is a social reality.

With all this in mind, I define *racism* as any and all attitudes, behaviors, or actions operating from the *conviction* that one race or races of people are entitled (often on the basis of biological inheritance of the group or groups) to occupy a superior station over another race or races, and/or they operate on the *desire* that such an established racial hierarchy should be the case whether the conviction itself is or is not shared. My definition would encompass people who do not actually believe that another race or races are inherently inferior but who support a system of thinking and behavior that renders benefits to their racial grouping.

Racism differs from *ethnocentrism*, which argues that a particular culture is superior to other cultures. While ethnocentrism can also be very detrimental, there might be a "paradoxical" desire of ethnocentrists to be culturally inclusive of other peoples, to encourage and sometimes compel them to adopt the ethnocentrist's culture. Unlike racism, ethnocentrism does not necessarily assume that other cultures have a genetic inferiority or claim natural or genetic inferiority of peoples from other cultures. Humanity reaching back to the Egyptians, Greeks, Romans, and others have long employed this way of thinking. It appears, however, that racism, based on a conviction of natural inferiority, has fairly recently—within the last five hundred years—appeared full bloom with the worldwide dominance of European cultures, though some might argue that clearly defined racism has existed much longer.

Relative to the discussion of racism, it is important to note that some people, both Black and White, argue that it is impossible for certain people—Blacks, for example—to be racist or practice racism because they lack the required social, political, and economic power to bring to fruition any racially adverse intentions toward other peoples. In other words, for people holding this view, racism is defined as exercising actual dominance or control over other races. Others say that sin is sin, whether imagined and talked about or whether one's desires or beliefs are concretized. Did not our Savior Jesus Christ say that as a person thinks in their heart so they are? That, for example, one does not have to commit adultery or murder physically to be an adulterer or murderer in the eyes of God? Besides, people who might today and in a current situation be unable to exercise power might tomorrow and in another context be in the position to effect their wishes. There was a time when the Nazi Party was a small group of people in pre-World War II Germany, but once they grew in numbers and acquired power, they conducted one of the most atrocious acts of genocide in human history in accord with the beliefs they had all along proclaimed. Also, sometimes people consciously or unconsciously appropriate negative views and actions that perpetuate racism against themselves. Therefore, I agree with the second perspective. Anyone can be racist, Black or White, powerful or powerless. Racism is something that should be totally uprooted from the *human* (not just White) experience; otherwise, we always risk its emergence or reemergence.

There are other terms relevant to our discussion of racial justice and racial reconciliation. One term is racial or *White dominance*. This term emphasizes the importance of actual social, political, and economic power residing in the hands of Whites that exercises an oppressive sway over Blacks and others. The term *White supremacy* in the broader sense refers to the belief and intentions of Whites to retain supreme power over non-White others. In a more contemporary, political sense it refers to White nationalism, the Ku Klux Klan, Neo-Nazis, and others who promote White racial superiority, support racist views about Blacks and Jews, and are willing to resort to violence and armed racial conflict to rid the nation of Blacks and others they consider undesirable. Fortunately, the racism confronted in the US for the most part is not currently the second variety of White supremacy.

Racial prejudice refers to prejudgments, biases, and false assumptions we harbor against people based on their racial grouping. There is *racial bigotry*, a kind of racial prejudice that is hardened, often unmovable, and strongly insistent on hating others and/or holding derogatory views regarding their worth. I believe no one is perfect and that everyone living in the United States with our long tradition of racial discrimination and the evisceration of Black/African history is subject to some expressions of racial prejudice, including the kind that might operate in a subtler and even unconscious manner. In other words, even those Whites who are generally good people and even fierce promoters of racial justice might find themselves saying, thinking, or doing things pertaining to Black people that run counter to their own professed and deeply held set of values and intentions. For example, it is a mystery why employees might be more likely to believe the accuracy of their Black manager's business observations if the recently hired White assistant manager affirms them. It is strange, a Black woman might think, that in a recent meeting she made a suggestion thirty minutes ago, but no one seemed to have thought it was a marvelous idea until it was stated two minutes ago by one of the White women in attendance. Again, people are imperfect, including on racial matters, and we can expect occasional failures or contradictions between their values and their behavior. But we also have the right to expect that people of genuine good will, when confronted with such inconsistencies or when they come to a realization of them, will amend their actions accordingly.

This discussion of unintentional or unrealized racial prejudice leads to the consideration of another term—*White privilege*. Hinted at in the above definition of racism and subsequent discussion, White privilege, which is not necessarily intended or embraced, refers to the reality that one's Whiteness automatically gives him or her advantages or privileges over those who are not White. A White teenager or young man will hardly fear that a minor traffic infraction, such as crossing the median or riding with a broken tail light, will result in a negative or even fatal encounter with a police officer of whatever race. A Black young man cannot be so sure.

IMPORTANCE OF BRINGING RACE
INTO THE PULPIT

Again, as Manis has demonstrated, there is no other social/political issue in our American past or present that is more divisive and volatile than race, particularly as it involves the interaction between Whites and Blacks.[57] Both as a society and as individuals, we face calls from many sectors to be fairer and more just in our dealings with others—the quest for gender equality, issues surrounding sexual orientation and sexuality, matters relating to immigration, challenges confronting the disabled, discussions regarding climate change, debates over religious identification and religious freedom, etc. But none of these or any other social concerns cause as much sustained, systematic, universal, intense, and great discomfort and pain as the issue of race—especially as it involves Blacks and Whites. As examples, we can consider differences relating to geography, political affiliation, gender, sexual orientation, religion, etc.; but none of them is a more accurate and consistent predictor of one's voting pattern in a presidential campaign and many other elections than racial identity. A clear majority of Whites vote Republican, and an even larger majority of Blacks vote Democratic. A majority of White Christians celebrated and thanked God for the electoral victory of Donald Trump as president in 2016; an even greater majority of Black Christians lamented the defeat of Hillary Clinton. Eight years earlier, a great majority of Black Christians praised God that God had allowed, and for some even moved in history to effect, the elevation of Barack Obama to the White House; whereas many of their White counterparts were deeply disappointed and perhaps some of them asked what was God's will in allowing the defeat of John McCain (and four years later the loss of Mitt Romney).

It is clear that there has not been as much discussion of race in the White pulpit as there should have been. Of course, one might push back and say that it depends on one's perspective about how we interpret when the issue of race is being treated and when it is not. One could argue that that the advocacy of certain political measures, such as state rights or smaller government, or the absence of criticism for certain other things, such as the support of comprehensive national health care, might be clear indications that race is being discussed—perhaps more subtly or tacitly and just not in the manner that many of us would like to see. But more pointedly, let us focus on the absence of a discussion of race as it pertains to reconciliation between the races and the support of measures that would empower Blacks and other racial/ethnic minorities.

OBSTACLES TO BRINGING RACE INTO THE PULPIT

Why is there an absence of discussion about racial justice and reconciliation in our churches? Andrew Manis has provided excellent, well-considered reasons. Allow me to offer these reasons in a somewhat different, but not antithetical, fashion. First, the professor is correct when he posits that many ministers, Black and White, approach issues of ethics and morality from an individualistic frame of mind; that is, they focus on the individual often at the expense of the collective behavior of groups of people and how that collectivity impacts the individual. Many ministers simply and sincerely assume that if people's hearts are right, they will sooner or later do what is right, however imperfect their actions might be. These clergy see racism largely as a spiritual failing of human nature that needs to be addressed at the individual level. They fail to comprehend or appreciate the magnitude of the limits those individuals face because of societal, historical, political, and economic factors, let alone see the impact that unchecked racial prejudice buttressed by these factors has on those suffering injustice.

Second, we should not underestimate the constraining influence of ministers' sheer discomfort and awareness of their own failings and inadequacies regarding racial matters that often hinder them from addressing the problem of race. I mentioned above the imperfectability of human beings. Conscious of their own limitations, some ministers are reluctant to "lecture" others about the sins of racism. As an analogy, consider the minister who wishes to discuss the need for the stability of the two-parent home but is painfully conscious that his or her own marriage might be in trouble or that he or she might have parented a child outside of a marital union. A positive, productive manner of dealing with this self-awareness of one's vulnerability and weakness is for the minister to own the fact that all of us are imperfect and that sermons preached to others are often most effective when we have developed them while looking into our spiritual "mirrors." That is, sermons and teachings should be directed not simply at the hearers but at the proclaimer; and the listeners should understand that when the minister or rabbi or imam says "we," they mean exactly that—a challenge is being delivered for both pulpit and pew.

Third, there is the matter of the priestly and prophetic approaches to religious preaching. Priestly ministry is understood as a form that deals with comforting people. Prophetic ministry, on the other hand, challenges people to tackle aspects of the faith and their own behavior that are uncomfortable. Understandably, as advocates of racial justice often point out, religious leaders can be so attuned to comforting people facing problems, such as those pertaining to finances or drug addiction, that they lose sight of the duty to challenge them to do what is right in terms of addressing discrimination in the community, especially when doing right causes conflict with their own comforts and that of fellow believers. We need bolder teachers and preachers who push Christian people to take up the cross of sacrifice, encourage practitioners of Judaism to embrace the covenant of God and faithfully follow the law of God wherever it leads them, and call Muslims to have faith in God and do what is right regardless of the consequences.

We can understand the failures of the "priestly" ministers to address problems of race from the pulpit. Yet we must also comprehend that they are often dealing with people in the pews who—as someone has said—are barely holding on. Sometimes the attention to the individual and to families and other groupings is required, given that people do deal with personal and individual challenges that can lead in the direction of despair and even suicide. Many religious leaders may feel that overarching social-economic-political problems are not ones that the average individual, including the average minister, can control or to which they can make any profound contribution. On the other hand, individuals and particularly families can be guided successfully through death and tragedy, given counsel on seeking financial help or advice, or helped with loneliness and depression. The answer, of course, is what Professor Manis has provided: there must be an endeavor to balance and sometimes link individual and social concerns, to practice both priestly and prophetic ministries.

In addition to the reluctance to appear hypocritical or the concern about dealing with more immediately pressing personal and family problems, the White rabbi, minister, or imam might also be facing dangers regarding his or her own inclusion within his or her own racial community. All people like to belong to some type of family or community. Preaching and doing other ministry relative to an often explosive, controversial issue like race might cost one a clerical appointment or promotion, something that entails financial loss. Even if one retains his or her ministerial appointment, the clergyperson might encounter social exclusion that can also be painful. Many clergy today will note that the Black pulpit has always been freer than the White pulpit when it comes to discussing racial injustice. One might say that for many Black clergy, the preaching of racial justice is a message and a goal shared by the congregants among whom they labor. Indeed, it is often in the interest of the Black minister to voice the message of liberation that members of his or her congregation might not feel at liberty to address. It is often not in the material interest of the White minister to approach issues of racial inequity because in many instances such might appear as racial betrayal to his or her White parishioners.

For White ministers, dealing with race has always been a challenge. During the colonial and pre–Civil War eras, many White ministers, such as David Barrows of Virginia in the 1700s, risked bodily harm and even death for daring to speak out against slavery.[58] During the civil rights protests in 1963 Birmingham, Fred Shuttlesworth, Baptist pastor and president of the Alabama Christian Movement for Human Rights, as noted by Manis in the preceding chapter, demanded that White clergy be willing to risk all to struggle for justice, which indicates that Shuttlesworth did realize that there were real dangers involved for even Whites engaged in the quest for racial equality. King, interestingly, showed in the 1950s some reticence in harshly condemning White pastors who equivocated in the intensity of their civil rights stands. In his book, *Stride toward Freedom*, largely an account of the Montgomery Bus Boycott, King noted that ministers, including Whites, had a mandate to stand against injustice. He noted how this was problematic for some White pastors. Some of those supportive of civil rights preferred to work in quieter ways to bring their congregations to a more Christian perspective on race and in that manner advance the cause of justice, rather than standing more boldly and losing their positions only to be succeeded by segregationist pastors who would set back the cause of justice. King wrote with empathy of such clergy, "There is no single right strategy." Yet he cautioned that no strategy should be employed as an effort to avoid the furtherance of justice, as an excuse to do nothing. There were many things, such as having interracial ministerial fellowships, that could advance the cause without the loss of pastorates. Racially progressive White ministers standing together and in concert with their Black counterparts would contribute immensely to the realization of a more just society. "If ever the white ministers of the South decide to declare in a united voice the truth of the gospel on the question of race, the transition from a segregated to an integrated society will be infinitely smoother." Even when White ministers were not actively marching and protesting publicly, King believed they should still find ways to push the boundaries so as to promote the cause of freedom.[59]

In the classic essay, "Letter from a Birmingham Jail," written in 1963, King[60] was insistent on the mandate of ministers to stand for what is right. He expressed grave disappointment with "white moderates" who were not more strongly pushing against the boundaries of the old segregated establishment. King wondered if White moderates were even greater obstacles to racial change than the White supremacists such as those associated with the White Citizens Councils and the Ku Klux Klan. These White moderates whom he was addressing, according to King, preferred social order absent tension over the advancement of racial freedom, trusted too much that time itself would advance productive change, and paternalistically sought to establish the timing of others' liberation. One could argue that some things in King's letter directed toward these particular moderate Birmingham Christian and Jewish clergy, who had called for him not to conduct civil rights marches in the city at that designated time, are exaggerations or caricatures. Even should we allow this, however, it remains the case that King deals accurately with the obstacles that sometimes even good people place in the way of progress.

In King's day, not only White ministers but also Black clergy were sometimes reluctant or noncooperative in the quest for social change. It is generally a minority of people anywhere in the world who lead the forces for progressive change, risking their lives and reputations and sometimes those of their loved ones as well. The same is true of Black church people in the South during the Civil Rights Movement in that it was a minority of clergy and laity that took active lead in challenging the established segregationist order. Some Black ministers, like their White counterparts, favored racial change but feared (with reason) the cost should they openly declare their support for civil rights. Not only ministers but Black folks generally in small towns and rural areas were often at the mercy of

White landowners and the White economic and political power structure. Standing up for justice could mean the loss of life, property, home, or one's freedom.

One minister in 1963, the same year that King was upbraiding moderate White Birmingham clergy, wrote King stating his concern for the dangers of standing publicly and forthrightly for the cause of freedom. He could be killed or run out of town. King responded and conceded that his fears had solid foundations. The minister, said King, had three choices: leave Mississippi for a more racially just environment; go along with the system of racial apartheid in the South; or stand with courage for what is right and deal with whatever the consequences are. King recommended the third of these because "as a Christian minister and symbol of the New Negro," the pastor's primary concern was not being chased from his home or saving his life. His main concern should be standing for "truth, justice, and freedom," being willing to bear the cross knowing that redemption derives from unearned suffering. "This is hard to do, but it is a sacrifice that we must make if we are to be free."[61]

One might wonder why King's response to the Black pastor, who faced far more immediate danger, was more non-compromising and "absolute" than his position toward the White ministers in the Montgomery area. King approved the latter moving more cautiously and seeking changes in less direct or challenging approaches. But he insisted that the Black minister, because he was a minister "and a symbol of the New Negro," stand forthrightly even if it meant the loss of life or exile from the area. Is this difference explained at least in part by the fact that King was speaking of White ministers in the context of the Montgomery Bus Boycott in 1955, whereas his reply to the Black minister took place later in 1963? Perhaps the stronger insistence on standing boldly is related to the belief that African Americans have to take the initiative to free themselves and that for Blacks there can really be no middle ground for ministers or pastors who must lead and set the proper examples. In other words, Black people, especially ministers, have to be willing to die or face exile because it is their agency that is the central human agency in gaining their freedom. It is interesting that Shuttlesworth's 1963 statement to Whites demands the same willingness to bear the cross as King's statement to the Black pastor in 1963.

Finally, another issue that inhibits some White ministers from bringing race into the pulpit is that they themselves do not see racial prejudice as a major theological concern. Sometimes matters of racial justice are seen as social or political issues that are best dealt with in venues outside of the institutional church. In the past, people, especially those supportive of the status quo or reluctant to challenge it, have contended that racial matters will not find solution in political efforts but by a change of individuals' hearts. "One cannot legislate morality" is often the manner of summing up this perspective. But we cannot so easily separate racial justice as a purely "moral" or "spiritual" concern that is not affixed to any political and economic efforts.

In the previous chapter, Manis did a magnificent job pointing out how inseparable from the teachings of Moses, Christ, and Muhammad is the admonition to love and do justice to one's neighbor regardless of race. Let me underscore and add to my colleague's exposition that racial slavery and segregation have done deep damage to social relations involving Blacks and Whites, both in society at large and in the church itself. Relegating slavery for the most part to African Americans, segregating people from personal and social contact with each other on the basis of race, and promoting the corollary doctrines of racial inferiority and racial superiority have sketched into the minds of Americans serious obstacles to a sense of genuine racial inclusion and equality. While we understand what people mean when they exclaim, "I do not have a racist bone in my body," the reality is that it is difficult for any

American to escape the stain of racial prejudice. Hence, some people have blind spots when it comes to facing the problem of race, and others have sometimes quite overtly embraced a racist approach to Christianity, Islam, or Judaism that in some instances fosters rather that contradicts racial prejudice.

SOME CHALLENGES FOR
AFRICAN AMERICAN CLERGY:
TERMS AND HISTORICAL BACKGROUND

Black clergy must continue to do what they have historically done so well: emphasize both liberation from oppression and reconciliation between the races; the universality of the Gospel and the particularity of Black people's struggle in the context of the Gospel; the promotion of racial progress along with the affirming love for all of God's peoples. Let us define and give some background for these terms: liberation, reconciliation, universality, particularity, love of God, love of neighbor.

When we think about racism and the quest for racial justice in this country there are two words that are helpful: *liberation* and *reconciliation*. In the late 1960s, the late James H. Cone pioneered the academic study of Black Theology in part by the publication of a book, *Black Theology and Black Power*, which was followed by other publications from Cone and other theologians and ethicists. Similar to the earlier Social Gospel Theology heralded in the late nineteenth and early twentieth century by notables such as Walter Rauschenbusch and Washington Gladden, Black Theology believes that the construction of a just social order is central to the Christian mission, that Christianity is not just a matter of an individual's relationship with God but also that Christians have the obligation to construct a just social order. More specifically, Black Theology asserts that at the heart of the Christian gospel is the mandate to work for the freedom of Black people from all social, political, and economic oppression. Cone, as other Black Theologians, claims that any version of the Gospel that does not address as a vital concern the freedom of Black people from oppression is not true to the Gospel of Christ. One of the greatest indictments Black Theologians have made against the church and the nation is that Christian leaders have spent so little time and energy dealing with the central social issue in American history and culture—race—as a biblical, theological, and ethical concern, especially pertaining to the treatment of Blacks. The White Christian churches have not condemned racism or provided guidance to the church and the nation about obliterating it.[62]

There were many responses to the theological claims of Cone, from Whites and Blacks, from those supportive of this type of liberationist approach to the gospel and those who opposed this interpretation of the Christian message. One reply to Cone came from a fellow Black Theologian, J. Deotis Roberts, who seconded Cone's understanding that Christianity calls for the liberation of Black people but who also maintained that his theological colleague had omitted sufficient emphasis on another aspect of the Christian message—reconciliation. In addition to the liberation of people from oppression, according to Roberts, the goal of Black Theology must be reconciliation of the oppressed and the oppressor.[63]

This same model of liberation versus liberation-and-reconciliation is informative for our purposes regarding Black clergy bringing the issue of race into the pulpit. On one hand, Black ministers have to be concerned about liberation, freeing people from the racially oppressive structures of society; on the other hand, they must be true to Christianity's call for reconciliation between the races. In some instances there is the need to address first and foremost liberation, freedom from injustice. At other times there is the need to emphasize the unity of humanity, oppressed and oppressor, Black and White. To phrase it another way, Black clergy and other Christians must deal with the particularity of

Black people's concerns; concomitantly, they must remember the universality of the Gospel that includes all of humanity. Some people would say that we cannot focus so much on liberation, placing particular emphasis on freeing Black people, that we lose sight of the universality of the Gospel, the need for humans to reconcile with each other in recognition of their common humanity. Likewise, others would say we should not focus on reconciliation or the universality of the Christian message while ignoring particular needs of Black people. It is possible to concentrate our attention so much on a particular people that we begin to advance a racialism at odds with the Gospel or our expressed political goals. Similarly, it is possible to focus on the universality of the Gospel in a manner that ignores pressing needs of Black people.

Historically, and I believe currently, the Black church tradition has overwhelmingly maintained the universality of the Gospel even amid the most intense struggles for particular racial justice concerns. The overwhelming goal of most Black Americans, historically speaking, has been inclusion within the general body politic rather than separation from it, though there have been separatist movements. For the most part, Black Christians, in the words of the African Methodist Episcopal Church's official motto, have embraced the principle, "The Fatherhood of God and the Brotherhood of Man," or, using more inclusive language, the common parentage of God and the siblinghood of all humanity. Actually, the current motto, which maintains the same commitment to humanity's commonality and siblinghood, is "God Our Father, Christ Our Redeemer, the Holy Spirit Our Comforter, and Humankind Our Family."[64]

Before, during, and especially after the Civil War, many Black Christians believed that they could not remain in the same local congregations as Whites. They refused to continue under the same racially discriminatory conditions that entailed things such as reluctance to ordain Blacks as clergy, segregation in worship service, and inattention to the spiritual and temporal needs of Blacks. Though they established separate congregations, associations, conventions, and denominations, Black church people always remained open to interracial cooperation in religious affairs, such as mission work. Black Christians took pride in saying that they did not practice a *caste* Christianity that permitted treating people differently on the basis of race, color, and other physical traits. Far from seeing themselves as imitators of White Christianity, Black Christians understood themselves as practicing true Christianity and pursuing genuine democracy. In perhaps the greatest, most effective movement toward racial justice and equality in the US, the modern Civil Rights Movement, leaders such as Martin Luther King Jr. were able to bring together Black Christians and many White Christians based on the principles of universal siblinghood.

Even Malcolm X in his later years demonstrated universality in his approach to religion. Prior to 1964 he was a dedicated member of the Nation of Islam, which at the time advocated racial separation on the basis of the inherent "devilishness" of White people and the inherent (though not always practiced) "Muslimhood" or righteousness of Black people. Later, however, Malcolm X embraced traditional Islam, which like Christianity and Judaism denounces racism of any type. He remained a Black nationalist calling for the solidarity of Black people and respect for Black history and culture both globally and in the US, as expressed in the formation of the all-black Organization of Afro-American Unity. Yet he rejected earlier racist teachings regarding Whites and Blacks and founded the Muslim Mosque, Inc., which was inclusive of all races. On the one hand, he emphasized the need for racial particularity; on the other hand, he embraced the principle of universal siblinghood of humanity.[65] The point, again, is that the Black church and more broadly the Black religious tradition have generally practiced a non-racist interpretation of faith.

Another approach to the discussion of Black clergy and race is to understand the solution to the problem of combatting racism in terms of external and internal dynamics. Externally, race impacts the Black community as a force acting upon it. The American economic and political establishments have generally been external to the Black community. Hence, to remove oppression it is necessary to contest external powers, that is, Whites. Yet there is also an internal dimension to our struggle, dealing with those actions, attitudes, and conditions within the Black community that militate against liberation and those that serve no helpful function in securing freedom. Black clergypeople have little difficulty bringing race into the pulpit relative to preaching racial reconciliation and advocating efforts to secure racial freedom. But there are internal challenges facing the Black church and community that need addressing more forcefully should we wish to maximize the church's potential in liberating Black people.

CHALLENGES FOR AFRICAN AMERICAN CLERGY: SOME SPECIFIC ISSUES

Perhaps the major issue facing the Black church is the same problem facing practically all other American religious bodies: falling memberships and participation. Official statistics inform us that overall, 75 percent or three-fourths of adults in the US identified Christianity as their religion. This is certainly a large share of the population, but two points bear noting. First, this 75 percent represents a steady decline in Christian identification in the US: it was 78 percent in 2012, which was a decrease from 81.6 percent in 2001 and 85 percent in 1990. Over a fifteen-year period there has been a decrease of 10 percentage points of adults self-identifying as Christians. Second, identification with Christianity does not necessarily equal intensity of faith commitment. If congregational membership is a vital indicator of faith intensity, then we should note that there is a minus 13 percentage points between those who self-identify as Christians and those who affiliate with specific church congregations. If we add to church membership the question of regular attendance, we are likely to see another declining percentage. Of course, those of us who attend church regularly have observed what statistics affirm: church attendance is declining in many churches, particularly among those under 50 years of age.[66]

There are many reasons for this declining identification with and participation in church, including a rise in agnostic and even atheistic beliefs; a preference for what is often termed a "spiritual" rather than a more "institution-affiliated traditional" approach; and alignment with other religions. There could in future years be a return to organized Christianity because of a general revival; and often people return to more formalized religion as they grow older. But we must ask ourselves, specifically as it relates to the Black community, what is the impact of declining church affiliation and attendance? There is of course the question of people's spiritual well-being and the quality of their personal and family lives. Will there be an increase in rates of depression or suicide? Will the family structure (understood here as the two-parent, heterosexual unit) continue to fracture? Even more specific for our purposes in these pages, how will declining church affiliation and participation affect the quest for racial justice and interracial reconciliation?

Whatever one's personal religious views, historical and sociological analyses clearly reveal that church life for African Americans, among other things, has been (a) central to quests to end or deal with the effects of racial slavery; (b) an alternative institution wherein Blacks affirmed their identity, purpose, and worth in the midst of a larger society that militated against the integrity of Black humanity; (c) key in formation and maintenance of institutions and activities for social, economic, and political advancement, including educational institutions, fraternities and sororities, banks, insurance companies, newspapers, racial improvement associations;

and (d) a crucial support for political campaigns with agendas deemed beneficial to racial advancement and interracial relations.[67] Some of us who are Black Southerners from small towns and rural areas (and I suspect some Whites as well) are old enough to remember attending grade schools whose lands and properties were owned by the local church or church conference though the instructional staff received compensation from the state. How could we possibly explain the organization, execution, and successes of the modern Civil Rights Movement apart from the faith, courage, organization, and material support of the church? With a continuing decline in church affiliation, will the economic and political progress of Blacks continue, or will even the current status of Blacks—however far from our goals of a free and equal society— face peril?

The Black church remains one of few Black institutions in society that African Americans own and operate. If fewer people affiliate with the Black church, how will that affect their freedom to exercise racial identity and solidarity? One could argue that there are indications that the future promises an increase in the number and membership of mainly Black Islamic congregations and, consequently, a greater social, economic, and political role for them that will offset such loss of influence of Black churches. But I wonder if Islam in America, Black and non-Black, is not also facing a decline of membership, and even if not, whether the increase will match the decline among Christian congregations.

A second major problem facing the Black church and community is the breakdown of the Black family, a momentous problem to which Black clergy and the African American church must speak much more forcefully than they have to this point. J. Patrick Moynihan, a member of the administrative team of President Lyndon B. Johnson and in later years a distinguished United States Senator from New York, warned during the middle 1960s that the Black family was headed toward a matriarchy with the high rate of out of wedlock births, which at that time stood around 20 percent. Many if not most people in the civil rights community dismissed his report as racist or insulting to the Black family, as a matter that was being exaggerated to the detriment of Black people. During an age when the nation was passing from legal segregation to greater desegregation, many Blacks and White liberals did not want to concede that Black family life was different from White family life. Even if one is successful in finding in Moynihan's writings and methodology some reflection of racial bias or insensitivity, that would not change the truth of his overall observation—the two-parent Black family is disappearing.[68]

As affirmed by the 2010 study, the *Moynihan Report Revisited*,[69] the rate of out of wedlock births among non-Hispanic Blacks had risen to 73 percent. Of course, the *Revisited* report revealed that Black people are not the only racial-ethnic group struggling with this problem. Around 29 percent of White and about 53 percent of Latino/Hispanic babies were born to single parents, both of these also representing significant increases since the 1960s. Given the systematic racial bias against Black people and the fact that the single-parent birth rate is so much higher for them than for either of the other two groups, this problem has a larger negative impact on the Black community, which among the three racial-ethnic groups can least afford more obstacles on their road to justice and equity.

As suggested above, we cannot totally separate the single-parent household problem among Blacks from the context of the larger American society. Beginning in the 1960s there was a significant change in sexual mores and expressions from former decades. For example, unwed motherhood became less of a stigma than in previous times. Artificial birth control in the 1960s and legalized abortion in the 1970s became more accessible and normative among Americans. The women's or feminist movement underscored a more open approach to sexuality and, with additional and more equitable employment opportunities, rendered women more financially independent and therefore afforded them more flexibility regarding marriage and family. With greater educational attainment along with these other factors, it is not surprising that more women would opt to remain single, delay marriage, or be more particular with their choices. The same factors that contributed to greater freedom, flexibility, delay, and reticence on the part of women applied in some degree to men as well. In addition, especially in the African American community, increased rates of incarceration—because of higher levels of poverty and fewer employment opportunities, discrimination by law enforcement and in the criminal justice system, over-policing of Black communities, and laws that disproportionately targeted Black populations—reduced the availability of marriageable males.

We must face the tragic fact that the two-parent Black family in the United States is suffering immensely because of internal, external, and societal factors. An alternative to the above argument is that it overlooks the obvious: the American family, Black and White, is not necessarily disappearing but diversifying. There are equally satisfying alternatives, this position holds, to the traditional heterosexual, two-parent family, which is often oppressive to women and non-heterosexual people. For example, some religious people and organizations endorse the moral acceptability of same-sex marriages and unions.[70] Many religious opponents who raise moral objections to such relationships nonetheless champion the constitutional rights of people so inclined and, hence, the necessity for government recognition of such marriages and unions. But even allowing for the existence of same-sex households does not solve the problem of single-parent families. Consistently practicing homosexuals are numerous but still a small percentage of the overall population, Black or White. Unmarried heterosexual parents of children do not for the most part enter into same-sex relationships subsequent to giving birth. Rather, those who remain unmarried choose one or more of the following heterosexual paths: remain single with few or no romantic engagements, enter long-term unmarried relationships, or have serial relationships. To be sure, children from single-parent homes often do well, some exceedingly so, according to accepted indicators of success; and having two parents does not exempt some children from personal, legal, and societal problems.

Still, a strong correlation exists between single parenthood and conditions such as poverty, low educational attainment, legal difficulties, and certain antisocial or counterproductive behavior. Statistics and experience, not to mention religious teaching, tell us that children desire and need two-parent, stable homes. Boys require fathers to model manhood; girls need to experience the unconditional love of males in the form of fathers. Girls require mothers to model womanhood; boys need to experience the unconditional love of females in the form of mothers. It is the position of this writer that if we are to maximize opportunities for advancement toward racial justice and equity, the Black community will have to address this issue. Though many who do not see the imperative of two-parent homes may continue to register their opposition, ministers must courageously and consistently address this major problem of the Black family, prescribing and endorsing religiously acceptable solutions.

A related problem to the decline of the two-parent family is the perilous state of Black men and boys in our society. It is often an accepted truism that Black women are doubly oppressed—as Blacks and as women—and, hence, they face altogether more oppression than their male counterparts. That is debatable. One thing statistically clear, however, is that considering some of the major indicators of achievement, girls and women generally fare much better than boys and men: in terms of educational achievement, such as high school graduation rates, college attendance, and the attainment of bachelors, masters, and doctorate degrees; negative encounters with law enforcement and the criminal justice system; victims of homicide; and police shootings and other violence perpetuated against them. Many of the above points regarding the manner in which males are losing or have lost ground compared to females are also descriptive of Whites and other racial-ethnic groups in the US. Something perhaps statistically harder to pinpoint that signals the precarious state of being a Black male is general society's greater fear and loathing of the African American male's presence in a variety of contexts.

This disparity between males and females is also found in the church. As has been true in Christian congregations historically, there continues to be a gender imbalance with greater numbers of females in church attendance and participation. I would not be surprised if this lack of male affiliation is even greater among Black Christians compared with White counterparts. Up to and including the present day, males generally exercised higher, more authoritative offices in the churches, such as pastors, priests, bishops, and convention presidents. Yet this situation is changing, with greater numbers of women entering the ordained ministry in both historically Black and non-Black denominations. Just as women have advanced considerably in the educational realm, it is possible that the same is occurring in religious institutions, Black and White. The question is, will we see an even greater decline of male presence and influence in the churches, particularly Black churches? How will the absence of male presence affect family, society, and quests for racial justice and equity? How does the absence of males at the current levels impact family, society, and the church's role in seeking racial advancement?

Why do we have such an absence, and perhaps a growing absence, of males in our churches? More specifically for this chapter section, various explanations can be advanced for the absence of males in Black churches. A more general observation, one indicated above, is that Christianity has long seemingly attracted more women than men. Is there something about the manner in which the faith is presented that does not attract men as readily as women? Around the beginning of the 1800s, American religious leaders were moving away from an earlier idea that women were often not as good at being Christians as men and were embracing the contrary position that women were more suited for religion than men. The roles of the Christian wife and mother became key in the American Christian tradition during the nineteenth century. As the century wore on, females and males embraced the concept of "the cult of true womanhood," believing that Christian women not only played special roles in family and church but had unique contributions to make in the public sphere, such as in temperance reform efforts and in foreign or overseas missions. While many of these advocates were not feminists, or even suffragists, they vigorously supported women's activities in church and society. Desiring greater male participation in the churches, some clergymen in the late nineteenth and early twentieth century America argued for a presentation of the faith with more direct appeals to masculinity, though their position does not appear to have dislodged the idea of the vital role of Christian women in the family.[71]

Perhaps illustrative of some of the discussion above, American Black males appear to be more attracted to Islam than Black females. Whether they embrace Islam or not, maybe many Black males, particularly in contexts where they more often encounter violence from criminals or the police, are not inclined to the Christian virtues of forgiveness, nonviolence, and humility. At any rate, Black clergy need to address much more specifically and systematically this gender imbalance in their churches. First, they should do so out of pastoral concern for the entirety of the people, both males and females. Second, I suggest that greater gender balance influences how and to what extent the church addresses all the problems facing the whole Black community.

To reiterate, the war against racial prejudice in the US has to be continually fought along two fronts: externally and internally. Externally, Blacks and White supporters must continue to challenge the social, economic, and political structures that oppose, hinder, and seek to overturn efforts to eliminate racial oppression, including but not limited to continued job discrimination in hiring and promotion, low levels of support for Black education, disparate and selected law enforcement and police brutality, and voter suppression. But this chapter has also attempted to demonstrate the internal challenges Black people face, problems that require much effort to fix from the inside. Above we have discussed declining church attendance and participation, the breakdown of the two-parent Black family, and the situation facing Black boys and men. There are a host of other issues deserving attention, including alcohol and drug addiction, racial identity and solidarity, education, employment, poverty, homelessness and hunger, crime and violence.

The problem with being racially self-critical about the community or religious and other forms of leadership in general is that one involuntarily invites attacks both externally and internally. Externally, opponents of racial justice and advancement can utilize discussion of weaknesses and need for corrections as indicators of Black unworthiness or as confirmation of their racism. Internally, there are problems as well. One in particular I wish to address is the charge from Black people and liberal Whites often directed toward other Blacks advancing internal critiques—that they are pushing "the politics of respectability" or "respectability politics." Crudely put, it is a criticism similar to a situation wherein one Black child says to another who is studious, appropriately dressed, or well behaved, "You are acting White."

The concept of the politics of respectability or respectability politics seems to have its origins in the work by Evelyn Brooks Higginbotham examining the women's movement among Baptist church women between 1880 and 1920. In chapter 7 of that excellent study, now a classic, Higginbotham sets forth a major underlying theology and philosophy behind the feminist or women-affirming movements and activities of leaders and spokespeople such as Nannie Helen Burroughs. Black and White Christians shared the same beliefs, ideals, and goals regarding the importance of Christianity and the usefulness of the faith in terms of morals and ethics to uplift humanity in political and economic as well as spiritual terms. Honesty, hard work, appropriate dress, high morals, education, etc. were key elements for achieving practical success and progress, both for individuals and for races of people. Higginbotham seems to suggest that the perspectives and actions of these early Black women leaders were open to the critique that they did not understand, fully appreciate, or fail to communicate that overarching sociopolitical structural aspects of society could blunt individual and racial progress even when people embraced the ideals of Christianity or demonstrated their moral worth as individuals. Furthermore, individuals and groups espousing such a politics of respectability often adopted an elitist attitude toward the masses of the people and themselves exercised some social oppression toward their fellow Blacks. In other words, behaving like Whites or in ways that Whites approved was no guarantee of success and could even be a means of maintaining an oppressive social structure within the race.[72]

Of course, there is much truth in Higginbotham's historical and analytical study. But I would argue that subsequent scholars, community leaders, and others have taken this critique far beyond the author's original point(s). The critiques made in opposition to those placing great emphasis on the quest for educational excellence, worthy ambition, appropriate dress, and respectful behavior have gone from the original, "No matter how much our behavior mirrors that of Whites, there is no guarantee of Black acceptance by Whites" to "If Black people's goals and behavior mirror that of

Whites, then something is wrong." Education excellence, ambition, proper attire, and decent behavior do not guarantee personal success or racial liberation, but they do help! Educational indifference and poor performance, unworthy ambition, improper and inappropriate attire, and indecent behavior must assuredly make both the personal and racial struggle for success and freedom much more difficult. Randall Kennedy's article in *Harper's Magazine*, published in October 2015, made a compelling case for a "progressive defense of respectability politics." One of his most piercing points was that some who decry respectability politics, such as college professors and media commentators in their personal and professional lives, do in fact abide strictly by respectability elements, such as achieving academic excellence, having superb command of the English language, and wearing proper and acceptable attire.[73]

Our Black clergy must continue to proclaim and reiterate that there are certain values and behaviors that are universally respected and expected around the world. The early Black women leaders whom Higginbotham studied did not promote hard work and high moral character simply because they were attempting to impress White people based on the belief that they would thereby gain acceptance by Whites. Yes, there is something to be said about modeling correct behavior as a demonstration that Blacks could be just as upright as any other race. But more than that, these mothers (and fathers) believed in certain bedrock principles because of their worldview, their religious outlook on life. In other words, they taught the principles of respectability not primarily because they wanted to please Whites but because they wanted to obey and glorify God. In many ways—such as the rejection of racism and the embrace of human siblinghood—they were hoping that Whites would imitate them! I agree with these women leaders that when people divorce moral character and initiative from the racial struggle or any other endeavor, then any success or freedom will have much emptiness and lack of direction. That is an ongoing danger posed by critics of the politics of respectability.

To conclude, this chapter has attempted to underscore Professor Manis's preceding chapter arguing the absolute necessity of bringing the discussion of race and racial justice into the pulpit. It is imperative that Black and White clergy, Christian and Jews and Muslims, make more intentional, concerted efforts to bring their congregants into a stronger focus on the matter of race because of its social, economic, political, and religious importance. In terms of addressing racial injustice and devising and following courses of action that derail prejudice, misunderstanding, segregation, and economic injustice, White clergy perhaps face the greatest challenges inside their churches. Black clergy, however, have their own challenges inside the churches, a few of which this chapter has briefly outlined: declining church attention and participation (as with other racial-ethnic groups), the breakdown of the two-parent Black family, and issues facing Black males in particular. In addition to these issues and others—such as crime and violence, domestic abuse, attaining educational parity, and the high rate of incarceration—Black clergy must be prepared to resist efforts to walk away from historically demonstrable solutions because of criticisms leveled at them for practicing respectability politics. Of course, many problems regarding the fight against racism faced by White and Black clergy overlap and transcend racial lines. A central point of this chapter is that bringing race into the pulpit is a challenge for all clergy, but one that must be met if we are to have a more just society and more righteous religious communities.

PART II

PROPHETIC UTTERANCES ON RACE: MINISTRIES OF RACIAL RECONCILIATION

3

A Fire No Water Can Put Out

The Reverend Dr. Tim Bagwell, Pastor of
Centenary United Methodist Church

Derwin Gray writes that, if you want to see racism and oppression, all you have to do is look at the culture in which Jesus grew up. In the mind of the Jew living at the time of Jesus, Gentiles (Africans, Romans, Greeks, Syrians, Asians, etc.) were going to burn in the fires of hell. If a Jewish person married a Gentile person, the Jewish parents held a funeral service for their child because, in their minds, the child had died. There was no mixing of different peoples without severe consequences.

There was enough hatred for all to be touched by it. Jews hated the Gentiles. Gentiles hated the Jews. Jews hated the Samaritans. Samaritans hated the Jews. Society was divided. The side of the tracks you lived on defined your hopes and dreams. Jews profiled those who were different. And in return, Jews were profiled by all those they profiled. Jesus grew up in an incredibly racist culture...not unlike our culture in modern-day Macon, Georgia.

Our beloved Macon—my, how we have struggled with racism! We don't have time to tell the whole story today, but let's look at part of the story. Macon high schools from the past: Miller, Lanier, Willingham, McElvoy, Ballard Hudson. Divided by race. There was fear and mistrust. Neighborhoods were destroyed in

Macon because of racism. We are worshiping today in one of those neighborhoods. At one time, Centenary Church was one of the largest in this city. Six hundred people once regularly worshiped here. In the original architectural design of this building, this wall was removed so the crowds would spill out into what we call the round room. Who worshiped here? White people. Centenary was not inclusive, just as the city was not inclusive.

Huguenin Heights, Beall's Hill, Pleasant Hill, and Intown Macon were once flourishing communities. I-75 was built in the 1960s. While improving national transportation and access, I-75 cut a canyon through Macon, Georgia, that destroyed neighborhoods and accelerated the racial divide. There was an exodus of White people because of fear. Racism gripped the heart of our city. White people fled to sub-south and north and west, seeking what they thought was the Promised Land. They were afraid to live with Black neighbors. Beall's Hill was essentially abandoned. It became the most notorious crack community in Macon. Centenary Church became a mere shadow of what it was formerly, one of the many victims of White flight.

Now, back to Jesus and racism. Early Christians often bore the name "People of the Way." These Christians emerged in the first century living into a different racial ethic. They were radically different from the culture around them. The most noticeable difference between the early church (People of the Way) and the surrounding culture is that the Christians rejected racism and profiling as the standard on which their lives would be built. The early Christians viewed themselves as part of the same family…a family made up of Jews, Gentiles, slaves, free, rich, poor, male, female. They gathered together, ate together, partied together, worshiped together. What prompted the tearing down of the walls in the early church? It was Jesus! Jesus lived his life reaching across barriers and inviting those outside to come inside. Jesus developed meaningful relationships with Gentiles, Samaritans, women, the outcast, the poor, the rich. Everyone was welcome! Doors were thrown open! Jesus never shut the door in anyone's face because to him EVERYONE was welcome.

August is the fiftieth anniversary of the Poor People's March. Campaigning at the historic 1963 March on Washington, Dr. Martin Luther King Jr. delivered his most famous speech in Washington, DC, on August 28, 1963. The words of the "I Have a Dream Speech" were eloquent and unforgettable. Give ear as Joel Chambliss and I take you on a journey with just an excerpt of that famous speech. [From this point, the preacher and musician will alternate the Word spoken with the Word sung.]

TIM: King's voice rings out—I am not unmindful that some of you have come here out of great trials and tribulations. Some of you have come fresh from narrow cells. Some of you have come from areas where your quest for freedom left you battered by the storms of persecution and staggered by the winds of police brutality. You have been the veterans of creative suffering. Continue to work with the faith that unearned suffering is redemptive.... Go back to Mississippi, go back to Alabama, go back to Georgia, go back to Louisiana, go back to the slums and ghettos of our northern cities, knowing that somehow this situation can and will be changed. Let us not wallow in the valley of despair.

JOEL: *We shall overcome. We shall overcome. Oh, deep in my heart, I do believe, we shall overcome someday.*

TIM: I say to you today, my friends, that in spite of the difficulties and frustrations of the moment, I still have a dream. It is a dream deeply rooted in the American dream....I have a dream that one day this nation will rise up and live out the true meaning of its creed: "We hold these truths to be self-evident: that all men are created equal."

JOEL: *We are not afraid. We are not afraid. Oh, deep in my heart, I do believe, we are not afraid today.*

TIM: I have a dream that one day on the red hills of Georgia the sons of former slaves and the sons of former slave owners will be able to sit down together at a table of brotherhood.
I have a dream that one day even the state of Mississippi, a desert state, sweltering with the heat of injustice and oppression, will be transformed into an oasis of freedom and justice.
I have a dream that my four children will one day live in a nation where they will not be judged by the color of their skin but by the content of their character.
I have a dream today.

JOEL oel: *Ain't gonna let nobody turn me 'round, turn me 'round, turn me 'round. Ain't gonna let nobody turn me 'round. I'm gonna keep on walkin', keep on talkin', marchin' up to Freedomland.*

TIM: I have a dream that one day the state of Alabama, whose governor's lips are presently dripping with the words of interposition and nullification, will be transformed into a situation where little black boys and black girls will be able to join hands with little white boys and white girls and walk together as sisters and brothers.

JOEL: *We'll walk hand in hand. We'll walk hand in hand. Oh, deep in my heart, I do believe, we shall overcome someday.*

TIM: I have a dream today.
I have a dream that one day every valley shall be exalted, every hill and mountain shall be made low, the rough places will be made

plain, and the crooked places will be made straight, and the glory of the Lord shall be revealed, and all flesh shall see it together.

JOEL: *Ain't gonna let nobody turn me 'round, turn me 'round, turn me 'round. Ain't gonna let nobody turn me 'round. I'm gonna keep on walkin', keep on talkin', marchin' up to Freedomland.*

[Now **TIM** resumes his sermon.] The values of the Civil Rights Movement are the values of Jesus and the early church. The values of the Civil Rights Movement are the values of the Apostle Paul, who wrote, "There is neither Jew, Gentile, slave, free, rich, poor, male, female…all are one in Jesus Christ" (see Gal 3:28). Christians cannot be Christian apart from an acceptance of a diverse community. This is what defined the early church: Jews and Gentiles and Samaritans eating together, working together, greeting one another with a holy kiss, raising their children together, taking care of one another, marrying one another, and burying one another. Classes and differences disappeared.

We long to live into a new day in Macon. Why are Stacey Harwell and Helen Willoughby teaching a course about Dr. Martin Luther King Jr. during the months of August and September? Because we are seeking to live into the Kingdom of God! Why do I preach this sermon? Because the subject matter cannot be ignored. Jesus lived in an incredibly racist culture, but he refused to be defined by it. We live in an incredibly racist culture! But this is Centenary United Methodist Church, where we refuse to be defined by the culture! We reach for diversity. We want to include all! And all means all. We are defined by the dialogue! In the heartbeat of Centenary is a fire that no water can put out! Thanks be to God.

(1) Hear this, all you peoples; give ear, all inhabitants of the world, (2) both low and high, rich and poor together. (3) My mouth shall speak wisdom; the meditation of my heart shall be un-

derstanding. (4) I will incline my ear to a proverb; I will solve my riddle to the music of the harp. (5) Why should I fear in times of trouble, when the iniquity of my persecutors surrounds me, (6) those who trust in their wealth and boast of the abundance of their riches? (Psalm 49:1–6)

Out of what does this conversation about racism come? How do we face what seems to be a paralyzing and overwhelming issue: racism in our lives and racism in Macon? What is our starting point? First, meditation. The psalmist says, "the meditation of my heart shall be understanding... I will solve my riddle to the music of the harp."

Let's hear a little harp music from Jerry and Philip. We are in the process of meditating on the issue of racism in Macon. Is it ludicrous, insane that meditation and worship is the beginning? Maybe, but it is the starting point according to the psalmist. Worship brings us close to the heart of God. When you are standing close to the heart of God, there is no room for racism! Jesus stood close to the heart of God...that is why he invited everyone to the party. Robert Frost stated that the most profane word in the English language is "exclusive." Martin Luther King, Fred Shuttlesworth, and most of the heroes of the Civil Rights Movement came out of the church. Standing near to the heart of God enabled them to call us to a new racial ethic. How is the riddle to be solved? To the music of the harp. Racism and the walls that divide us are spiritual issues. "My mouth shall speak wisdom; the meditation of my heart shall be understanding.... I will solve my riddle to the music of the harp."

In February of 1968, shortly before his assassination, King returned home to Montgomery, Alabama, where his career in the Black freedom struggle had begun. Addressing a mass meeting, he fell into reverie and memories of Birmingham and the battle with Bull Connor, who abused the freedom marchers by turning dogs loose on them and spraying them with fire hoses. Here is what

King said: "...And then ol' Bull would say as we kept moving, 'Turn on the fire hoses,' and they did turn 'em on. But what they didn't know was that we had a fire that no water could put out."

JOEL: *Woke up this morning with my mind stayed on freedom. Woke up this morning with my mind stayed on freedom. Woke up this morning with my mind stayed on freedom. Hallelu, Hallelu, Hallelujah!*

4

Reconciliation: An Islamic Perspective

Imam Adam Fofana,
Islamic Center of Middle Georgia

بسم الله الرحمن الرحيم
In the Name of Allah the Merciful the Beneficent

First Khutbah (Sermon): The word *reconciliation* means reestablishment of friendly relations after the period of misunderstanding. It also means to end the estrangement between humans and their Creator (Allah SWT the Almighty God), between human and human, and between humans and the rest of the creations of (Allah SWT the Almighty God).[74]

According to the *Merriam-Webster* dictionary, the word *reconciliation* means the act of causing two people or groups to become friendly again after an argument or disagreement.[75] The Qur'anic word for the reconciliation in Arabic is (المصالحة Al-Musalahah). The root word is (صلح: salaha), meaning to improve something and make it better. It is from this root verb that the word (صالح) with the letter Alif (ا) was developed. Adding the Alif signifies that two parties simultaneously were engaged in making this effort to improve the situation and make it better.[76] In the terminology, it means to pardon your right or part of it in order to establish a new relation and friendship.

According to Islam, humans were created by (Allah SWT the Almighty God), and their creator put in their DNA from day one the principle of making a mistake and learning from their mistakes. It is due to this quality that humans become the best among all the creations of (Allah SWT the Almighty God), and because of this fact humans were given the leadership over the rest of Allah's creations.

Islam teaches us that there are three conscious creations of (Allah SWT the Almighty God). The first category is the creation that cannot make a mistake because they don't have free will and they are called Angels (الملائكة). The second category is creations that make mistakes because they have free will but never seek to correct their mistakes or learn from them. These creations are called Shayateen (الشياطين), the devils. The third category is the creations that make mistakes and continue to make mistakes, but they learn from them and make changes. These creations are (الإنسان), the humans. Therefore, these last creations are the ones who can make sense of life and make life better because of this unique ability.

The first ever incident Qur'an narrated about this was the case of the first man Allah created, Adam (AS).[77] The Holy Qur'an says:

> Behold thy Lord said to the angels: "I will create a viceregent on earth." They said "Wilt thou place therein one who will make mischief therein and shed blood? Whilst we do celebrate Thy praises and glorify Thy holy (name)?" He said: "I know what ye know not." (30) And He taught Adam the names of all things; then He placed them before the angels and said: "Tell Me the names of these if ye are right." (31) They said: "Glory to Thee: of knowledge we have none, save that Thou hast taught us: in truth it is Thou who art perfect in knowledge and wisdom." (32) He said: "O Adam! tell them their names." When he had told them their names, Allah said: "Did I not tell you that I know the secrets of heaven and earth, and I know what ye reveal and what ye conceal?" (33) And behold We said

to the angels: "Bow down to Adam"; and they bowed down: not so Iblis: he refused and was haughty: he was of those who reject Faith. (34) We said: "O Adam! dwell thou and thy wife in the Garden and eat of the bountiful things therein as (where and when) ye will; but approach not this tree, or ye run into harm and transgression." (35) Then did Satan make them slip from the (Garden) and get them out of the state (of felicity) in which they had been. We said: "Get ye down all (ye people) with enmity between yourselves. On earth will be your dwelling place and your means of livelihood for a time." (36) Then learnt Adam from his Lord words of inspiration and his Lord turned toward him; for He is Oft-Returning Most Merciful. (37) We said: "Get ye down all from here; and if, as is sure, there comes to you guidance from Me" whosoever follows My guidance on them shall be no fear, nor shall they grieve. (38) "But those who reject Faith and belie Our Signs, they shall be Companions of the Fire; they shall abide therein." (39) (Qur'an, Surah Al-Baqarah 2.30–39)

So by deceit he brought about their fall: when they tasted of the tree, their shame became manifest to them, and they began to sew together the leaves of the Garden over their bodies. And their Lord called unto them: "Did I not forbid you that tree and tell you that Satan was an avowed enemy unto you?" (22) They said: "Our Lord! we have wronged our own souls: if Thou forgive us not and bestow not upon us Thy Mercy we shall certainly be lost." (23) (Qur'an, Surah Al-Araf 2.22–23)

Islam does not believe in original sin, but it believes in original mistakes that took place in the beginning of the creation and the original reconciliation that followed it immediately with (Allah SWT the Almighty God). It was this unique ability of humans' father Adam to reconcile his differences with (Allah SWT the Almighty God) that made him better than Shaytan (Satan)—the cursed devil—who never seeks to reconcile with his Lord; therefore, he and whoever follow his example were cursed forever. As a result of this incident, (Allah SWT the Almighty God) promised Adam and his children his forgiveness and endless love as long as they make mistakes, learn from their mistakes, and reconcile with Allah. It is based on this principle that human life continues to evolve and improve, and the endless love of (Allah SWT the Almighty God) continues to accompany us to the new discoveries, new improvement, and new life.

You may want to look back to the past hundred years and see how far we have come, from tools to the wheels, to the machines, to the computer and smart phones, from the error of one man trying to jump from the top of the building to a five hundred passenger jumbo airplane in the sky—all are based on trial and error. The question is: "When did the first error take place?" It took place against (Allah SWT the Almighty God), and therefore he made it our destiny in life that we will continue to make mistakes. But as long as we are willing to learn from them, the Almighty will show us the way to do better. As this is true in the material world, it is also true in the spiritual world. The concept of forgiveness and redemption are means to create anew a spiritual human who is willing to do it better till he meets his Lord in paradise.

RECONCILIATION AMONG HUMANS

If humans can make mistakes against (Allah SWT the Almighty God), it is possible that they can also make mistakes toward their fellow human beings. If the humans can reconcile with (Allah SWT the Almighty God), it is also true that they can reconcile with one another about their past mistakes. The types of errors that humans commit against their fellow humans are varied. The list includes, but is not limited to the following:

Human rights abuses
Oppression
Aggression

Slavery
Exploitation
Injustice
Torture
Wrongful imprisonment
Wrongful seizure of money/property etc.
Internal fights
Civil war (which may involve killing innocents and
    causing destruction)

Historical accounts have shown us many examples of the above-mentioned errors. However, these accounts also proves to us that each time such mistakes were corrected and lessons were learned, human life has always improved and become better. Each time such mistakes were ignored and not corrected, human life suffered. The best example that Qur'an teaches in this regard is the story of prophet Yusuf (AS) or Joseph. Surah 12 of the Qur'an, which is about 111 verses, explains specifically about this incident. In this story, Joseph was wronged by his own brothers who were jealous of him, plotted against him, tried to kill him, threw him in a well, and eventually sold him into slavery in Egypt. To hide their crime, they lied to their father about what they had done, and the father had no other option but to be patient and put his trust in (Allah SWT the Almighty God).

In Egypt, Yusuf (AS) or Joseph was again wronged by the wife of the king who seduced him and failed to convince him, but ended up accusing him of attempted rape in the presence of her husband. Therefore he was wrongfully sentenced to prison for a crime he did not commit. The best part of the story is when Yusuf (AS) met with his brothers after being freed from prison and eventually became the person in charge of the food supply of Egypt.

The kind of reconciliation that took place between Yusuf (AS) and his brothers is a life lesson for all of humanity to learn from. The Qur'an says:

Then when they came (back) into (Joseph's) presence they said: "O exalted one! Distress has seized us and our family; we have (now) brought but scanty capital: So pay us full measure, (we pray thee) and treat it as charity to us: for Allah doth reward the charitable." (88) He said: "Know ye how ye dealt with Joseph and his brother, not knowing (what ye were doing)?" (89) They said: "Art thou indeed Joseph?" He said: "I am Joseph, and this is my brother: Allah has indeed been gracious to us (all): behold, he that is righteous and patient, never will Allah suffer the reward to be lost, of those who do right." (90) They said: "By Allah! Indeed has Allah preferred thee above us, and we certainly have been guilty of sin!" (91) He said: "This day let no reproach be (cast) on you: Allah will forgive you. He is the Most Merciful of those who show mercy!" (92) (Qur'an, Surah Yusuf 12.88–92)

These Divine words in narrating the process of this reconciliation involve the key elements of any successful reconciliation:

1. This involves the acknowledgement of the mistake and the admission of an error and being willing to say, "Yes, I was wrong and I am sorry."

2. This involves the willingness of the aggrieved party to accept the apology and be ready to pardon and forgive, even though he may not forget.

3. This also involves the willingness of two parties to open a new page in the relationship and work together to establish a new common good.

Most modern attempts at reconciliation have failed because they lack these three principles. The wrongdoers never admit their mistakes and the party that was wronged never gets their right, and therefore are not ready to pardon, and the two parties do not have genuine intentions to open up a new chapter in their relationship.

Another interesting point happens when Yusuf's brothers (Joseph's brothers) came to reconcile with their ill and aging father who suffered a great deal from their plot and lies. They simply admitted their mistake and said:

"O our father! Ask for us forgiveness for our sins, for we were truly at fault." (97) He said: "Soon will I ask my Lord for forgiveness for you: for he is indeed Oft-Forgiving, Most Merciful." (98) Then when they entered the presence of Joseph he provided a home for his parents with himself, and said: "Enter ye Egypt (all) in safety if it please Allah." (99) And he raised his parents high on the throne (of dignity), and they fell down in prostration, (all) before him. He said: "O my father! This is the fulfillment of my vision of old! Allah hath made it come true! He was indeed good to me when he took me out of prison and brought you (all here) out of the desert, (even) after Satan had sown enmity between me and my brothers. Verily my Lord understandeth best the mysteries of all that He planneth to do: For verily He is full of knowledge and wisdom." (100) (Qur'an, Surah Yusuf, 12.97–100).

At the end of the story the family was reunited once again, not as enemies, plotters, and liars against their brother but as best friends and best family living in peace, harmony, and prosperity. This is the true worldly paradise.

RECONCILIATION BETWEEN PROPHET MUHAMMAD (*PRAISE BE UNTO HIM*) AND MECCA

The example of our beloved Prophet Muhammad (PBUH) was not different from that of prophet Yusuf (AS) or Joseph. He the Prophet Muhammad (PBUH) was tortured, prosecuted, plotted against; he survived many assassination attempts, and eventually he was kicked out of his hometown Mecca by his own uncles and cousins. Not only that but also wars were waged against him in his new homeland Medina. This continued for twenty-three years and the result was the failure of the entire plan of the Meccan people. Eventually the Prophet (PBUH) emerged as the victor. During the conquest of Mecca, he entered the city of Mecca with no resistance and did not seek any revenge; instead, he asked them, "What do you think I am going to do to you today?" They said, "You are a kind brother and a son of a kind brother." He replied, "I'll do to you what Yusuf (Joseph) did to his brothers; I'll set all of you free and guarantee your safety and security over your life and proper-ties."[78]

RECONCILIATION WITHIN AMERICAN SOCIETY

Second Khutbah: Fellow Americans, America is home to many great innovations in our lifetime, from iPhone to Boeing, from the Wright brothers to F-35, from George Washington to Barack Obama; however, it is also home to many mistakes that have hap-pened in the past. What has made America a great nation is not only those great innovations but also the fact that it learned from its mistakes and emerged a better nation each time. Or perhaps we may say it is the land of possibilities where the concept of trial and error is more possible than in any other part of the world. It was once the nation of slaves and slave masters, but as soon as the shame of that practice became obvious, the practice was abolished and the mistake was corrected, and from that point all its citizens became free men and free women.

Once again it became the nation of segregation in schools, buses, and public parks, but as soon as the shame of this practice became obvious, the practice was abolished and civil rights were introduced. American had been a nation where women and other minorities did not have rights to vote, but as soon the shame of this practice also became noticed, the practice was abolished and voting rights were established. We can count more and more such examples in American history. The point is, this nation is more willing to make changes for the betterment of the future than any other nation I have seen. Therefore, God has granted the leadership of the world in our time to this nation, simply because we possess more of this unique human quality than other nations. This is not to say that we Americans are perfect, but we seek perfection in everything we do, and we do it through learning from our mistakes and promising ourselves never to repeat them again.

Among the recent mistakes that have rocked our nation are the slaying of two New York police officers, Officers Wenjian Liu and Rafael Ramos,[79] and the killing of Eric Garner, Michael Brown, and Trayvon Martin.[80] These are all part and parcel of the historical mistakes we continue to make. We should be able to draw lessons from them, be able to forgive and reconcile as we have always done. Such a process will shape our future and make us a better nation. We should not seek revenge or remain irreconcilable. This is against our true nature as a nation and against our true nature as humans as well.

Dr. King once said:

> There are certain things we can say about this method that seeks justice without violence. It does not seek to defeat or humiliate the opponent but to win his friendship and understanding. I think that this is one of the…basic distinguishing points between violence and non-violence. The ultimate end of violence is to defeat the opponent. The ultimate end of non-violence is to win the friendship of the opponent. It is necessary to boycott sometimes but the non-violent resister realized that boycott is never an end within itself, but merely a means to awaken a sense of shame within the oppressor; that the end is reconciliation; the end is redemption. And so the aftermath of violence is bitterness; the aftermath of non-violence is the creation of the beloved community; the aftermath of non-violence is redemption and reconciliation. This is a method that seeks to transform and to redeem, and win the friendship of the opponent, and make it possible for men to live together as brothers

in a community, and not continually live with bitterness and friction. (from "Justice without Violence," 3 April 1957)

But the end is reconciliation; the end is redemption; the end is the creation of the beloved community. It is this type of spirit and this type of love that can transform opposers into friends. The type of love that I stress here is not eros, a sort of esthetic or romantic love; not philia, a sort of reciprocal love between personal friends; but it is agape which is understanding goodwill for all men. It is an overflowing love which seeks nothing in return. It is the love of God working in the lives of men. This is the love that may well be the salvation of our civilization. (from "The Role of the Church in Facing the Nation's Chief Moral Dilemma," 1957)[81]

My fellow Americans, learning from the past mistakes means not to keep repeating them. One of the definitions of insanity is "to keep repeating the same and expecting different results"; therefore, we cannot abolish slavery and be caught in the sex slavery in all major cities around the country, and we cannot abolish segregation and be caught in the exploitation of illegal immigrants. We should not abolish gender inequality in voting and yet be caught in gender inequality in paychecks, and the list goes on and on. The point I am establishing here is we have come long way but we have a long way also to go. The future is promising. As long as we are willing to learn from our mistakes, draw meaningful lessons from our past, try to make things better, and reconcile among ourselves, we shall remain the greatest nation we strive for, and that is what God has destined for us. Let me conclude with these verses of the Qur'an that teach us the virtue of forgiveness and reconciliation and place them at a level that no other virtues can be compared to. The Qur'an says:

Whatever ye are given (here) is (but) a convenience of this Life: but that which is with Allah is better and more lasting: (it is) for those who believe and put their trust in their Lord; (36) Those who avoid the greater crimes and shameful deeds, and, when they are angry even then forgive; (37) Those who harken to their Lord, and establish regular prayer; who (conduct) their affairs by mutual Consultation; who spend out of what We bestow on them for Sustenance; (38) And those who, when an oppressive wrong is inflicted on them, (are not cowed but) help and defend themselves. (39) The recompense for an injury is an injury equal thereto (in degree): but if a person forgives and makes reconciliation, his reward is due, from Allah: for (Allah) loveth not those who do wrong. (40) (Qur'an, Surah Al-Shuraa 42.36–40)

5

Can We Talk?

The Reverend Dr. Jarred Hammet,
Pastor of Northminster Presbyterian Church

Note: Since preaching this sermon in Macon, Dr. Hammett has assumed the pastorate of the First Presbyterian Church, Tifton, Georgia

(8) Let no debt remain outstanding, except the continuing debt to love one another, for whoever loves others has fulfilled the law. (9) The commandments, "You shall not commit adultery," "You shall not murder," "You shall not steal," "You shall not covet," and whatever other command there may be, are summed up in this one command: "Love your neighbor as yourself." (10) Love does no harm to a neighbor. Therefore love is the fulfillment of the law. (11) And do this, understanding the present time: The hour has already come for you to wake up from your slumber, because our salvation is nearer now than when we first believed. (12) The night is nearly over; the day is almost here. So let us put aside the deeds of darkness and put on the armor of light. (13) Let us behave decently, as in the daytime, not in carousing and drunkenness, not in sexual immorality and debauchery, not in dissension and jealousy. (14) Rather, clothe yourselves with the Lord Jesus Christ, and do not think about how to gratify the desires of the flesh. (Romans 13:8–14)

In Mark 10 there is a story about a blind beggar who kept shouting out to Jesus, "Son of David, have mercy on me!" Preaching on this episode, Bishop T. D. Jakes was moved to comment, "I am so glad I am not part of some silent church. I want a noisy church. I want a church that lets God hear them...."

I don't want part of a silent church. Oh, you know the church. Some of the members drive to church in silence. They sit in the church in silence. Then they leave the church in silence. You know some churches are like that, right?

I know some Presbyterians who would be thinking, "Gosh, I miss the good old days when we were silent in church."

Now let me tell you about two people—Barbara Smith and Bill Bowden.[82] You know that old song, "If you're happy and you know it, then your face will surely show it"? Miss Barbara had a happiness inside, I think. But somehow it got lost on the way to her face. Now Bill Bowden, on the other hand, he was all face. And the two of them were kind of unspoken archenemies in the church. Bill was always in the vestibule of the church, cutting up and acting a fool. Laughing, slapping people on the back, telling jokes. Shaking hands, hugging. Giving or collecting kisses. Miss Barbara was in her pew, no later than nine minutes before worship, near the front, sitting quietly, checking the bulletin to see what hymns we were singing, looking for misspelled words, looking over the responsive reading, being a good Puritan—no I didn't say that...ok, but she was.

And after about forty-five seconds, she would turn around and look with disdain towards Bill Bowden. She would try to get quiet and collected again, and then forty-five seconds later, her head would turn back. That Bill Bowden—wearing loud pants and talking even louder, making people have an unfit frame of mind to worship the God of majesty and glory. Getting people all stirred up.

"Where is the solemnity, Reverend Hammet, where? Where is the respect for Almighty God? And that Dickie Felder doesn't even have the decency to pipe down once the prelude starts. And he has gotten worse! He's gotten worse since his daughter died, so I forgive him. But you need to talk to him. You."

That's what the Bible says, right? If there is someone in the church who has something against you, send the preacher to talk to them, right? But I digress.

One day, the secretary told me, "Miss Barbara would like to visit with you at 10:30. She says she is bringing bulletins to prove her point." At 10:26, she walked in. Bulletins from 1955, 60, 65, 70. We went into my study. "Reverend Hammet, I know you've heard me, and I know your hands are rather tied, but something has got to stop. So I am bringing you examples of how to get a handle on this problem. Because, if unchecked, people are going to quit coming." She showed me the way, at the top of each bulletin, printed in Old English (the official font of the Puritans), it had a psalm and a citation. Do you want to guess which psalm? Psalm 46 and verse 10—"Be still and know that I am God...." She continued, "If we would just print this at the top of the bulletin, I think we could solve our little problem. I know you don't want people staying away from church."

So there's Bishop T. D. Jakes with a noisy church in one corner. And in the other corner is the dour Miss Barbara Smith, who wanted a silent church. Miss Barbara being a bit like the people in the crowd in Mark's Gospel, trying to shush the blind man and his expressiveness, his excessive emotion.

At a Unity Service at Vineville Methodist a year or two ago, I started forming a question: What is "church"? And as I pondered that question, two people came to mind: the late Reverend Doctor Lonzy Edwards, longtime pastor of Mt. Moriah Baptist Church in Macon, and, of all people, Comedienne Joan Rivers.

Some years ago, the Reverend Edwards and I were in a conversation at an interracial breakfast when he surprised me by saying, "I am growing weary of gatherings where we sit together, Black and White, and that's about all that we do. We don't really get to solutions.... Occasional proximity doesn't address the issues."

And then Joan Rivers, just before she was about to rake someone over the coals, would ask, "Can we talk?" I think it is the Northern, Jewish equivalent to what we Southerners mean when we say, "Bless her heart." When Joan Rivers asked, "Can we talk?" you knew it was not going to be pretty. But it's a good question—Can we talk?

You see, on that Sunday evening at Vineville Methodist some months ago, I wasn't exactly sure I plugged into what was going on in the worship service. I saw some people fully enjoying it. There was a palpable joy and energy.

But now, for real, can we talk? In some ways, it felt like I was watching a sociological film of a different culture. Or like a field trip in seminary. And that was when my esteemed colleague, the Reverend Cliff Little, asked a rhetorical question—you know, one when the asker really isn't looking for an answer. "Haven't we had church tonight?" he asked. I heard several responses: "Yes, Lord," "Amen," "My, my, my." But in my head, I heard, "I'm not really sure."

Yes, some people had church. I wasn't sure what I was feeling. I now know, with T. D. Jakes's help, that I was a bit like Miss Barbara. So that morning at Centenary, as Reverend Edwards and I were eating grits and talking about worshipping together, and what progress might look like, we were being terribly polite. And speaking in generalities. But I heard Reverend Edwards in my head. And I heard Joan Rivers in my head. "Can we talk?"

We started a very good conversation that morning. And we started by admitting that we didn't know much about each other.

We liked each other, but we didn't know how many children people had...if they had them. We didn't know where others lived. But we started learning more about each other that day in some simple ways.

So here's what I have been wondering ever since the invitation to speak tonight came to me: on a scale of one to ten, ten being the highest, what chance does a Caucasian, a somewhat closeted Puritan, have of bringing a message that will lead my Methodist friends to think we had church, and then my AME friends to think we have had church tonight, and my Baptist friends— whether Cooperative, Foot Washing, Primitive, Free Will, Southern, or Two-seed—and my friends from the General Missionary and New Era Baptist denominations to think we have had church? I figured I would start, at best, with about 2.8–3.1 points on the scale. With anointed blessing, maybe end up at a 4?

Can we talk?

If it is hard work for the clergy to really talk, what's our best shot at worshipping together in some kind of way that paves a little bit more of this new road? You know, I found myself divided...do I simply come in tonight with minimal expectations? Do I come in with delusional expectations? Do I simply hope to cause no offense, kick a field goal, and put three on the board?

But you know, ultimately, the only person we can be is who we are. We can smell a fake a mile away. And where there is a connection to be made, we should make it. And where there is a bridge washed out, we should acknowledge it.

Have any of you seen the show *Black-ish*? Ruby, Dre's mom, brilliantly played by Jenifer Lewis, realizes that in certain situations she needs more help. In those moments, you know who she calls on? Black Jesus. So can we talk? Can a Caucasian call on Black Jesus?

Our scriptures tonight all focus on one common theme: what are we wearing? Joan Rivers, so nosey, so pushy and so brash and shamelessly pointed, asked four little words. Those four little words changed what we commonly call the red carpet. "Who are you wearing?" she asked. And every designer wanted the person interviewed to answer with their name: Prada. Givenchy. Chanel. Michael Kors. Valentino. Jerome Lamar. Versace.

But long before Joan Rivers started asking that question, the New Testament was already calling us on the carpet about our lifestyle. When you are baptized, there is supposed to be something different about you. You are supposed to be a changed person. In the early church, when you came out of the water you were given a new piece of never-worn-before cloth. You were wrapped in it, still wet. Paul is saying that when we receive that sign and seal, when we put on not our Sunday best but our Sunday newest, there is to be something different about us.

We don't just play by the world's rules. We don't put justice aside even though it makes good business sense. We no longer live comfortably and separately with slave and free, Gentile and Greek, male and female. Because in Christ we are made one.

So who we are wearing has something to do with how we relate to each other. And sometimes, the faith life is a hard life. The Spirit is willing, but our flesh is weak.

Any museum worth its salt has a suit of armor in it. In the New York Metropolitan Museum of Art, there is an enormous section that starts out with swords, then there are shields, then there are breastplates, and you move on to spears, and javelins, and crossbows, and then helmets, and then, when you think you are done, you come to whole suits of armor. Eighty pounds of protection.

Paul understood what it was like to feel under siege. People disparaged him and his ministry. In prison, he watched the Roman soldiers take care of their gear. They would lay it out, and he would see them practice moving forward together. He would see them soak their leather shields in water so they wouldn't catch fire from a flaming arrow. He saw what they were wearing so as to not be taken down. He would ask, in a sense, What are you wearing? Whose armor are you wearing?

It seems to me that we need to acknowledge two things this evening. One, we have so up-armored ourselves historically as the races that we need to take off some armor and get to know each other. And on the opposite side, when things would divide us, we need to be like the Roman soldiers, shields held up over our heads, in tight formation, because if one falls, we all fall.

And as I prepare to make my way towards a seat, I ask that we look at the book of Romans. There, Paul talks about our old nature—the way we were raised. Our biases, prejudices, mistrusts, suspicions. Who are you wearing? I'm wearing George Wallace. I'm wearing some vintage Lester Maddox. I'm wearing a young designer Dylann Roof. I'm wearing Malik el-Shabazz.[83]

I want to say tonight that those designers, those rags, are not appropriate attire. They are the rags of the flesh. You know what hand-me-downs are? There is nothing wrong with some hand-me-downs, but what hand-me-downs are we wearing? The old rags of racism or pieces worn before by those who can see a better way forward?

Some things were wrong to be worn in the first place. Joan Rivers would say so in a minute. "Why? Why are you wearing that?" The lifestyle given to us in Romans exhorts us to shop. We are to fill our closet with Christ's clothes.

And that's not something they sell at a local Christian bookstore. And as I recall, his clothes, Christ's clothes, he gave up to wash people's feet, and those clothes were hung up, gambled for, as he was on the cross. Christ's clothing can cost you. Dearly. Who are you wearing?

Lastly, I think part of my trouble with the question about whether we've truly had church is that it cuts against my Calvinistic tradition. The question was really an innocent question, and yet it hit my ears as "What did I get out of going here?"

And John Calvin, our chief character in church history or sixteenth century history, insisted that the real question to ask is this: What does God get out of our having come to church? Is God praised? Was scripture valued? Did all the glory go to God? Not the choir, not the preacher, not the evangelist, not the exhorter, not the wealthiest member, not the most charismatic member, not the person with the strongest voice, but did the glory go to God?

I know this could be dangerous. I am not so sure that any of us should care if we had church tonight or not. It's not like a football game where we say, "that wasn't much of a game" or "it was a great game." It's worship, and what matters is whether God feels that he was worshipped tonight. Because if I had to make a choice of being present at a service that didn't feel right to me but gave God great happiness, and the choice of what felt wonderful to me broke God's heart, I would want to be on the side where God says, looking over to Jesus and the Holy Ghost, "I think we had church tonight." Because it's God's question to answer, not ours. And I suspect that all of you have desires and strong leanings towards a worship that has the greatest chance of pleasing our God and a worship that is not about judging each other by the color or shade of the skin.

Paul says, "Make no provision for the flesh." Your attire is to be based on the one who claimed you in those baptismal waters. You went down a sinner and came up clean. There are plenty of people who wear the rags of racism and hatred. And some of those rags are tailored. Custom made. They need to be burned like a leper's cloak. No need holding on to rags like that in your wardrobe. They will not come back in style...indeed, they never were.

So, are you leaning towards putting on Jesus Christ? Are you leaning towards having awkward but truthful conversations? Can we simply get to know each other better, like the Paired Clergy are trying to do?[84] For the sake of our city, can we find a way forward?

Are you leaning towards having church in a way that warms God's heart? Those are good leanings...it's a choice we make every day. So which way are you leaning? Do you need some strength as we carry on? Are you leaning on the arms of the one who is ever-lasting?

6

Laying Down, Taking Up

The Reverend Cassandra Howe,
Former Pastor of High Street
Unitarian Universalist Church in Macon[85]

The hymn "Gonna Lay Down My Sword and Shield" is set in the Peace section of *Singing the Living Tradition* (the Unitarian Universalist hymnal) but is probably more appropriately placed in the Freedom section. Its pacifist imagery made it a great song for Anti-Vietnam War protests, where many middle-class White folks first heard the song.[86]

> Gonna lay down my sword and shield,
> Down by the riverside,
> Down by the riverside,
> Down by the riverside.
> Gonna lay down my sword and shield,
> Down by the riverside,
> Ain't gonna study war no more.
>
> I ain't gonna study war no more,
> I ain't gonna study war no more,
> I ain't gonna study war no more.

Gonna lay down my burden,
Down by the riverside,
Down by the riverside,
Down by the riverside.
Gonna lay down my burden,
Down by the riverside,
Ain't gonna study war no more.

I ain't gonna study war no more.
I ain't gonna study war no more,
I ain't gonna study war no more,

Gonna shake hands around the world,
Everywhere I roam,
Everywhere I roam,
Everywhere I roam.
Gonna shake hands around the world,
Everywhere I roam,
Ain't gonna study war no more.

I ain't gonna study war no more,
I ain't gonna study war no more,
I ain't gonna study war no more.

But that was the song's second coming. It was originally sung before the Civil War as an African American spiritual whose singers dreamt of achieving earthly freedom.[87] How, then, does one achieve freedom? Every spiritual will offer a way specific to the time and the place of the person who wrote it.[88] As a White upper-middle class woman singing this song from within Unitarian Universalist congregations in the twenty-first century, I have found great meaning in the song's lyrical rhythm. It is a rhythm that offers a pathway to freedom for people outside the condition of slavery—namely, the slave masters and their White descendants.

Singers of this song will sing their way through two very different physical acts: letting go and taking up. We let go, or lay down, our sword and shield. We take up the action of shaking hands "around the world." This makes sense when you think about it: if you really wanted to shake hands around the world, you would have to lay some things down in order for your hands to be free.

So often we in the West emphasize the things we gain. Having to lose something, however, or having to "die to something" runs counter to much that our consumer culture holds sacred. But as Bishop Desmond Tutu has written, "Liberation is costly."[89] What, we might ask, do White folks need to lay down? What are the "swords and shields" of those with race privilege?

My first experience giving up a sword and shield happened just after college. I had invited my friend Stephanie over for lunch and a walk. Stephanie is a Filipina American. I was living with my parents at the time in a mostly White suburb. I didn't think anything of it. When Stephanie arrived, I could tell she was a little uneasy. I asked if everything was OK and she said that as a person of color she felt really self-conscious driving through my neighborhood. She knew this was a covenanted community, one where, not that long ago, people of her skin color had been prohibited from purchasing property. She was aware of the police officer following her down the road. She was so uncomfortable that she was not sure if she would be able to come back.

I was surprised, to say the least. I thought, "Well, this is a great house and a great neighborhood!" My parents had just moved to this house a year ago, and I was enjoying my time living there while I figured out what to do next. They were in the middle of a green belt. They had a private trail to a beach, together with the neighbors. My favorite berry, thimbleberries, were just coming out.

My friend's news was disappointing. I had been so excited to welcome her to my home.

We went for our walk and had our lunch. After she left I did a little research. I looked up the bylaws of the covenanted community in which my parents lived. Sure enough, they were still there: rules about not selling to any families of color. The board hadn't even gotten around to removing this part since redlining became illegal. It was not only worse than I thought; it was worse even than my friend had described!

I had loved the idea of my home and my family as living in this land of paradise. I had loved the idea of being free from the marks of racism, being innocent. But now it was more complicated than that. It was still my home, for sure. It was still a life-giving place for me and my family. But it was no longer perfect. It was no longer void of the errors of the past. So I had a choice: keep the glass case that I had constructed around my parents' house, or allow for a more mature, more complicated view of my home. I decided to let the glass case go.

The illusion of innocence is part of my friend Tara's story as well. She is White while her partner is Black. Recently they received two foster kids—a two-year-old and a four-year-old, African American boys. My friend Tara has been texting me lots of pictures of her two boys. It is wonderful to see how excited she is.

One thing that Tara was really looking forward to was reading to her kids before going to bed. She pulled out her old favorites: Laura Ingalls Wilder's Little House series and started to read them again. Disappointment set in. Reading them as an adult, she quickly realized how racist these books are. She set them down, knowing she could not in good conscience read them to her two sons, at least not until they were old enough to also talk about the author's context and the history of White supremacy in the United States.

Like the glass case of innocence around my parents' house, Tara's glass case around her beloved Laura Ingalls Wilder was shattered. But as she looks at her dark-skinned wife and children, she realizes this is a small price to pay for being part of an authentic relationship with people she loves.

In *Soul Work: Anti-Racist Theologies in Dialogue,* the Rev. Dr. Rebecca Parker shares a story of something that happened to her on her way to seminary. In 1976 she and a friend were driving across the country, on their way to theological school. They had time on their hands and decided to take back roads. One afternoon, late in the day, they descended from hill country into a valley. It had been raining hard, and as they neared a small town they noticed blinking yellow lights signaling danger. They looked to the left and saw a field covered in standing water. The roads to the right were blocked off with signs saying, "Road Closed." As they crossed a bridge and looked over the railing, they saw high muddy water, flowing fast.

They started their way out of town. But at the next bend in the road they were stopped in their tracks by a quickly rising wall of muddy water swallowing up *their* road. They turned their car around only to find the water also rising behind them.

At that point they realized they were contending with a flood in real time, not in the safety of the past. With dry ground disappearing before their eyes, they quickly got out of the car and scrambled to higher ground. Soaked to the bone, they huddled under a fir tree. Outside of their familiar vehicle, the cold water from the storm poured down on them, as Parker describes in first person, "baptizing us into the present—a present from which we had been insulated by both our car and our misjudgments about the country we were traveling through." Parker continues:

This is what it is like to be a white person in America. It is to travel well ensconced in a secure vehicle; to see signs of what is happening in the world outside the compartment one is traveling in and not realize that these signs have any contemporary meaning. It is to be dislocated—to misjudge your location and to believe you are uninvolved and unaffected by what is happening in the world.[90]

She had to let go of her car in order to reach true safety. To stay accountable to my friend, I had to let go of the image of innocence around my parents' home. My friend, Tara, let go of the innocence of her childhood books. She had to let it go to experience the fullness of love in her multiracial family.

We in the United States have experienced our own innocence shattered—the glass case represented by the Confederate battle flag. Those who want to keep the flag up in public places say it is about preserving our history. I wonder, though, if it is less about protecting our history and more about protecting that idea of innocence we have placed around our history.

If there is anything citizens across the United States can agree on, it is that we are a country called towards freedom. It would serve us well, then, to listen more closely to "Down by the Riverside." What do we need to lay down in order to take up the physical and spiritual freedom we so deeply desire?

If there is any place that offers physical and spiritual freedom, it is heaven. Heaven, it has been said, looks a lot like hell. In both you will find the long table filled with food: fresh fruits and vegetables, sauces, breads and meats. You will find people sitting on both sides of the table. In hell people sit at tables overflowing with food, but they are starving. They cannot eat because their elbows will not bend. They cannot reach their hands to their mouths in order to eat. Likewise, in heaven the people sit at tables of abundance. Their elbows don't bend, either. But they have discovered the key to freedom: they feed one another from across the table.

Lay down your sword and shield! What are you willing to lay down in order to climb to that mountaintop? In order to arrive in that freedom land where black and white, brown and yellow and red, gay and straight and transgendered, rich and poor, temporarily abled and disabled, old and young, conservative and liberal people all sit down together at the table of fellowship?

Let's sing "Gonna shake hands around the world" one last time, but this time, let's do it—shake hands with someone you haven't yet met! Amen.

7

We're Much Too Smart

The Reverend Julie Whidden Long,
Former Minister of Children and Families at
First Baptist Church of Christ[91]

(26) So in Christ Jesus you are all children of God through faith, (27) for all of you who were baptized into Christ have clothed yourselves with Christ. (28) There is neither Jew nor Gentile, neither slave nor free, nor is there male and female, for you are all one in Christ Jesus. (29) If you belong to Christ, then you are Abraham's seed, and heirs according to the promise. (Galatians 3:26-29)

One of the joys of working with children and having children of my own is that I have once again immersed myself into the world of children's books. I love reading children's literature. Children's books have a way of telling a story or illustrating a truth plainly, of getting to the heart of the matter both concisely and imaginatively. They often remind us of the simplest but most profound of life's lessons.

As I browsed through the children's section in our church library recently, I ran across one such book. The title is innocent enough—*What If the Zebras Lost Their Stripes?* by author John Reitano—but listen to this powerful cultural critique:

What if the Zebras lost their stripes, and some lost black and some
    lost white?

Would they think that it's all right, or would the Zebras start to
    fight?

Would there be separate Zebra "types" if the Zebras lost their
    stripes?

Would different colors be the end of living life as loving friends?

Would Zebras see themselves as Zebras?

Or would their colors make them start to only see the black and
    white—and not what lives within their hearts?

Would there be separate Zebra lands? Could black and white
    friends still hold hands?

Would Zebra children be okay to join together, laugh and play?

I know why God gave Zebras stripes—so that there'd be no black or
    white!

But, Zebras would be much too smart to let their colors tear them
    apart![92]

Reitano calls us to use our imaginations. How would our
world be if black and white didn't matter? What if we did all look
alike, people all one shade of brown, or even, like zebras, with
stripes of dark and light?

The image reminds me of something I experienced as an undergraduate student at Mercer University. As a junior, I signed up
for a class in Christian Social Ethics taught by one of Mercer's leg-
ends, Dr. Joe Hendricks. "Papa Joe," as he was known on campus,
had served as Dean of Students at Mercer during the years surrounding the university's integration and had been a force for
equality between the races. The course was required for Christianity majors such as myself, but students from across the university
competed for seats in the class to listen to Papa Joe tell his stories.

One day in class, Papa Joe shared his hopes for racial reconciliation in the South. "Imagine this: One person attends the wed-

ding of a friend and comes back to tell a mutual friend about it. She describes the ceremony, the reception, and all the festivities. The friend who stayed behind asked, 'Well, what color was the groom?'"

At this point, I thought the story was finished. In my experience of growing up in South Georgia, it was generally accepted that one married another of the same race. This story was shocking enough in that the friend did not assume that the groom's color matched that of the bride. But Papa Joe continued. "Well, what color was the groom?" the friend asked. And the person who attended the wedding answered, "I don't know. I didn't even notice."

It's powerful, isn't it, to imagine a time when we didn't even notice another's skin color? Is this what racial reconciliation means? To not notice? To refuse to see the traits that distinguish us from one another?

> What if the Zebras lost their stripes, and some lost black and some lost white?
> Would they think that it's all right, or would the Zebras start to fight?
> Would there be separate Zebra "types" if the Zebras lost their stripes?
> Would different colors be the end of living life as loving friends?[93]

In his letter to the Galatians, Paul wrote about the divisions that took place between Jewish and Gentile Christians. Paul challenged them not to let these distinctions divide them:

> For in Christ Jesus you are all children of God through faith. As many of you as were baptized into Christ have clothed yourselves with Christ. There is no longer Jew or Greek, there is no longer slave or free, there is no longer male and female; for all of you are one in Christ Jesus. And if you belong to Christ, then you are Abraham's offspring, heirs according to the promise. (Galatians 3:26–29, NRSV)

Paul called the church at Galatia to become unified in spirit and in message. As redeemed children of God, baptized in the name of Christ Jesus, they were one. But Paul did not mean that the Christians at Galatia should ignore what made them different. Being one in Christ does not do away with one's identity as Jew or Greek, male or female. A person can't erase his or her background or gender or ethnicity. And who would want to? The truth is that our different colors, our unique heritages, make the world a more beautiful place.

For Paul, and for God, unity does not mean uniformity. Being one in Christ means that we celebrate the uniqueness of each individual and see the beauty in each person. It means that categories and stereotypes are irrelevant. It means, like Papa Joe implied, that the categories of race or class or gender or ethnicity are not the first things we notice about each other.

What if the Zebras lost their stripes, and some lost black and some lost white?...

Would Zebras see themselves as Zebras? Or would their colors make them start to only see the black and white—and not what lives within their hearts?[94]

The First Baptist Church of Christ has been a beacon of light in this community since 1826. Admittedly, we have had our darker moments when it came to taking notice of race and social status. From our pulpit, at least one pro-slavery sermon was preached. Those of the African American race were kept "in their place" for many years, before we helped them to move on to a place of their own down the street. African Americans have been employed as "the help," and while we hope they were treated with kindness and respect, we definitely took notice of their differences from the majority of the congregation.

Now, in 2014, some things have changed. We have ordained African American deacons. We welcome into our church family people from countries all over the world to learn skills in our English as a Second Language program. Our children's ministry reflects the beauty of a rainbow, with children of parents who hail from Guatemala, Mexico, Brazil, Scotland, and Japan, as well as those who are African American or biracial. On a recent Wednesday night, only two of the nine boys in our elementary school boys' class had two White, American parents.

As individuals, we are all in different places in our perspectives on race, based our varied backgrounds and experiences. But as a congregation, in many ways we consider ourselves sophisticated and progressive on the issue. While most of us still "notice," we try our best to suppress our prejudices and to be loving and fair to all people. So what does racial reconciliation mean for this congregation? To where does God call us now?

There's another children's book that I've fallen in love with, one that I pick out to read to my daughter as often as I can. It's called *God's Dream,* and it's written by Archbishop Desmond Tutu along with Douglas Carlton Abrams. "Do you know what God dreams about?" it asks.

God dreams about people sharing. God dreams about people caring. God dreams that we reach out and hold one another's hands and play one another's games and laugh with one another's hearts....God dreams that every one of us will see that we are all brothers and sisters—yes, even you and me—even if we have different mommies and daddies or live in different faraway lands. Even if we speak different languages or have different ways of talking to God. Even if we have different eyes or different skin.[95]

Many of us share God's dream already. We dream of a day, like Martin Luther King Jr. dreamed, when justice prevails and our children are judged for their character and not for their skin color. But how do we make God's dream come true?

"It's really quite easy," the book says. "As easy as sharing, loving, caring. As easy as holding, playing, laughing. As easy as knowing we are family because we are all God's children."[96]

Dreaming God's dream is not enough. Our dreaming must move into action. Sharing, caring, holding, playing—living out these verbs requires the hands and the feet. They are active, not passive.

This, I believe, is our congregation's challenge: to get our hands dirty and our feet moving. We don't have to be convinced to dream God's dream. We dream, and we believe. But how many of us take an active role in making this dream come true?

Let's use our imaginations again: what would it be like if every individual in this congregation chose to do one intentional, practical thing to break down the racial barrier? How would that impact this community, so fraught with racial tensions?

And now, use your imagination to come up with the one thing that you will do. Invite someone you know whose skin is a different color than yours to join you for dinner at your home. Sit and listen to another person tell his story. Vote for a candidate of another race in the next election. Get involved in a public school where you are the minority, and perhaps even think of enrolling your child there. Write your legislator about an issue or bill that you feel is unjust toward a particular group of people. Use your imagination, but know that you don't have to work hard to be creative. When you open your eyes to the people around you and try hard to see them as God sees them, opportunities to do something different will abound. But whatever you do, don't sit idly by simply dreaming of another day. Don't grow more complacent about the way things are. Do something!

I know why God gave Zebras stripes—so that there'd be no black or white!

But, Zebras would be much too smart to let their colors tear them apart![97]

No, God didn't give us stripes like the zebras. God made us black and white and all shades of brown. Certainly God knew we'd be more beautiful that way. And surely God dreamed that we'd be much too smart to let our colors tear us apart.

8

A Response to Injustice

The Reverend Dr. Ike Edwin Mack,
Unionville Baptist Church, Macon, Georgia

(1) Let brotherly love continue. (2) Be not forgetful to entertain strangers: for thereby some have entertained angels unawares. (3) Remember them that are in bonds, as bound with them; and them which suffer adversity, as being yourselves also in the body. (Hebrews 13:1–3)

Are there some things that challenge your sense of justice and fair play? Most of us become angry when we see someone cheated out of an opportunity or robbed of their liberty. When we watch the news and view men being released from prison after serving decades on bogus charges, our sense of justice is utterly disturbed. When people are prosecuted without reason and unreasonably persecuted, we become angry!

Everyone has a breaking point. Even Jesus himself had a breaking point. Usually soft-spoken and philosophical in his demeanor, he reportedly became angry when he saw the moneychangers in the temple. He turned over the tables and shouted, "It is written that my father's house is a house of prayer, but you had turned it into dens of thieves." (See Mark 17.) Jesus was visibly angry.

There was never any other occasion where Jesus expressed so much rage, but on that day the presence of so much sin made Jesus quite angry. Sin pushed Jesus' buttons! Many times, we're the same way. We tried to hold our peace on some issues, but every now and again one subject or another literally touches that very last nerve. Injustice has a way of challenging our sense of order; it stirs our anger and then we must struggle rather hard to remain cool, calm, collected, and in control.

This is the feeling many people have and maintain with regard to the aftermath of the slaying of Trayvon Martin in Sanford, Florida, on February 26, 2012. Trayvon Martin, a 17-year-old African American high school student, was fatally shot by George Zimmerman. Zimmerman is a late 20-something-year-old, multiracial, Hispanic American who was a semiautomatic-gun-toting neighborhood watch coordinator of a gated community in Sanford.

Trayvon Martin was armed with a can of Arizona iced tea and a package of fruit-flavored Skittles candy. George Zimmerman killed Trayvon Martin, a 17-year-old boy trying to get home after going to the store.

Zimmerman immediately claimed self-defense. Yet the multitude of the facts paint a vastly different picture. George Zimmerman, one hundred pounds heavier and ten years older, followed Trayvon Martin for several minutes while calling 911. He continued following even after emergency dispatch personnel advised him not to do so. He was advised to fall back and wait for the police. But George Zimmerman, armed with a semiautomatic 9 mm handgun, continued in his pursuit, ignoring the dispatcher's demands. He accosted the teenager, gunning him down in what Zimmerman claimed was self-defense, and he immediately defended his dubious deed with Florida's Stand Your Ground law.

This Florida statute defines justifiable use of force, or standing one's ground, in defense of one's person, saying that one is justified in using force, except deadly force, against another when and to the extent that the person reasonably believes that such conduct is necessary to defend himself or herself or against the other's imminent use of unlawful force. However, a person is justified in the use of deadly force and does not have time to retreat if he or she reasonably believes that such force is necessary to prevent imminent death or great bodily harm to himself or herself or another.

When George Zimmerman was brought to trial on second degree murder charges, the jury of five White women and one Hispanic, upon reviewing the evidence and a daylong deliberation, found George Zimmerman not guilty on all charges and released him into society as a free man.

Such incidents are so frustrating, and their injustice is quite clear. Although President Barack Obama originally identified with Trayvon's parents, saying, "If I had had a son he would look like Trayvon," the President later identified with Trayvon himself, saying, "He could have been me thirty-five years ago."

The national sense of fair play and justice has been assaulted by the cries of protest, and outrage is spilling from all sectors of this nation. Many African Americans have concluded that there is simply no real justice!

However, according to our text, the Christian community is given directive on how to respond or react to injustice. The passage indicates that God is concerned about any injustice inflicted on the believer. Furthermore, the text declares that we are to be empathetic towards the victims of any injustice, while seeking justice for anyone suspected of infringement.

As we carefully note in Hebrews 13, the writer is discussing a list of miscellaneous items. Some of the items include hospitality, marriage, church officers, and the imprisoned. In the Bible, there is no division between doctrine and duty. Revelation and responsibility for the two always go together, for the book of Hebrews is also known as "the Faith book." In chapter 11, the author writes of examples of faith, while chapter 12 is the encouragement to faith. In chapter 13, the writer speaks of the evidence of faith.

The evidence of faith is exhibited in our lives daily as we walk, talk, and fellowship with our fellow man. The first verse of chapter 13 focuses on how the evidence of our faith will be expressed to those who have suffered injustice, and we will empathize with them because we have been there or will be there one day ourselves.

So let us observe what our responses should be to injustice. The first response to injustice is "let brotherly love continue." The phrase "let brotherly love continue" means keep being concerned about each other as the Lord's followers should.

The writer of Hebrews encourages each believer to promote present love for one another. The admonition to continue implies that brotherly love already exists. There are several factors to promote brotherly love, and it is when we understand each other, listen to each other, and appreciate one another's differences. We create atmospheres were brotherly love can exist, and conversely, there are many factors that threaten brotherly love.

In America, racial hatred has been one of the most divisive traits of our national character. It has cost us to imprison, enslave, kill, and destroy each other mercilessly. Even as the bigotry and hatred raised their bitter heads, there were voices in the faceless masses that cried out, "Let brotherly love continue!" In every struggle, we view and witness the real culprit that divides us, and ironically it is not color. It is the presence of evil showing itself in the form of greed, envy, jealousy, hatred, tragedy, and the hurting all over the world. This is a work of love that must continue even in the face of injustice. It is not a call to ignore the billboards of injustice, but it is rather an invitation to increase our efforts to "let brotherly love continue!"

Church, it is tempting to let incidents like the tragic slaying of Trayvon disrupt efforts to build and rebuild bridges between the races. This must not happen, for it would prevent us from speeding up our efforts to change unjust law and become more sensitive to the rights of others. While the nation is disturbed over the injustice we see all around us, we are still compelled to "let brotherly love continue."

The second response to injustice is "be careful how you respond to strangers." In the second verse, the author advises us: "Be not forgetful to entertain strangers; for thereby some have entertained angels unawares." Be sure to welcome strangers into your home. By doing this, some people have welcomed angels as guests even without knowing it.

The writer of the epistle to the Hebrews cautions those of the faith not to forget to entertain strangers. Our society often paints caricatures of people who are different. We tend to use racially descriptive terms to describe or label those of other places or cultures. Often these mental images are offensive and negative. Even worse, we tend to categorize, stereotype, and label people without ever bothering to discover the potential differences that might exist. Thus, we believe that anyone living in the housing project is a drug dealer, drug user, or low achiever. We often idealize those of Hispanic origin as illegal immigrants, and every Black man or boy that walks into a store is coming to rob or steal.

The second verse of our text compels us to be careful how we respond to strangers, to those who are different from us. We cannot assume that every White man is a Klansman, or that every Democrat is good and that all Republicans are evil. We should never assume anything about anyone, but we are to keep a watchful eye of spiritual discernment in regards to others, their actions, and their behavior.

Jesus taught the greatest example of how to deal with those who are different. He also made no judgment about them and did not buy into the custom that he should avoid contact with the Samaritans, publicans, or sinners who were looked upon by society as tainted people. While Jesus followed that principle, the world didn't respond to him the same way as before. He was now a stranger among many. But they didn't know they were entertaining the Son of God.

The tragedy of young Trayvon Martin's slaying is a clear example of what happens when our hidden prejudices and stereotyping cause us to respond out of fear rather than respect for one another. Trayvon, 17, was an innocent young boy who appeared strange and out of place, and for that lone perception, he died. It is an injustice that screams to the throne of God, and as juror B9 stated, "Zimmerman got away with murder." But you cannot get away from God, and surely heaven will respond.

The third response to injustice is to "share the sorrow of victims." Verse 3 tells us to "remember them that are in bonds, as bound with them; and with them who suffer adversity, as being yourselves also in the body." We are to remember the Lord's people who are in jail and be concerned for them. Don't forget those who are suffering, but rather imagine that you are there with them.

In verse 3 of Hebrews 13, the author entreats believers to have a sympathetic heart toward the victims of injustice. An injustice is an action that has defied all the rules of fair play. Injustice leaves its victims wounded, troubled, and unsettled. All too often, injustice leads to death. We have seen too much unjustified death in such a respect. Victims include Emmett Till, Medgar Evers, Malcolm X, John F. Kennedy, and Martin Luther King Jr., just to name a few who were all victims of hatred, bias, and inequality.

Church, too many times we have seen sorrowing mothers, crying sisters and brothers, and grieving dads holding their hearts in their hands. The word of God says we who have walked in their footsteps and have felt the sting of tragedy ourselves should be sympathetic to those who are now victims of injustice. That feeling of concern should go well beyond compassion; it should be galvanized into the energy necessary to make something good come out of an unjust deed.

Conditions that allow racism to flourish must be improved, and there must be a resolve never again for the innocents of our nation to be lost to something senseless the way a teenage boy vanished because he chose to wear a hoodie for the day and drape it over his head because it was raining, for a teenage boy naïvely looking to buy a drink and candy to vanish. Those of us who have experienced the pain should help bear the pain of the victims of oppression, prejudice, and inequality everywhere. We should lift them up in prayer and call upon the God we serve to wipe away their tears. Sisters and brothers, I ask you to leave here today knowing that we are all compelled to display the evidence of our faith by responding to any injustice by putting it all in God's capable hands. If the hearts and souls of those who have been mistreated are to be repaired and reborn, then it will only start by putting it all in God's hands. No wonder the scripture of Hebrews 11 declares, "Now faith is the substance of things hoped for, and the evidence of things not seen." When we can't see justice and fairness, just put it in God's hands.

Church, in all of our responses we must never lose the capacity to love. That is why Ephesians 4 tells us, "Be angry and sin not; Let not the sun go down on your wrath."

Martin Luther King Jr. reminds all of us that while we, as a people, are angry with the racism of the American system, we should not lose our capacity to love every American. God set the example on how to love the sinner but hate the sin.

God was angry when Israel sinned and began to follow Baal, but he loved them anyway! God told the prophet Hosea to dramatize his love by marrying a wife of whoredom, who cheated and who was unfaithful; but Hosea's call to his wandering bride was, "I don't like what you are doing to yourself, but I still love you!" That call is still going out from the throne of God today. Yes, I'm angry with sin, but I love the sinner anyway! I don't like what the world is doing, but I love the world anyway! No wonder John 3:16 declares, "For God so loved the world that he gave his only Begotten Son, that whosoever believes him should not perish, but have everlasting life!"

Our responses to injustice must be much like God's response to our sins; we were sinners, but God still loves us!

Love says, "Pass me your guilt, and I'll give you my grace."

Love says, "Pass me your meanness, and I'll give you my meekness."

Love says, "Pass me your badness, and I'll give you my goodness."

Love says, "Pass me your faults, and I'll give you my favor."

Love says, "Pass me your vices, and I'll give you my virtue."

In order to get justice, we must be willing to be washed in the blood of Jesus.

What can wash away my sin? Nothing but the blood of Jesus.

What can make me whole again? Nothing but the blood of Jesus.

Oh precious is the flow that makes me white as snow

No other fount I know, nothing but the blood of Jesus.

9

Wrestling and Reconciling with Race

Andrew M. Manis

Behold, how good and pleasant it is for brothers and sisters to dwell together in unity. (Psalm 133:1)

(22) That night Jacob got up and took his two wives, his two female servants and his eleven sons and crossed the ford of the Jabbok. (23) After he had sent them across the stream, he sent over all his possessions. (24) So Jacob was left alone, and a man wrestled with him till daybreak. (25) When the man saw that he could not overpower him, he touched the socket of Jacob's hip so that his hip was wrenched as he wrestled with the man. (26) Then the man said, "Let me go, for it is daybreak."

But Jacob replied, "I will not let you go unless you bless me."

(27) The man asked him, "What is your name?"

"Jacob," he answered.

(28) Then the man said, "Your name will no longer be Jacob, but Israel, because you have struggled with God and with humans and have overcome."

(29) Jacob said, "Please tell me your name."

But he replied, "Why do you ask my name?" Then he blessed him there.

(30) So Jacob called the place Peniel, saying, "It is because I saw God face to face, and yet my life was spared." (31) The sun rose above him as he passed Peniel, and he was limping because of his hip. (32) Therefore to this day the Israelites do not eat the tendon attached to the socket of the hip, because the socket of Jacob's hip was touched near the tendon. (Genesis 32:22–32)

(1) Jacob looked up and there was Esau, coming with his four hundred men; so he divided the children among Leah, Rachel, and the two female servants. (2) He put the female servants and their children in front, Leah and her children next, and Rachel and Joseph in the rear. (3) He himself went on ahead and bowed down to the ground seven times as he approached his brother.

(4) But Esau ran to meet Jacob and embraced him; he threw his arms around his neck and kissed him. And they wept. (5) Then Esau looked up and saw the women and children. "Who are these with you?" he asked.

Jacob answered, "They are the children God has graciously given your servant."

(6) Then the female servants and their children approached and bowed down. (7) Next, Leah and her children came and bowed down. Last of all came Joseph and Rachel, and they too bowed down.

(8) Esau asked, "What's the meaning of all these flocks and herds I met?"

"To find favor in your eyes, my lord," he said.

(9) But Esau said, "I already have plenty, my brother. Keep what you have for yourself."

(10) "No, please!" said Jacob. "If I have found favor in your eyes, accept this gift from me. For to see your face is like seeing the face of God, now that you have received me favorably. (11)

Please accept the present that was brought to you, for God has been gracious to me and I have all I need." And because Jacob insisted, Esau accepted it.

(12) Then Esau said, "Let us be on our way; I'll accompany you."

(13) But Jacob said to him, "My lord knows that the children are tender and that I must care for the ewes and cows that are nursing their young. If they are driven hard just one day, all the animals will die. (14) So let my lord go on ahead of his servant, while I move along slowly at the pace of the flocks and herds before me and the pace of the children, until I come to my lord in Seir."

(15) Esau said, "Then let me leave some of my men with you."

"But why do that?" Jacob asked. "Just let me find favor in the eyes of my lord."

(16) So that day Esau started on his way back to Seir. (17) Jacob, however, went to Sukkoth, where he built a place for himself and made shelters for his livestock. That is why the place is called Sukkoth.

(18) After Jacob came from Paddan Aram, he arrived safely at the city of Shechem in Canaan and camped within sight of the city. (19) For a hundred pieces of silver, he bought from the sons of Hamor, the father of Shechem, the plot of ground where he pitched his tent. (20) There he set up an altar and called it El Elohe Israel. (Genesis 33:1–20)

Now for the psalmist to speak a word of unity into a room full of the sons and daughters of Africa and Europe...in America...in Georgia...and in Macon. Wow! I suppose the best you can say is that the psalmist "wasn't just whistlin' Dixie." And it certainly doesn't take a rocket scientist or three Baptist historians to discern why he puts a premium on fraternal oneness. It's simple supply and demand—we prize it so highly because we encounter it so rarely—especially in the world we live in, where petty disagreements almost automatically escalate to murder and cultural rivalries morph into ethnic cleansings and holocausts and genocide.

And the world of the Bible? Forget about it! Bible brothers seem torn apart by sibling rivalry much more often than they dwell in unity. Cain and Abel. Shem, Japheth, and the accursed Ham, who according to many of our Antebellum Southern forebears was elected with all his descendants to be the wood-hewing, water-drawing servants of his brothers and the rest of us White folks. There are Moses and Aaron, Absalom and Amnon, John and James, the thundering sons of Zebedee, scrambling respectively (if not respectably) to be at Jesus' right and left hands. Why, even the brief peek the Gospels give us of Jesus and his siblings shows us anything but brothers dwelling in unity.

Here we sit today, on a continent where the culture clash began.

> ...where sons and brothers of Europe showed up along the James River in a colony known as Virginia aboard the *Susan Constant*, followed shortly by twenty sons and brothers of Africa on a Dutch man-o-war.

> ...where a little bit later and a bit farther south, other sons and other brothers settled with a third set of sons and brothers who named our own river Ocmulgee.

> ...where Maconites for four long years lived out the true meaning of *the Confederate* creed—according to its vice-president, that "its foundations [were] laid, its cornerstone rest[ed] upon the great truth that the Negro is not equal to the white man, and that slavery—subordination to the superior race—is his natural and normal condition."[98]

> ...where 106 years later, and 16 years after the *Brown* ruling, White Maconites demonstrated by the hundreds at Judge William Augustus Bootle's house when he finally ordered the schools integrated not just because it was now legal but because

it had always been fitting, proper, and just.[99]

Yes, here we sit, almost four centuries later, and we find ourselves, in one way or another, still fighting the Civil War, still
wrestling with that war's most basic cause, our own hell-conceived,
self-imposed enmity over pigmentation.

I.

Now please, let us not be fooled into believing the wishful thinking
that with the election of a Black American to the presidency we
have arrived at some millennial post-racial America. Instead, let
everyone be aware that race still matters and racism still exists, is
still in the air we breathe, and still infects everyone in America.
And not America alone.

One day during his own lifelong wrestling match with apartheid, Archbishop Desmond Tutu sat in a South African airport
awaiting his next departure. Coming through the gate, the flight
crew noticed the international celebrity among their passengers
and went over to greet the archbishop. Tutu noticed that both the
pilot and the co-pilot were young Black South Africans, a demo-
graphic that until very recently had been barred from holding or
even training for such occupations. So in his typically jovial manner, Archbishop Tutu congratulated them for their accomplishments and told them they were living symbols of their movement's
success. But later, after the plane had reached cruising altitude, it
was hit by what the archbishop called "the Mother of all Turbulence." There, while his fellow passengers wept and prayed and
promised God everything, the Archbishop was dismayed to discover that at the very moment that the turbulence made itself felt,
the first thought that entered his mind was, "Hey, there's no white
men in the cockpit. Are those blacks going to be able to make
it?"[100]

Whether we are Klansmen or civil rights activists or anything in between, racism is within us, lurking and looking for those knee-jerk situations to leap visibly to the surface. And when we do self-consciously wrestle against it, more often than not it turns people on either side of the color line into strangers or enemies rather than allies or brothers.

II.

When we look closely at our fraternal history together on this continent, we White and Black Americans start to look quite a bit like Jacob and Esau. As "twins," we both arrived in the New World at roughly the same time. But we Whites have been Jacob, the favored one. We've done all we could to make sure of it, after all. Like Jacob, we came out of the womb and into the New World wrestling, grabbing at Esau's heel to get around him and into first place.

As our American story has unfolded, Jacob has been the brains—the pampered, softer, indoor person; Black Americans playing Esau have been the brawn, the hunter, the one living closer to the earth.

A 400-year interaction on this continent tells us unquestionably that the American Jacob has been the trickster, the cheater, the supplanter, the schemer, building an entire social system deliberately designed to put Jacob in front and Esau, as Stevie Wonder once sang, "at the back of the line when it comes to getting ahead."

For the biblical Jacob, the name of the game was first Esau's birthright and then his father's dying blessing; for the American Jacob and Esau, it was a two act drama—*first* there was 250 years of slavery and then another hundred years of Jim Crow; first the whip and then the abominable lynching tree. All played out with a musical score composed of the spirituals and the blues. Like Billie Holiday who sang:

Southern trees bear strange fruit
Blood on the leaves and blood at the root
Black bodies swinging in the southern breeze
Strange fruit hanging from the poplar trees

Pastoral scene of the gallant south
The bulging eyes and the twisted mouth
Scent of magnolias, sweet and fresh
Then the sudden smell of burning flesh[101]

Good thing we have the power to change the final act in this drama. But in America's drama of race, the lingering mystery is whether we will find a way to choose wisely and do the right thing.

You may not know that in Richmond, Virginia, a short distance from where that Dutch man-o-war first delivered its African cargo, there is a bronze statue called Reconciliation that abstractly depicts two unrecognizable people in an embrace. Unveiled in 2007, the Reconciliation Statue was the last of three sculptures created. The first stands in Liverpool, England, and the second in the west African city of Cotonou, the capital city of the Republic of Benin. Three cities who had been partners in the infamous triangular trade that brought slaves from Africa to the New World. All three issued apologies for their foreparents' involvement in human trafficking. In solidarity with each other, all three declared to slavery what the world has said to the Holocaust: "Never Again!" In the example of those three cities, along with the story of Jacob and Esau, I believe we can detect a recipe for reconciliation.

III.

Remembering is the starting point. Remembering means facing up to the truth of our history. As Jacob refocused his life away from that which he knew under Laban, his wily father-in-law, he turned toward an honest-to-God encounter with himself, and all the ways he had cheated his brother came rushing back. Acknowledging our active role in making chattel slavery a human reality is as easy as looking into a mirror.

So let us remember vividly the role of the churches and the Bible in defending slavery. By far the largest subcategory of pro-slavery literature was religious in nature and written by no less than 275 clergymen, most of them Evangelical Protestants. Of all these writings, the one written by Baptist minister and editor of Virginia's *Religious Herald*, Thornton Stringfellow, was clearly the best-selling, most widely distributed, and "vastly the best" in the opinion of some of his contemporaries.[102]

But five years after the publication of Stringfellow's work, Frederick Douglass told a London audience: "...the pulpit and the auctioneer's block stand in the same neighborhood; ...We have men sold to build churches, women sold to support missionaries, and babies sold to buy Bibles and communion services for the churches."[103]

It is true that many factors contributed to the success of Evangelical Christianity in nineteenth century America, but one factor almost always overlooked is the willingness of our pastors and laypeople to sacrifice prophetic preaching on the altar of evangelism and ever-enlarging memberships. To realize this historic reality is for Evangelical Christians in America to understand that we owe the very existence of our churches—not to mention their numerical and institutional success—to the shedding of blood. Not the shed blood of Jesus, but rather the African blood of an estimated six million slaves in the entire history of slavery in the United States.

IV.

But beyond remembering his transgressions against his brother, Jacob also began to catch on to the depth of devastation his actions had caused to Esau. Here's a life lesson that, of all people, conservatives ought to understand: actions have consequences. Thus, how can 250 years of slavery, followed by another hundred years of Jim Crow and lynch law, not also have consequences that have lasted into our own times?

Thus, we are still a society:

...where if you are born White, you can expect to live 4.5 years longer (76.5 years) than if you are born Black (72.0 years).[104]

...where 76 percent of college professors are White.[105]

...where you are 50 percent more likely to be called for a job interview if your resume bears the name Brad or Jennifer rather than the name Quintarius or LaKeisha.[106]

...where a Black person is more than twice as likely to be unemployed (14.6% of Blacks compared to 9.4% of Whites).[107]

...where the median household income for Blacks is $41,361, only 59 percent of the median White income of $70,642.[108]

...where the median net worth for Blacks ($20,000) is 8.5 times less than for Whites ($170,000).[109]

Millions of us White Americans—especially conservative ones—regularly say that we are, were, or should return to being a "Christian nation." But anyone who thinks we are a Christian nation in matters of race simply hasn't taken a long, hard look at our history and the legacy of the slave ship, the auction block, the overseer's whip, and the lynching tree. AME Bishop Reverdy Ransom once wrote that despite being faithful Christians and loyal Americans, Blacks had never gotten much justice out of Christian America. Not even Jesus had been able to break the color line. Then he said, "If Jesus wept over Jerusalem, he must have wept for America an ocean of tears."[110] The first step toward reconciliation is some deep remembering.

V.

Jacob's next step was a *deeper repentance*. A good deal of that work has been done by the Southern Baptist Convention. In 1995, the

SBC became the first denomination to issue a formal apology for its role in both slavery and Jim Crow. And in 2011, they went another step down that road by electing the first African American as SBC president.

These are important steps toward reconciliation. But a deeper repentance would, as John the Baptizer said, "bring forth fruits worthy" of the word repentance. Deeper repentance means fixing what we broke. And we don't fix it necessarily because you and I or our foreparents individually perpetrated the offense. We fix it because good Christian citizenship should clean up an environment that is dangerous to everyone living in it.

So on the night before Jacob was scheduled to meet an aggrieved brother Esau, he decided on a deep repentance: He set aside a rather hefty total of livestock to the tune of 550 rams, goats, cows, and donkeys. Not chump change by any means. More like Zacchaeus's giving back fourfold the amounts he had extorted from his clients. Jacob gave back enough to affect Esau's material well-being. And according to the Hebrew word chosen by the author of Genesis, his intention was not "to appease" Esau, as most translations render it, but rather "to atone" for his previous misdeeds.[111]

Have things changed for the better since the civil rights era? Yes, of course. But in 1968, the year King was murdered, Black per capita income was 55 percent of White income (55 cents per $1.00); in 2001 it was 57 percent. At that pace it would take 581 more years to equalize. In 1970, 65 percent of Whites in America owned their homes compared to 42 percent of Blacks; in 2001 the figure was 75 percent of Whites compared to 48 percent of Blacks. Progress, yes, but at this rate it would take 1,664 years to close the gap.[112]

But to speed up the process, and to fix what we White people broke, we ought to lead a movement of Evangelical churches to establish an Evangelical Trust Fund and a campaign to solicit every

White Evangelical church in America to raise an average of, say, $2000–$3000 per congregation for an endowment that would exclusively make grants of up to $100,000 to qualified African American applicants. These grants could be for the exclusive purpose of enabling applicants to buy their first home or start new businesses, enterprises that enable those families to accumulate wealth—putting back with a little extra thrown in—what Whites allowed slavery and Jim Crow to take away.

Will it work? Will it create the sort of harmony that finally enveloped Jacob and Esau? Who knows? Jacob wasn't absolutely certain about it. He tried to sleep on it, but there was too much to wrestle with. His conscience. His fears for his life. His hopes that his brother's anger could be overcome. But he wrestled with it all and wouldn't let go until he had his brother back again.

Now to tell you the truth, I wrestled with whether or not to talk about this today. When I decided to do so, I contemplated changing the title of this address to "I Have a Pipe Dream." But if we don't aim for the impossible, I doubt human beings will ever accomplish the difficult. Historian Mills Thornton may have said it best: "More often than not, nobility lies precisely in being unwilling to accept reality. Because a community where no one was willing to work to make it truly Beloved would be a place too awful to contemplate."[113]

But then I always have believed in fairy tales. Like this one the rabbis used to tell: Once upon a time before time, say the rabbis, there were two brothers. Each day they ground their grain together and each night they evenly divided it between them. One day one brother thought, "It's not really fair to divide the grain evenly. I only have myself, but my brother has a large family to feed." So each night he secretly put some of his grain into his brother's granary.

But the other brother thought, "It's not really fair to divide the grain evenly. I have children to provide for me in my old age, but my brother is alone." So each night *he* put some of his grain into his brother's granary.

Then one night the brothers unexpectedly met each other halfway between their two houses. They suddenly realized what had been happening, threw their arms around each other, and embraced in love. It is said that God witnessed this meeting and proclaimed, "This is a holy place. Here is where my Temple shall be built." And so it was. The holy place where God is made known is the place where brothers and sisters discover each other and embrace in love.[114]

Much like Jacob and Esau. Like their story, our own American drama has a final act. It's name is Reconciliation, and "how sweet" the soundtrack—music by a slave named Unknown, familiar lyrics by a former slave-trader named John Newton.[115] The program says it's time to sing them. Will you join me?

> Amazing grace, how sweet the sound
> That saved a wretch like me.
> I once was lost, but now am found.
> Was blind, but now I see.

10

Carrying Your Corner of the Blanket

Jason McClendon, Pastor of Community Church of God, Macon, Georgia

(1) At Caesarea there was a man named Cornelius, a centurion in what was known as the Italian Regiment. (2) He and all his family were devout and God-fearing; he gave generously to those in need and prayed to God regularly. (3) One day at about three in the afternoon he had a vision. He distinctly saw an angel of God, who came to him and said, "Cornelius!" (4) Cornelius stared at him in fear. "What is it, Lord?" he asked. The angel answered, "Your prayers and gifts to the poor have come up as a memorial offering before God. (5) Now send men to Joppa to bring back a man named Simon who is called Peter. (6) He is staying with Simon the tanner, whose house is by the sea." (7) When the angel who spoke to him had gone, Cornelius called two of his servants and a devout soldier who was one of his attendants. (8) He told them everything that had happened and sent them to Joppa.

(9) About noon the following day as they were on their journey and approaching the city, Peter went up on the roof to pray. (10) He became hungry and wanted something to eat, and while the meal was being prepared, he fell into a trance. (11) He saw heaven opened and something like a large sheet being let down to earth by its four corners. (12) It contained all kinds of four-footed animals, as well as reptiles and birds. (13)

Then a voice told him, "Get up, Peter. Kill and eat." (14) "Surely not, Lord!" Peter replied. "I have never eaten anything impure or unclean." (15) The voice spoke to him a second time, "Do not call anything impure that God has made clean." (16) This happened three times, and immediately the sheet was taken back to heaven.

(17) While Peter was wondering about the meaning of the vision, the men sent by Cornelius found out where Simon's house was and stopped at the gate. (18) They called out, asking if Simon who was known as Peter was staying there.

(19) While Peter was still thinking about the vision, the Spirit said to him, "Simon, three men are looking for you. (20) So get up and go downstairs. Do not hesitate to go with them, for I have sent them."

(21) Peter went down and said to the men, "I'm the one you're looking for. Why have you come?" (22) The men replied, "We have come from Cornelius the centurion. He is a righteous and God-fearing man, who is respected by all the Jewish people. A holy angel told him to ask you to come to his house so that he could hear what you have to say." (23) Then Peter invited the men into the house to be his guests.

The next day Peter started out with them, and some of the believers from Joppa went along. (24) The following day he arrived in Caesarea. Cornelius was expecting them and had called together his relatives and close friends. (25) As Peter entered the house, Cornelius met him and fell at his feet in reverence. (26) But Peter made him get up. "Stand up," he said, "I am only a man myself." (27) While talking with him, Peter went inside and found a large gathering of people. (28) He said to them: "You are well aware that it is against our law for a Jew to associate with or visit a Gentile. But God has shown me that I should not call anyone impure or unclean. (29) So when I was sent for, I came without raising any objection. May I ask why you sent for me?" (30) Cornelius answered: "Three days ago I was in my house praying at this hour, at three in the afternoon. Suddenly a man in shining clothes stood before me (31) and said, 'Cornelius, God has heard your prayer and remembered your gifts to the poor. (32) Send to Joppa for Simon who is called Peter. He is a guest in the home of Simon the tanner, who lives by the sea.' (33) So I sent for you immediately, and it was good of you to come. Now we are all here in the presence of God to listen to everything the Lord has commanded you to tell us."

(34) Then Peter began to speak: "I now realize how true it is that God does not show favoritism (35) but accepts from every nation the one who fears him and does what is right. (36) You know the message God sent to the people of Israel, announcing the good news of peace through Jesus Christ, who is Lord of all. (37) You know what has happened throughout the province of Judea, beginning in Galilee after the baptism that John preached— (38) how God anointed Jesus of Nazareth with the Holy Spirit and power, and how he went around doing good and healing all who were under the power of the devil, because God was with him.

(39) "We are witnesses of everything he did in the country of the Jews and in Jerusalem. They killed him by hanging him on a cross, (40) but God raised him from the dead on the third day and caused him to be seen. (41) He was not seen by all the people, but by witnesses whom God had already chosen—by us who ate and drank with him after he rose from the dead. (42) He commanded us to preach to the people and to testify that he is the one whom God appointed as judge of the living and the dead. (43) All the prophets testify about him that everyone who believes in him receives forgiveness of sins through his name."

(44) While Peter was still speaking these words, the Holy Spirit came on all who heard the message. (45) The circumcised believers who had come with Peter were astonished that the gift of the Holy Spirit had been poured out even on Gentiles. (46) For they heard them speaking in tongues and praising God. Then Peter said, (47) "Surely no one can stand in the way of their being baptized with water. They have received the Holy Spirit just as we have." (48) So he ordered that they be baptized in the name of Jesus Christ. Then they asked Peter to stay with them for a few days. (Acts 10:1–48)

Beloved, you need not have lived in Macon for very long, or turn on CNN or Fox or MSNBC, whatever you want to watch, to be informed about what's happening in the world. But we are seeing something that is impacting the church and our community even here today. We are seeing a resurgence of racism. It's very peculiar because we see Jesus having been raised from the dead and ascended to the Father making intercession for his people for about fourteen days. Then in the second chapter of Acts we learned that the church was experiencing exponential growth and the Lord was adding those who were being saved every day.

But it's easy to have rapid growth when you have Jews worshiping with Jews. It's easy to have growth when everyone is working with their own people and with their own neighbors. It's really hard to do something that you've never done before. But it's time to let the world know the full reason why Jesus died. It's time for us to do some work in our community.

So if I could just pose a question to you today: Can saved people be prejudiced? There are several reasons we have to deal with prejudice today. People differ, number one. There are different nationalities, colors, religions, beliefs, looks, behaviors, abilities, energy, social status and position, possessions, wealth, and birthplaces.

The other reason we see prejudice in our communities is that mistreatment causes prejudice also. When someone mistreats others, his nature is inclined to become even more prejudiced and judgmental. The mistreatment that gives rise to prejudice includes a wide variety of behaviors: ignoring, neglecting, joking, gossiping, opposing, cursing, abusing, persecuting, passing over, even segregating and enslaving.

Acts 10 delivers a fatal blow and says "Enough is enough." Here is some background on what the Jews had to deal with. The Jews had always been mistreated and enslaved and persecuted—much more than any other people of the Earth. They had always been conquered by various armies. They had been scattered abroad. One of the things that made the Jewish people so strong was their religion. Religion held them together. It was their religion that taught people to respect their father and mother. It was their religion that taught them how to love one another. We can never forget the story of the prodigal son that helps us always remember that our God is a loving God and he's forgiving.

But the problem was that the Jews did not fully understand God's word. God chose them just like Abraham to be ambassadors to the rest of the world. But because of their persecution and because of their oppression, and they let their religion stay inward instead of sharing it freely. They kept it to themselves. And they got themselves into a position that implied, "We are better than you because we worship the true and living God."

I don't know how things are where you live, but there's a spirit in the world today that tries to separate us and says, "You need to stay with your own people. Don't you go on that side of the aisle." In my denomination, the Church of God, we are so proud to claim that we are people who accept everybody, but we've got a deep dark secret. And that is that we have two assemblies: a White assembly and a Black assembly.

This goes back to the 1920s and the denominational meeting in Anderson, Indiana, where large numbers of Whites in our sphere of influence were associated with the Klan or some other White nationalist groups. When Blacks from the South came to the conference, they were told it would be better if they were gone. The assembly was trying to get these Klan members saved. But they wouldn't come to the conference if Black people were included.

Maybe you've received some type of oppression. Maybe you've felt some type of micro-aggression. But let's get into the Word because Jesus wants to break down walls of prejudice. In the first place, God loves people of influence. In order to effect some kind of change, you have to have some influence over somebody else. The passage says there was a large number of priests—people of influence. There was Dorcas, the Ethiopian eunuch, and Simon the sorcerer—all people of influence. Very peculiar that God uses people of influence.

So what are the prerequisites for you and me to carry our part of the blanket? In the vision, God is sending down a huge table-cloth large enough to carry by the corners. But to change the church for the better will take Peter and his group along with Cornelius and his group. The problem in the text is that Cornelius is from Caesarea. That is a geographical area that Jews avoided at all costs. So what are the prerequisites to allow us to carry a corner of the blanket?

Number one, God says to Cornelius, "your alms have come up as a memorial." God chooses Cornelius because he is an individual who is willing to give to charity without himself controlling what happens to the money. Did you know that some people give to charity without having a heart of charity? There are some people who give to the poor, but they never have the poor with them. It is impossible to fully fellowship somebody that you will not share a meal with. You cannot have fellowship with anybody if you are not willing to sit at the same table with them. How can you fellowship with somebody when you won't even let them come into your home? One prerequisite is almsgiving. How can we be saved, live lives of luxury, and not be concerned about the poor?

The next one is your prayer life. When was the last time you prayed to the true and living God? When Cornelius prayed that God would use all that he was and all that he had for the upbuilding of the Kingdom, there came a knock at his door. God had prepared his heart.

But next God had to prepare us religious people. The story of Peter and Cornelius is the longest discourse in the book of Acts. From part of the ninth to the early part of the eleventh chapter of

Acts, God gives extra detail to the story because it revolutionized the church! It could revolutionize our communities also.

But we've got to deal with our prejudices. Take, for example, Simon the tanner. He is an outcast from Jewish society because of his work with animal skins. And it's a violation for Peter even to be staying in Simon's house. Can you imagine Simon the tanner trying to serve a meal to Peter and cooking food, and Peter saying, "I don't eat this and I don't need that." Simon might respond, "OK, I'm good enough for you to stay in my house, but I'm not good enough for you to eat my food?"

The thing we need to learn is that a lot can happen between us over a table just fellowshipping and eating together. But God has to work on Peter. He sends him a vision with all these different foods and a command to eat. But Peter objects, "Not so, Lord. I've never eaten anything unclean. God and my mama taught me never to eat unclean food!" Sometimes the way we were raised can thwart our spiritual receptivity to hear the direction that God wants us to go.

Back when I was doing my clinicals in school, there was a multicultural congregation in Texas, and I went down to interview for a position there. Naturally, my preference is to dress up, but from the pulpit I could see that the men in the congregation were dressed casually. And I heard a woman moan that with a Church of God minister, "We gon' be speaking in tongues." But when I got in the pulpit, I decided to try to help the congregation lighten up a bit. So I took my jacket off, unbuttoned my shirt, and rolled up my sleeves. At once, I saw the people start smiling. Why? Because they saw me trying to identify with their culture. And God is trying to help you and me identify with the cultures that are around us, just as God was working on Peter to get beyond some of his preconceived notions.

The problem is that we are not faithful in holding our corner of the blanket and in proclaiming that our God loves all people. As a member of the beloved community, we were asked to let a Caucasian preach at our church. But some in the congregation felt some misgivings. Some asked, "Pastor, do you know what you're doing?" And I felt some pressure. But after it was over, you know what the church said, right? "Pastor, when are we going to do it again?!" Sometimes we are afraid of things because we just don't know any better.

But when Peter finally gets it, he says, "Lord, I will not call something that you have made unclean or uncommon." And once he realized that, in his spirit he took hold of his corner of the blanket and helped the church become what God intended it to be.

It's amazing that we can do so much work, but we dropped our corner of the blanket. With God's discipline and with his help, let us commit ourselves to take up once again our corner of the blanket. And let us pray that God will make us into the church and the beloved community he intends for us to be. Amen.

11

On Religion, Race, and Reconciliation

Father Allan J. McDonald, St. Joseph Catholic Church[116]

(13) You say, "Food for the stomach and the stomach for food, and God will destroy them both." The body, however, is not meant for sexual immorality but for the Lord, and the Lord for the body. (14) By his power God raised the Lord from the dead, and he will raise us also. (15) Do you not know that your bodies are members of Christ himself? Shall I then take the members of Christ and unite them with a prostitute? Never! (16) Do you not know that he who unites himself with a prostitute is one with her in body? For it is said, "The two will become one flesh." (17) But whoever is united with the Lord is one with him in spirit. (18) Flee from sexual immorality. All other sins a person commits are outside the body, but whoever sins sexually, sins against their own body. (19) Do you not know that your bodies are temples of the Holy Spirit, who is in you, whom you have received from God? You are not your own; (20) you were bought at a price. Therefore honor God with your bodies. (1 Corinthians 6:13–20)

(35) The next day John was there again with two of his disciples. (36) When he saw Jesus passing by, he said, "Look, the Lamb of God!" (37) When the two disciples heard him say this, they followed Jesus. (38) Turning around, Jesus saw them following and asked, "What do you want?" They said, "Rabbi"

(which means "Teacher"), "where are you staying?" (39) "Come," he replied, "and you will see." So they went and saw where he was staying, and they spent that day with him. It was about four in the afternoon. (40) Andrew, Simon Peter's brother, was one of the two who heard what John had said and who had followed Jesus. (41) The first thing Andrew did was to find his brother Simon and tell him, "We have found the Messiah" (that is, the Christ). (42) And he brought him to Jesus. Jesus looked at him and said, "You are Simon son of John. You will be called Cephas" (which, when translated, is Peter). (John 1:35–42)

By a very fascinating coincidence of history, the day after Dr. Martin Luther King's national holiday on Monday, January 19, 2009, the United States of America experienced an orderly transition of power on Tuesday, January 20, 2009, when Barack Obama became the forty-fourth American but the first *African* American to be inaugurated President of the United States of America.

Dr. Martin Luther King, both in life and death, paved the way for the historic inauguration of the first African American president. Some in Christian America believe that presidents are called by God to continue the great tradition of the Declaration of Independence and our United States Constitution.

In a religious way, we feel that God has made us a chosen nation, a people set apart for a specific mission of freedom and justice in the world. We prayed that President Obama would continue to lead our nation in the ways of God's divine will. We wanted him to succeed and to lead our nation in the ways of respect for human life, especially the unborn, which in the twenty-first century is clearly an agenda for civil and human rights. We wanted God to anoint him and to make him wise in all his decisions. President Barack Obama was called by Americans through our election process and by God to the vocation of being a world leader. As such, he would seek to draw the nations, religions, and races of the world together under the umbrella of respect for one another. We felt he could assist our nation in the struggle for racial equality and brotherhood. Only time and 20/20 hindsight will tell how history will evaluate President Obama's presidency. We prayed that he would succeed and do so masterfully.

With 2,000 years of 20/20 hindsight, salvation history has revealed that Jesus is God's Anointed One, the Christ, and the Lamb of God whose real presence in our lives will unite us and set us free.

Yet many of us remain shackled to sin and death. We refuse to grasp what it means to be a true follower of Jesus and learn from Him the two greatest commandments—loving God and loving our neighbors. Instead, we sometimes treat people as second-class citizens and do not realize how God's grace can transform our prejudices and change us into who we are meant to be—people created in the image and likeness of God.

One of my first recollections about inequality or a lack of freedom for some in terms of civil rights was when I was a child of 3–5 years of age in Atlanta. We had just moved from Naples, Italy, in 1957, and my Italian mother who spoke broken English and did not drive would always take me with her on the bus to shop downtown. I noticed that the Black people always sat at the back of the bus, and I wanted to sit on the long back seat myself, but we were told that it was for Blacks only. I thought how lucky they were. Of course, I did not understand the prejudice and racism involved. But I did come to understand it more clearly one weekday afternoon when my mother's American friend from Ohio, the friend's Black housekeeper, and I went downtown together on the bus. We planned it so that the housekeeper could sit at the first seat for Blacks and we could sit at the last seat for Whites, and we could converse with the housekeeper.

Once the bus took off and arrived at the next stop, the bus driver got out of his seat and came to us and told us we could not talk to the housekeeper. My mother and her friend from Ohio were just plain shocked. Keep in mind my mother had lived during a time of Fascism in Italy.

I remember my parents talking about this incident and how horrible it felt that something like this could happen in the USA. Not to mention in the South of all places, known as the Bible Belt with its strong Protestant beliefs. How could Christians treat others in this manner?

Obviously the words to describe this treatment are *sin* and *evil*. There are many who, out of ignorance and sin and evil, do not see everyone as created in the image and likeness of God. They do not behold the Lamb of God in their neighbor, nor do they love their neighbor as themselves.

The apostles heard about Jesus from St. John the Baptist, who pointed them in the right direction. Then they dialogued with Jesus. This led them to recognize Jesus as Messiah and King, and Jesus would lead them to live as Jesus does and to love as Jesus does. He would lead them to form a community of people from every land and race, a community of faith, hope, and love that would continue forever. He would lead them to follow the two greatest commandments, love of God and love of neighbor.

Because Jesus Christ is God, the Second Person of the Blessed Trinity, Son of God and Son of the Blessed Virgin Mary, his leadership can be trusted and will never disappoint. He will lead us in the ways of the common good.

Dr. Martin Luther King is a hero for many people, and certainly his life and death have brought about seismic changes in American culture and society. He called us as God's voice to put aside prejudice, racism, and segregation and to focus on the content of our character. Dr. King through his eloquence did what John the Baptist does in today's Gospel reading: he points not to himself but to the Lamb of God, Jesus Christ, and says that we are to follow Him.

Saint Paul in his first letter to the Corinthians wanted the Corinthian community and us to know that by virtue of our baptism, we have become part of something greater than ourselves. We are incorporated into the life of Christ, the family of God, and the community of the church where no one is excluded by virtue of race or national origin. We are all brothers and sisters in the Lord.

We are no longer on our own but are a part of something much bigger than we are and led by Jesus Christ, the Lamb of God. Paul reminds us not to pollute the place where Jesus is encountered by using slogans and attitudes of the world that are opposed to life and unity.

In our struggles to overcome racism and prejudice and anything that compromises the dignity of the human being created in the image and likeness of God, we must go to the root of exclusion, of the throwaway culture that Pope Francis references, to the very heart of human life at his or her moment of conception. The culture of inclusion and unity that Pope Francis dreams about begins at the moment of any human person's conception. The new spiritual battle for civil rights continues for those races that know the sting of discrimination and prejudice built upon racism. Yet we know too that innocent human life, by law, can be snuffed out and completely excluded. There are no civil rights for the unborn. If we see the connection between this scourge of no legal protection for the unborn and the sad mentality of racism sometimes codified by law also, we will go a long way toward building a culture of inclusion and the unity that embraces with equal dignity all God has created, and we will protect God's children by law.

At Mass, when the priest says, "Behold the Lamb of God, behold Him who takes away the sins of the world," let us worship Jesus in spirit and truth. Let us recommit to following Him in all things. Let us see in Him our unity and dignity as brothers and sisters in the Lord.

12

We Need Each Other

Reverend Billy Graham McFadden,
Pastor of Greater Allen AME Church[117]

(12) Just as a body, though one, has many parts, but all its many parts form one body, so it is with Christ. (13) For we were all baptized by one Spirit so as to form one body—whether Jews or Gentiles, slave or free—and we were all given the one Spirit to drink. (14) Even so the body is not made up of one part but of many. (15) Now if the foot should say, "Because I am not a hand, I do not belong to the body," it would not for that reason stop being part of the body. (16) And if the ear should say, "Because I am not an eye, I do not belong to the body," it would not for that reason stop being part of the body. (17) If the whole body were an eye, where would the sense of hearing be? If the whole body were an ear, where would the sense of smell be? (18) But in fact God has placed the parts in the body, every one of them, just as he wanted them to be. (19) If they were all one part, where would the body be? (20) As it is, there are many parts, but one body. (21) The eye cannot say to the hand, "I don't need you!" And the head cannot say to the feet, "I don't need you!" (22) On the contrary, those parts of the body that seem to be weaker are indispensable, (23) and the parts that we think are less honorable we treat with special honor. And the parts that are unpresentable are treated with special modesty, (24) while our presentable parts need no spe-

cial treatment. But God has put the body together, giving greater honor to the parts that lacked it, (25) so that there should be no division in the body, but that its parts should have equal concern for each other. (26) If one part suffers, every part suffers with it; if one part is honored, every part rejoices with it. (1 Corinthians 12:12–26)

During the thirteenth century, the Roman Emperor Frederick carried out a rather cruel and evil experiment. He wanted to know what man's original language was: was it Hebrew, Greek, or Latin? So he decided to isolate a few infants from the sound of the human voice. No words were to be spoken at all. He reasoned that they would eventually speak the natural language of man. Other women were brought in to breastfeed the infants and sworn to absolute silence; although it was hard for them to do, they abided by the rule. The infants never heard a word—not a sound from a human voice. Within three months they were all dead. Beautiful people, write this down: it is one of the truths emerging from our text today. *God created us to live in relationships.* No man or woman is an island. We need each other.

As the text points out so vividly, whether you are the eye, the foot, or the hand, each needs the other in order for the whole to function well. Listen as the text announces its premise. If Foot said, "I'm not elegant like Hand, embellished with rings; I guess I don't belong to this body," would that make it so? If Ear said, "I'm not beautiful like Eye, limpid and expressive; I don't deserve a place on the head," would you want to remove it from the body? If the body was all eye, how could it hear? If all ear, how could it smell? As it is, we see that God has carefully placed each part of the body right where he wanted it.

But I also want you to think about how this keeps your significance from getting blown up into self-importance. For no matter how significant you are, it is only because of what you are a part of.

An enormous eye or a gigantic hand wouldn't be a body, but a monster. Just in case you didn't know, we've had enough monsters to last us a lifetime. We see firsthand the destruction that the monster mentality has brought our way. The segregated water fountains and lunch counters. The failed separate but equal doctrine that worked hard to justify the practice of segregation and Jim Crowism. Essentially, it was simply a practice of keeping people apart and alienating individuals of different and diverse human realities. Unfortunately, there are vestiges of this practice that still persist to this day.

This was not, however, God's best nor God's intention for human beings. From the beginning, God acknowledged that togetherness is a much better road to travel through life. The Bible declares that God said, "Let US make man in our image." Embedded in this statement was a unity among the heavenly hosts being modeled for humanity on how we should get along. Jesus even labored in prayer for humanity's state of togetherness when he prayed in the Gospel of John "that we would be one." The old Black spiritual picked up on the Lord's admonition to us in the words,

> Walk together children.
> Don't get weary.
> Oh walk together children.
> Don't get weary.
> There is a great camp meeting in the sky.

If in this world, we would simply learn to walk together, then perhaps there would be less war and more peace; less hate and more love; less division and separation and more unity. God declared in the book of beginnings, "It is not good for the man to be alone." Inherent in God's statement is the reality that "We need each other."

Brothers and sisters, I can't make it by myself. I need you. We each need one another. We can't make it alone. I need to hear your voice. I need to see your smile. Just as the parts of our own body works better with cooperation and assistance, the body of Christ also works better when we recognize and concede that we need all parts of the body working together.

First Baptist Church of Christ on High Place in Macon, Georgia, needs Steward Chapel African Methodist Episcopal Church on Forsyth Street in Macon, Georgia. Members of Macon's NAACP need members of the Macon Georgia Rotary. My friends, the light of God shines brighter through a body agreeing with God's assertion located in the text that says I want you to think about how all this makes you more significant, not less. A body isn't just a single part blown up into something huge. It's all the different but similar parts arranged and functioning together. Did you hear that? "Different but similar."

Psalm 139 declares that God fearfully and wonderfully put us together, and that brings me to my second point. God made us uniquely who we are and what we are. We are different but similar at the same time. Red and yellow, black and white, we are ALL precious in God's sight. God created us uniquely with differing skin colors, differing textures of hair, and differing physical characteristics. Yet to be so different we ALL still breath oxygen, we ALL still have a heart that pumps red blood, we ALL still have an eardrum that enables us to hear, ALL with two bean-shaped organs called kidneys that filters blood through our bodies. Look to your neighbor and say ALL.

We ALL have a stomach that stores food and emits a digestive substance to help digest our food. Each of these bodily functions are important and significant. We simply can't get along without them. They do what they do because this is their God-created function. I've never seen my kidney, never even given my eardrums much thought. But I'm here to tell you that life would be a mess without them functioning like they do. I couldn't make it without them. I thank God they function in harmony with each other. There is no one who can do what God created me to do. No one who can perform my function in the earth. Try as you will to be someone or something you're not, and you will fail every single time. There isn't but one Billy, only one Tammie, only one Betty Lowe, only one Louis Scott. And still we ALL belong to a loving, caring God who created us ALL in God's image to work and live in harmony with each other.

This is also the truth for larger society. When we intentionally alienate ourselves from each other and purposely discriminate between racial, social, and ethnic lines, we diminish the harmony and curtail the moment of reconciliation that is so badly needed for a well-functioning society. This directs me to my last point. We belong to each other.

Mother Teresa once said, "If we have no peace, it is only because we have forgotten that we belong to each other." People fall out and cuss and fuss and stop caring and talking with each other because we forget that we belong to each other. Crowds square off on opposite sides of the street, hurling insult after insult, forgetting entirely that we belong to each other. We quickly lift our constitutional rights of free speech and the right to assemble and protest, but even more quickly, we forget that we belong to each other.

There is something extremely unpleasant when others turn a blind eye to the march of justice that has been diverted and otherwise delayed for a people disenfranchised throughout history. On the morning before facing trial, Dr. Martin Luther King Jr. preached about the obnoxious peace on the University of Alabama campus that had so angrily rejected a Black student just days before. He said,

Yes, things are quiet in Tuscaloosa. Yes, there was peace on the campus, but it was peace at a great price: it was peace that had been purchased at the exorbitant price of an inept trustee board succumbing to the whims and caprices of a vicious mob. It was peace that had been purchased at the price of allowing mobocracy to reign supreme over democracy. It was peace that had been purchased at the price of capitulating to the force of darkness. This is the type of peace that all men of goodwill hate. It is the type of peace that is obnoxious. It is the type of peace that stinks in the nostrils of Almighty God.[118]

There is something obnoxious about working together from nine to five but condoning harmful hate speech in your personal, private circles. Just like I need you at work, I need you in life. Look to your neighbor and say, "I need you."

Beautiful people, I don't know about you, but I need you to encourage me sometimes. I need to hear some positive, optimistic, and uplifting admonition coming from you. Paul recognized just how important this aspect of unity is. He writes in the text, "The eye cannot say to the hand, 'I don't need you!' And the head cannot say to the feet, 'I don't need you!'" Why? Because we need each other. We are all important and significant. And God loves each of us so much that God emptied Godself of all heavenly glory and descended to a cold, sinful world and died for the likes of you and me: sinful man.

The Bible says that God was in Christ reconciling the world. The New Living Bible paraphrases it "restoring harmony in the world." If I declare I'm a child of God, then I must walk in harmony with you. Black, white, red, or yellow. Sin caused a great chasm between God's created beings. But the same Jesus who knew no sin became sin for us. He extended his love toward us while we were in sin.

I thank God for God's love and grace today. God's unmerited favor. I really didn't get what I deserved. The truth is none of humanity has gotten what we deserve. All because Jesus walked down the Via Dolorosa and up Calvary's mountain. There they hung him high and stretched him wide, and he gave up the ghost and then

he died. But early Sunday morning, just before the break of day, Jesus got up! The Bible says he led captivity captive and gave gifts to men. And today I'm glad to be a part of the family of God. God's family. Red and yellow, black and white family.
WE NEED EACH OTHER.

13

Making Bitter Water Sweet

The Reverend Jeff Morris,
Pastor of First Assembly of God Church

(19) The people of the city said to Elisha, "Look, our lord, this town is well situated, as you can see, but the water is bad and the land is unproductive." (20) "Bring me a new bowl," he said, "and put salt in it." So they brought it to him. (21) Then he went out to the spring and threw the salt into it, saying, "This is what the Lord says: 'I have healed this water. Never again will it cause death or make the land unproductive.'" (22) And the water has remained pure to this day, according to the word Elisha had spoken. (2 Kings 2:19–22)

Something had caused the water at Jericho to go bad, or to become bitter, and it was devastating the city. Everyone has probably heard of Jericho because of Joshua and the battle of Jericho, where the city walls fell down flat. That happened about five hundred years before Elisha's time, and God did say that whoever rebuilt Jericho would do so at the cost of his oldest and youngest son—and that actually happened! (See 1 Kings 16:34.)

But once the city was rebuilt, there was no command to destroy it again or for people not to live there. Elisha built a prophet school there. Jesus even visited there! It was at Jericho he met a little IRS agent named Zacchaeus.

So the prophecy came true, but there was no lasting curse on this city! It was just a city with a problem they couldn't fix themselves. All they knew was that they needed help. They needed God, and he came through for their city.

I don't know what caused the water at Jericho to go bad. But I do know what healed the water. It wasn't the salt! Salt contaminates water. Salt should have just made things worse. What healed the water was the word of God! Elisha said, "This is what the Lord says, 'I have healed this water. Never again will it cause death or make the land unproductive.'" God healed it; but he used the salt in the new bowl.

God didn't have to use the salt. That will be important to remember later. But he did use it, and he healed their water forever. The same spring waters Jericho today. It is called "Elisha's Spring."

Here is the message today: Macon is like Jericho. It is a well-situated city, but there is bitterness flowing here. And nothing is more counterproductive than bitterness. It destroys potential, and it is so senseless. Being bitter is like you drinking poison and hoping the person who hurt you gets sick.

Bitterness can kill you, and it can doom a community. But the word of the Lord can heal forever! So hear the word of the Lord today! Macon is a city that needs God's intervention. Like all cities we have problems here, but the one God is continually pointing out to me is racism.

I. RACISM CAUSES BITTERNESS

It is certainly causing bitterness in Macon. It causes people from different backgrounds to dislike and distrust each other. Through racism, Satan makes many White people think Black people are the problem; and he makes many Black people think White people are the problem. Church, Satan is the problem! Paul told the Ephesians, "For we wrestle not against flesh and blood, but against principalities, against powers, against the rulers of the darkness of this world, against spiritual wickedness in high places" (Ephesians 6:12). Satan is the problem! Satan is the enemy!

But not everyone knows who is causing the problem, just that there is a problem. And there is a racial problem in Macon. But God has the answer. He has the solution. And I want to be a part of God's solution to what may be the biggest problem in our community. So here are three steps we can take starting today to become part of the solution for racism.

1. Stop being part of the problem. God does not show favoritism. Neither should those of us in the church. James said simply, "Don't show favoritism" (James 2:1). James is talking to the church! Some New Testament churches were judging people at the door to determine where they would sit for the service: some up front, some in back, and some on the floor! If God's church doesn't get this right, who will?

It is soul-searching time for God's church in Macon. I already mentioned this about the water in Jericho—the Bible does not tell us why it went bad. It does not tell us whose fault it was. Did someone sin? Was God punishing them? Was an enemy contaminating their water supply? We don't know. The focus of the story in the Bible was not on the problem—the focus was on the solution!

So many people want to talk about who is at fault for the origins of racial strife in Macon, but there is a simple answer. Have you heard of slavery? How about Jim Crow? The origins of racial strife here are in White people sinning against God and against their fellow man. The problem is sin. So if the problem is and has always been sin, the solution can only be God! Let's move to step two in becoming a part of the solution.

2. Recognize that the problem is spiritual. This means the solution is not political. I appreciate people who are willing to be public servants; we should pray for them all, and they can certainly help. But politics cannot cure the root problem when the problem is spiritual.

The solution is also not economics. Money is not the answer to everything. I pray for better and higher-paying jobs for our community, but they will not cure sin! And the solution is not education. I believe in education! My degree is in education, but the root cause of racism is not ignorance, and our public schools are not equipped to handle spiritual issues. My own children are public school children here in Macon and are doing extremely well. Education will improve when families improve, and that is also church work. Government, jobs, and schools are important and can all help. But they are not the solution. The problem is sin. Racism is sin! And we need God.

"Righteousness exalts a nation (or a city), but sin is a disgrace to any people" (Proverbs 14:34). We need grace. We cannot continue disgrace. Communities and nations are like churches in that they are really people. They are not just geographical entities or institutions. God does not love or forgive institutions—he loves and forgives people. Then, led by God, people change their institutions, including their churches. And almost everyone in every church in town would admit that God can do anything, if we believe. That brings us to step three in being a part of the solution for racism.

3. BELIEVE! "Everything is possible for him who believes" (Mark 9:23). Ask God to heal our land. Ask by faith. If you believe, you will keep on asking. You stop asking when you stop believing. Ask God to forgive you for any part you have personally played in bringing division, because you absolutely cannot be part of the problem and part of the solution at the same time! You change first. Believe God to change you, then believe God to change Macon.

This is important: First believe in God. Then believe in Macon. If you have given up on Macon, you have given up on God.

You must believe in what God can do where he has planted you. That is what happened in Jericho. They knew they had a good city with potential. So they went to Elisha because they knew he would go to God. And Elisha said, "Bring me a new bowl."

II. "BRING ME A NEW BOWL"

I don't know why it had to be a new bowl. It was just a container, just a vessel. It seems like an old bowl would have worked. Maybe God was testing their obedience. When God speaks, do exactly what he says! Or maybe God was about to do something that had never been done before. At least not in Jericho. All I know is that part of God's plan to heal the waters of Jericho involved a new bowl, and I believe part of God's plan to heal the sin of racism in Macon will involve a new vision for his church here in our community.

Elisha said, "Bring me a new bowl, and put salt in it." Now that must have sounded ridiculous! How could salt in a new bowl cure anything? When the survival of a city is at stake, you'd think a smart man like Elisha could come up with a better plan than this. Rational people must have laughed. Educated people knew this was not a good idea. How could salt in a new bowl cure bitter water and save a city? The same way our small church can help bless this whole community. It will take a miracle!

We already know that. There is nothing about us that can change this community. This community is bigger than we are, and the problems in Macon have been here longer than our church has been here. What can a handful of believers in a small church building do about all the difficulties our community is facing? Not much. Not if all we ever do is done inside this building—secluded, concealed, and segregated.

But God did not heal the water while the salt was in the bowl. The healing was not in the bowl. The miracle did not happen in the bowl. The healing came when what was in the bowl got into the water. Elisha took the salt in the new bowl, and he threw the salt into the water.

III. HE THREW THE SALT INTO THE WATER

Now that's FAITH! It should have made things worse. There was no natural reason to do what he did. But as Christians, we don't live by natural principles; we live by faith! Faith is hearing and obeying God. It is not just believing something; it is doing something. "Without faith it is impossible to please God" (Hebrews 11:6). If we want to help heal our community, we must be willing to do something. So what should we do? As a church, we are intentionally becoming a model church of racial reconciliation for our community. We are intentionally interracial.

The Christian church should have been the first institution in Macon to integrate. Instead we are among the last. As far as I can see, there are few truly integrated churches in our community, and we can testify that it is not easy. But here—in the church—is where God can change people better than anywhere else, because the Bible says,

> Here there is no Greek or Jew, circumcised or uncircumcised, barbarian, Scythian, slave or free, But Christ is all, and is in all. Therefore, as God's chosen people, holy and dearly loved, clothe yourselves with compassion, kindness, humility, gentleness, and patience. Bear with each other and forgive whatever grievances you may have against one another. Forgive as the Lord forgave you. And over all these virtues put on love, which binds them together in perfect unity. (Colossians 3:11–14)

True forgiveness is our only hope for perfect unity in our community. For that reason, there will be no racial harmony in Macon until it is REAL at church.

Here is what we must do: First, forgive people who hurt you and ask for forgiveness from anyone you have hurt. If you don't forgive, you are not forgiven (Matthew 6:15). Second, look for someone who is not like you and who is not in church, and invite them to your church. Jesus said go! Go right into the bitterness! We must all personally be forgiving and intentionally interracial.

The key is getting church people out of their bowls and into the water, because we are the "salt of the earth" (Matthew 5:13). So let us go and trust God for the healing. There is no lasting curse on our city. Macon is just a city that has a problem we can't fix ourselves. We need God. And the same God who healed the waters of Jericho can heal all the bitterness that flows in Macon. God loves Macon. God believes in Macon! He wants us to prosper. He wants to replace the bitterness here with the sweetness of his Holy Spirit. Macon can become a model community. All it needs is some salt. I hear God saying, "Where's the salt? Someone pass the salt!" And you should say, "Here am I, Lord. Send me."

14

Where Are We and What Are We Looking For?

Rabbi Aaron Rubinstein of Congregation Sha'arey Israel

(6) When the woman saw that the fruit of the tree was good for food and pleasing to the eye, and also desirable for gaining wisdom, she took some and ate it. She also gave some to her husband, who was with her, and he ate it. (7) Then the eyes of both of them were opened, and they realized they were naked; so they sewed fig leaves together and made coverings for themselves. (8) Then the man and his wife heard the sound of the Lord God as he was walking in the garden in the cool of the day, and they hid from the Lord God among the trees of the garden. (9) But the Lord God called to the man, "Where are you?" (10) He answered, "I heard you in the garden, and I was afraid because I was naked; so I hid." (11) And he said, "Who told you that you were naked? Have you eaten from the tree that I commanded you not to eat from?" (12) The man said, "The woman you put here with me—she gave me some fruit from the tree, and I ate it." (13) Then the Lord God said to the woman, "What is this you have done?" The woman said, "The serpent deceived me, and I ate." ... (16) To the woman he said, "I will make your pains in childbearing very severe; with painful labor you will give birth to children. Your desire will be for your husband, and he will rule over you." (17) To Adam he said, "Because you listened to your wife and ate fruit from the tree about which I commanded you, 'You must not eat from it,' cursed is the ground because of you; through painful toil you

will eat food from it all the days of your life. (18) It will produce thorns and thistles for you, and you will eat the plants of the field. (19) By the sweat of your brow you will eat your food until you return to the ground, since from it you were taken; for dust you are and to dust you will return." (Genesis 3:6–13, 16–19)

Where are we? What are we looking for? Those two questions show up in interesting contexts in Genesis, and those contexts might shed some light on the character of our on-again/off-again national conversation around race.

Where are you?

Shortly after Adam and Eve ate of the forbidden fruit, God asked, Where are you? Adam explained that he and Eve were hiding out of shame over their nakedness. What a strange question for God to ask! It's not as if anyone could really play hide and seek with God. God doesn't need any clues about the whereabouts of Adam and Eve. Perhaps God is posing deeper questions: Where are you? Do you have a clue about where you're going and about what you're doing? If we read the text in that fashion and apply it to the arena of race relations and social justice, I believe God's question—Where are you?—speaks to us as Americans quite forcefully.

What are you looking for?

Jacob sent his son Joseph (Genesis 37) to check on his brothers. Joseph tells his father, Here I am! The brothers loathe and resent Joseph, and he's the last person they'd like to see. So Joseph is on his way and he gets lost. A stranger (the text isn't particularly interested in the man's identity) finds Joseph *to'eh basadeh*; literally, wandering in the fields. And he asks, *ma t'vakesh*; what do you seek? Joseph replies, I seek my brothers. We can read the words in their plain sense to be a snapshot of someone lost asking for directions, and we can dig a bit deeper and approach this fateful exchange as a moment of someone who is lost, stumbling without direction. And when asked what he's looking for, he says something much truer than he knows in that moment: I seek my brothers. I'm cut off from them. I am hated by them, but I want to connect to them.

How does this short but powerful conversation speak to us about Black and White America living in largely separate worlds? Because Black and White America seem millions of miles apart, it's not easy to know how folks living across the tracks see things. Viewing American culture through my White (and privileged) spectacles, where am I and what am looking for? As for where I am, I must start by acknowledging my privilege—the benefits of living in America while White. Actually, to be honest, it's more complicated. I wear Jewish spectacles, and, like many other Jews, my Whiteness is not so obvious.

Throughout the unfolding American story, Jews have been listed on the very same Keep Out signs that told Blacks they were not welcome in a certain neighborhood or university or country club. On those forms which instruct us to fill in our ethnic status, like many other Jews, I'm more comfortable with "other" than with White. That's because otherness has been part of my narrative. And yet I must also acknowledge the many ways in which Jews have made the way up the ladder. Still, the recent resurgence of hateful graffiti and cyber-bullying has targeted several minority groups. The haters let me know loud and clear that my tribe is not wanted.

What do I see when I lift my gaze beyond my small community? I see African Americans still segregated in terms of neighborhoods and schools. I see laws (voter ID laws, for example) that place roadblocks in their path. It doesn't surprise me that many folks grow up resenting Whites for the pervasive systemic injustice that stains our culture. I fear my brothers. When I occasionally walk in a Black neighborhood, I feel like I don't belong there, and the gazes of the people I pass by seem to ask, What are you doing here? But I also seek my brothers—I want to forge real relationships beyond my comfortable neighborhood.

And what does an African American reply to these same questions? It seems the height of presumption for me to pen an answer. Maybe I'd have to ask.

At the recent MLK church breakfast,[119] a colleague and friend offered an opening prayer which moved me with its bracing honesty. She spoke of being afraid. And I surely feel afraid in this age of terror, this moment in time when the dictionary, responding to our present cultural moment, has just added the phrase *post-truth*. I'm frightened by demagogues who belittle and ridicule and demonize minorities. I'm frightened by leaders—who should know better—who casually shrug off an incessant stream of fabrications as if lying is no big deal and truth is no big deal either. If God is asking us, Where are you, like God did with Adam and Eve, I'm also trembling and ashamed. I struggle with a sense of foreboding as we lurch into uncharted waters, clueless about what happens next.

But the imam who offered the closing prayer reminded us all that God is always in control and that hope and joy are not mere ephemera; they are intentional choices; they are strong and important tools for holding the torch aloft and facing the next chapter. I thank God for these much-needed rousing words of faith. Norman Rockwell would surely smile approvingly upon the scene of a Black imam, addressing a church hall filled with a diverse crowd (something painfully rare in our city), exhorting Christians—and a few Jews—to hold fast to America's greatness and to Dr. King's redemptive legacy.

Now consider two communal moments in our city. On the Sunday of this past MLK weekend I was privileged to take a small part in a warm and uplifting gathering at Daybreak,[120] and on Monday morning I was blessed to offer a few words at the 27th annual MLK breakfast at St. Peter Claver. You could feel the fellowship in the room, and you knew that everyone there brought a focused sense of mission to their presence. Beyond the celebration of Dr. King's work, in both programs that was a spoken and unspoken acknowledgment of the hard work ahead.

Rabbi Tarfon, a second century Talmudic teacher, speaks to us clearly: "It is not up to you to complete the task. Neither are you free to walk away from it."[121]

15

We Have Been There

The Reverend Eddie Smith, Pastor of Macedonia (Baptist) Church

(1) Shephatiah son of Mattan, Gedaliah son of Pashhur, Jehukal son of Shelemiah, and Pashhur son of Malkijah heard what Jeremiah was telling all the people when he said, (2) "This is what the Lord says: 'Whoever stays in this city will die by the sword, famine or plague, but whoever goes over to the Babylonians will live. They will escape with their lives; they will live.' (3) And this is what the Lord says: 'This city will certainly be given into the hands of the army of the king of Babylon, who will capture it.'" (4) Then the officials said to the king, "This man should be put to death. He is discouraging the soldiers who are left in this city, as well as all the people, by the things he is saying to them. This man is not seeking the good of these people but their ruin." (5) "He is in your hands," King Zedekiah answered. "The king can do nothing to oppose you." (6) So they took Jeremiah and put him into the cistern of Malkijah, the king's son, which was in the courtyard of the guard. They lowered Jeremiah by ropes into the cistern; it had no water in it, only mud and Jeremiah sank down into the mud.

(7) But Ebed-Melek, a Cushite, an official in the royal palace, heard that they had put Jeremiah into the cistern. While the king was sitting in the Benjamin Gate, (8) Ebed-Melek

went out of the palace and said to him, (9) "My lord the king, these men have acted wickedly in all they have done to Jeremiah the prophet. They have thrown him into a cistern, where he will starve to death when there is no longer any bread in the city." (10) Then the king commanded Ebed-Melek the Cushite, "Take thirty men from here with you and lift Jeremiah the prophet out of the cistern before he dies."

(11) So Ebed-Melek took the men with him and went to a room under the treasury in the palace. He took some old rags and worn-out clothes from there and let them down with ropes to Jeremiah in the cistern. (12) Ebed-Melek the Cushite said to Jeremiah, "Put these old rags and worn-out clothes under your arms to pad the ropes." Jeremiah did so, (13) and they pulled him up with the ropes and lifted him out of the cistern. And Jeremiah remained in the courtyard of the guard. (Jeremiah 38:1–13, NIV)

We Americans of African descent find ourselves in a land that was never designed or intended to be our own. Brutally and worse than being inhumanely treated, we were snatched from our motherland against our wills and forced to endure experiences that no words can truly describe. There has been nothing in American history that even remotely compares to what we have endured. We have endured heartache and hardships worse than any in human history. *Yet we are still here!*

Yes, with much thanksgiving, I report that we are still here, this first day of February. Thank God! As you know, February is set aside to celebrate Black people, and it is known as Americans of African Descent History Month. There are many in this day and age who question the relevance of this celebration. YES, it is relevant...now more than ever! We must *never* stop. If anything, we need to do it more often! Believe me, it is more than necessary that we never cease. We will continue to see how the hand of God has led, provided for, and protected us, just as he did in this passage for the prophet Jeremiah.

The God we serve is a God of providence. His gracious providence can be observed in his raising up the boy-king, Josiah, to execute reforms in an age emboldened by evil and destined for destruction. In the call of the boy Jeremiah, to the prophetic office, we find a similar gracious providence. For nearly twenty years, from the thirteenth year of Josiah's reign to his sudden and untimely death in 636 BCE, these young men, Jeremiah and Josiah, were a team in reforms and in holding the gospel of hope for all who would turn to the Lord.

Jeremiah continued to prophesy after Josiah's death under the successive reigns of his sons until the nation's end came in 586 BCE. Under Josiah, Jeremiah's ministry had the full support of the throne, but under the last few kings of Judah, the prophet was left to the unpredictability of headstrong but weak-minded boys.

Jeremiah was the son of Hilkiah, one of the priests of Anathoth.[122] Jeremiah was born to priestly rank. However, by the time he arrived on the scene, massive corruption had caused Yahweh to stop appointing priests as the chosen agency for communicating with his people. In mercy, God raised up prophets and continued to speak to his people. In no other generation had God been left without a spokesman.

In the call of the boy Jeremiah, we are struck by the care and precision God used to choose and prepare his instrument of guidance. Before Jeremiah was ever formed in his mother's womb, God had known him. God had sanctified and ordained him as a prophet both to Judah and to the nations.[123] His commission was twofold, involving destruction on the one hand and building and planting on the other. His messages must demolish the order of things fabricated by sin and declare the hope of an abiding order based upon a true recognition of God's sovereignty.

My brothers and sisters, it could well be that Jeremiah's messages were like the source of wisdom Shakespeare described: "Earthly power doth show itself the likest God's when mercy seasons justice." Certainly in Jeremiah's writings we have the record of a God whose sovereignty is ever based on his essential wisdom and beneficence. Truly Jeremiah had a job to do in a wicked and perverse generation.

Yes, he did have a great job before him, but Jeremiah could handle it, for he is declared to be the greatest of Old Testament prophets because he introduced the idea of the universality of God. Amos, Hosea, and Isaiah had dwelt upon the idea that God was a one nation God. They understood God to be the God of Israel alone. He had to descend and protect Israel from all other nations—from all of her enemies. But did his protection mean that He was only God for Israel?

Jeremiah proclaimed to the people that God was everywhere. He told the people that they did not have to worship the God of Babylon; that Yahweh, Elohim, the God of Israel, was everywhere and that He could hear and answer prayer anywhere, to all human beings wherever they were. He went on to declare that the earth was the Lord's, the world and all the people who dwell in it.

Where was God in the midst of all of this? First there is the Eternal Plan, a forewarning. Take a look at verses 1 and 2. Now in the story, Shephatiah, Gedaliah, Jucal, and Pashhur overhear Jeremiah speaking to the people of Jerusalem. The Eternal God forewarns the people that anyone who stays in the city will die by war, famine, or disease; but those who surrender to the Chaldeans will at least have some incentive to save their own lives. The Eternal God has proclaimed that Jerusalem will be handed over to the army of Babylon's king, who will capture it. God can reach into a mess and bring out a blessing!

Remember with me the story of Joseph and his brothers, who did everything they knew to remove him, short of killing him. In fact, they thought they had succeeded. They thought he was dead! Remember how later on Joseph looked back on all the trials and ordeals and exclaimed, "Oh brothers...."[124] Many years after Joseph said this, Paul echoed this same sentiment in his letter to the Romans. As *The Voice* Bible notes, "God can take even the meanest intention and make it work for good for his devoted followers." "Don't be afraid. Am I to judge instead of God? It is not my place. Even though you intended to harm me, God intended it only for good, and through me, He preserved the lives of countless people, as He is still doing today."[125]

Secondly, there is the enemies' plot. Truth has made enemies of God angrier than angry down through the years. They were angry because Jeremiah's words were hindering the war effort. So four of Zedekiah's officials banded together to urge the king to kill the prophet. We know nothing about Shephatiah. If Gedaliah was the son of Pashhur, who had put Jeremiah in the mud, he was certainly no friend to Jeremiah or to the truth. Jucal we met earlier in Jeremiah 37:3 (NIV). He may have been related to the guard who arrested Jeremiah.

When these officials heard Jeremiah's remarks, they advised the king:

> This man...should be put to death! His words border on treason; they are affecting the morale of what troops we still have in the city, as well as all the rest of the people. This man does not have the best interests of this people at heart—only their downfall.[126]

On the surface, this looks like patriotism. However, the truth is that not only is it not patriotism, but it is in opposition to God's truth, and it will never stand! Jeremiah told the truth. Jeremiah didn't just wake up one morning thinking to himself, "I think I feel like talking!" No. He had received the authority from God to say this. He knew it was true, and he never wavered or equivocated. Some people who claim to speak for God are actually saying what they want to say! Be very careful who you listen to!

God's Plan was the preservation from destruction. Those who had conspired to kill Jeremiah had destruction in mind, but God had a different plan. He was in charge. "So they [the conspirators] took Jeremiah and threw him into a muddy cistern in the court of the guard that belonged to the king's son, Malchijah. Rather than killing him immediately, these officials lowered Jeremiah by ropes into this deep, dark cistern where he sank into the mud. Now he would be silenced. Soon he would be dead."[127]

Jeremiah was lowered into a muddy cistern, where he sank into the mud and was left to starve. I wish I could get you to see Jeremiah...bogged down in the mud. He's stuck in the mud! Waiting to die, like many of us sometimes do. We wait for death! Whatever happens to you, don't ever lose heart: "A man who does what is right and good may have many troubles," says the Psalmist. "But the Lord takes him out of them all."[128] Oh, I feel reasonably sure that Jeremiah was pondering, and he was wondering if he'd ever make it out of the pit. But God had already figured it out!

The perpetrators had demanded and received from King Zedekiah permission to throw Jeremiah into an empty cistern covered with a thick layer of mud at the bottom, planning to leave him there.[129] Too weak to oppose his own princes, the king gave in to their request. Instead of simply having Jeremiah slain, which would have been shedding innocent blood, the men had him imprisoned in an old cistern, where he sank in the mire at the bottom. The officers hoped that the prophet would eventually be forgotten and would die.

Oh yes, the officials figured that they were through with Jeremiah. God, however, raised up the deliverer Ebed-Melek—a man from Ethiopia who became an Old Testament "Good Samaritan." God will deliver on time, the record reminds us in Jeremiah:[130] "But Ebed-Melek, a Cushite, an official in the royal palace, heard that they had put Jeremiah into the cistern." Note some different biblical renderings to describe Ebed-Melek in 38:7: *God's Word Translation* (GWT) says that he is an official in the royal palace. GWT goes on to say that Ebed-Melek from Sudan heard that they had put Jeremiah in the cistern. The *Living Bible Paraphrase* reports that "When Ebed-Melek the Ethiopian, an important palace official...." The Geneva Bible refers to him as "Black Moor...." Dr. Ironside, in his Bible, calls the faithfulness of Ebed-Melek "a Negro."

We have been there. Who knows what God is ready to do with Black people or how God plans to use them when He places us "there"? The God of the universe might be just about ready to turn this thing around right here in the USA! I know how wronged we've been feeling about recent events like Trayvon Martin's death. He was just 17 years of age! As a people, when we watched on international TV, we saw the life choked out of Eric Garner and George Floyd and heard their desperate cry—"I can't breathe." God just might be ready to get this nation out of the mud. Ebed-Melek means "servant of the king." God was getting ready to use his Black servant.

Jeremiah is interesting in this situation because he was thrown into a pit filled with muck and miry clay, left there to suffocate and die. But a Black man brought him back to the land of the living and enabled him to complete the work God had assigned his hands and the book which bears his name. The man who rescued Jeremiah was Ebed-Melek.[131]

In Jeremiah 38:7–13 (New International Version), it is written:

> But Ebed-Melek, a Cushite, an official in the royal palace, heard that they had put Jeremiah into the cistern. While the king was sitting in the Benjamin Gate, Ebed-Melek went out of the palace and said to him, "My lord the king, these men have acted wickedly in all they have done to Jeremiah the prophet. They have thrown him into a cistern, where he will starve to death when there is no longer any bread in the city." Then the king commanded Ebed-Melek the Cushite, "Take thirty men from here with you and lift Jeremiah the prophet out of the cistern before he dies." So Ebed-Melek took the

men with him and went to a room under the treasury in the palace. He took some old rags and worn-out clothes from there and let them down with ropes to Jeremiah in the cistern. Ebed-Melek the Cushite said to Jeremiah, "Put these old rags and worn-out clothes under your arms to pad the ropes." Jeremiah did so, and they pulled him up with the ropes and lifted him out of the cistern. And Jeremiah remained in the courtyard of the guard....

My brothers and sisters, let's observe the characters—preacher, perpetrators, pit, and the picker upper! Whenever the preacher is sent with the truth, wicked perpetrators refuse to hear the truth; they will place him in the pit, seeking to destroy the preacher. But the Lord will always have a picker upper. I believe that you can understand that were it not for this Ethiopian benefactor, a picker upper, the world would have been robbed of the knowledge of the great prophet Jeremiah and the great theology found in his book. We would have truly missed something very special!

Note that the word Ethiopian means burnt face. "Ethio" means "burnt" and "op" means "face." Thus, the word Ethiopian literally means one whose face has been burnt by the sun. There-fore, Ebed-Melek was a Black man. Thank God that Ebed-Melek was there. Praise God that Ebed-Melek was there to intercede with the king on Jeremiah's behalf. He was there and was the means by which Jeremiah was saved from death by famine.

And *we of African descent* have *also* been there! The African was brought to this country against his will. He was ripped from his native land. He was chained and crowded into boats, packed like sardines and brought to this country. Families were separated. Yet we have been present in the development of world civilization. We have been instrumental in every facet of this society.

Black people have been present even if the truth about their presence was strayed, stolen, or hidden. Carter G. Woodson, a Black Baptist layman, saw the need to create a way to ensure that we hear the truth; that we create a way to remember; that we tell our children so they can tell their children that we are here. Carter G. Woodson raised our story from the cistern through what we now celebrate as Black History Month.

This is a time when we remember that we were here through the many contributions that have been made by Black educators like Mary McLeod Bethune, Alain L. Locke, Robert R. Moton, Booker T. Washington, and R. J. Martin. We remember the Black military figures like Henri Christophe, Benjamin O. Davis Jr., Martin R. Delany, and Crispus Attucks. We have been there. Some of the world's greatest contributions to science have come from people like Daniel Hale Williams, Theodore K. Lawless, Charles R. Drew, George Washington Carver, Benjamin Banneker, and Percy L. Julian. We have been there in medicine through Wade and Brian Scott, George Johnston, and many others.

We have been there as writers like Phyllis Wheatley, Maya Angelou, Richard Wright, Ralph Ellison, Paul L. Dunbar, Gwendolyn Brooks, James W. Johnson, Arna Bontemps, Langston Hughes, James Baldwin, Alice Walker, and Toni Morrison. As political figures like Adam Clayton Powell Jr., Edward W. Brooke, Shirley Chisholm, Maynard Jackson (the first Black mayor of Atlanta), Jack Ellis (the first Black mayor of Macon, GA), and William H. Hastie. Thurgood Marshall, Constance Baker Motley, and Johnnie Cochran were there in the legal arena.

We've been there as entertainers like W.C. Handy, Bessie Smith, Billie Holiday, Duke Ellington, Louis Armstrong, Sam Cooke, Ossie Davis, Brock Peters, Richard Pryor, Ray Charles, Luther Vandross, Nipsey Russell, Ronald Winans; athletes like Jack Johnson, Muhammad Ali, Colin Kaepernick, Althea Gibson, Wilma Rudolph, Serena and Venus Williams. In the civil rights and social justice arena, we've been there like Sojourner Truth, Fannie Lou Hamer, A. Philip Randolph, Walter F. White, Roy Wilkins, W.E.B. DuBois, Bill Randall, Rosa Parks, and M. L.

King Jr. In the church we've been there like Jack Smith Jr., Ben Johnson, E. J. Calhoun, E. S. Evans, and many more; time will not permit me to call a complete roll. But we have been there.

Is a study of Black history still relevant? Has the world reached a point where we no longer need to learn about the many valuable contributions of Black people in a society that forgets, ignores, or writes us out? Are you tired of learning about yourselves? Did you answer, "Yes"? Shame on you if you did! Never forget that we can never catch up with all of our history that has been omitted from annals of American history! A people who know not their history or forget are bound to repeat it. Perhaps that's why we are slipping back.

Years ago, Dr. L. K. Williams said, "It is clear that the Negro has made valuable and substantial difference to the material progress of mankind; but these have not been the best of his gifts. For he has injected into the world something more tangible and something far more spiritual." My brothers and sisters, the Americans of African descent, in one way or another, have been the central prey of history. We have affected outcomes of elections—sometimes for the good of the people and at other times to our disadvantage. Black people have elected more people to office or have had more laws passed or enacted than any other racial group in the world.

My brothers and sisters, you know, I feel that it is by nature that Black people are a people best suited for Christianity. Howard Thurman captures this clearly in *Jesus and the Disinherited*. The Black race has come through the storm and rain; but through it all we have tried to keep our faith in God, to live peacefully with all humankind, and to share those gifts and talents that God has given us.

America was founded as a refuge for the oppressed, a place of religious liberty and freedom. Providence was in the midst of the African coming to America, and through his undying optimism, his ability to exist on meager things and yet be happy, the American of African descent has helped the world to know beyond a shadow of a doubt that it is not the abundance of earthly and material things that bring joy and happiness. It is spiritual depths and a relationship with God at the core of our past.

The American of African descent has done many amazing and outstanding things. He has given from the depth of his soul.

As I hasten to conclude the message, I want to share the story about the Mississippi River running wild. Levees here and levees there were all trying to stop the weight of the added volume of water. When the levees would show signs of breaking, the enslavers would have the Black enslaved people fill bags of sand as the water continued rising and the levees began to give away. The owners of the enslaved Black people demanded them to give their bodies to fill in the holes that had developed in the wall.

Thousands upon thousands of Black people gave their bodies freely to hold the waters, to save the lives and property of the enslavers. The Black man has given of himself, given of his genius, his creativeness through all of the years he's been on these shores. Once again, he might be called on to help hold back the waters of hate, ignorance, prejudice, injustice…fill up the hole where all of these are creeping through from outside, expecting the destruction of civilization as we know it.

Yes, the Lord has uniquely made the Black man and put within him something that sets him apart. If destiny calls on the American of African descent, he'll give of himself. Think about the song the whole world is singing: "Oh, swing low, sweet chariot, coming to carry me home." Think about the dark days when our mothers and fathers went for many days without food to eat. I can almost hear them now singing, "I'm going to eat at the welcome table, feast and never get tired." One of these old days…

I can almost hear them singing, "Steal away, steal away to Jesus, Steal away home. I ain't got long to stay here." They go on to say, "One of these old days, I'm going to put on my long white robe." One of these days...we have been there!

16

A Change of Heart

Acts 1:8; 10:9–48; Ephesians 4:29–32

The Reverend Gail Tolbert Smith,
Pastor of Universal Light Christian Center,
Macon, Georgia

We began this year studying the book of Acts. In our examination of Luke's fascinating book, we have focused our attention on the launching and movement of the early church, honing in on the manner in which the Holy Spirit moves and expands the church. As we notice how the Holy Spirit guides the church in addressing critical issues that set them apart from any other religion, we get a sense of what is in the mind of God concerning his church, the Body of Christ.

Today, I want to pick up where we left off last Sunday when we looked at the Apostle Peter, who experiences a paradigm shift after seeing a vision during the time he is temporarily residing with Simon the Tanner. Not long after the vision, Cornelius, the God-fearing Gentile, summons the Apostle Peter. We may also consider that this event takes place in the city of Joppa, the same area where Jonah boarded a ship attempting to escape the call of God to minister to the people of Nineveh. You may think of these as minor details, but we should keep in mind that every detail in scripture is important and necessary. I love the way the New Living Translation captures what the Apostle Paul says in 2 Timothy 3:16 about the nature of the scriptures. It says, "All Scripture is inspired by God and is useful to teach us what is true and to make us realize what is wrong in our lives. It corrects us when we are wrong and teaches us to do what is right." Today we draw usefulness from this passage as we consider how Peter is staying with Simon the Tanner while being sent for by Cornelius, the Gentile centurion.

Last week in our review of Jewish history, we found that no good Jew would ever dwell with a tanner. Jews had no dealings with tanners because they handled dead animals, making them ceremonially unclean. We also discussed how Jews viewed Gentiles with disdain—as an inferior race of people, "dogs," who were unacceptable to God. As horrible as this all sounds, it reminds us of the history of our nation, how we are separated by racism. If only this could be a world problem or a societal ill only! Sadly, that is not the case because racism is also a church problem.

Many Christians find themselves like Peter. They are wonderful people who say they love God, but they practice racism and prejudice. They are generous supporters of the cause of Christ yet adhere to racism and prejudice. They are anointed preachers and teachers of the Word, but in their hearts they hold to racist and prejudiced beliefs. They are even pastors and church leaders, yet they promote and justify racism and segregation. Perhaps we have stumbled upon a concept we could call "Christian racism." You know what kind of racism that is, don't you? It's the kind that causes us to attempt to justify our picks and choices of those with whom we will mix and minister. It's a kind of undercover segregation. It's the kind of segregation that keeps us thinking our churches must be separated along racial lines. You know how we do it with the White church over here and the Black church over there. You know how we do it around here—the White church moves to the north part of town or the suburbs while the Black churches remain in the inner city. It's easier for us to cross racial lines when it comes to missions than it is when it relates to collaborative ministry and worship. It's okay for Peter to live with Simon the Tanner because it's related to his mission work in that area, but going to Cornelius's house means Peter must have real fellowship and engage in real ministry with Cornelius. And that involves an authentic connection with a different group of people who are thought to be inferior. Peter was able to do what God called him to do, but only after he had a change of heart. In fact, Peter needed to be transformed just as much as this Gentile who sent for him.

This causes me to revisit the promise Jesus makes to his disciples just before his ascension: "But you will receive power when the Holy Spirit comes on you; and you will be my witnesses in Jerusalem, and in all Judea and Samaria, and to the ends of the earth." This verse blows my mind every time I read or hear it. This promise is for the people of God even today—that we will receive power after the Holy Spirit comes upon us and we will be witnesses everywhere. I don't know whether people really get what the Master is saying here, but let's look at it closely for just a moment.

Notice that this is what we call a compound sentence, meaning there are actually two sentences joined by a conjunction. The conjunction is there to serve as a bridge bringing together two concepts. The first concept is there's a power that will come along with the Holy Spirit coming upon you. The second concept indicates what happens after the power comes. There is a direct connection with the power and witnessing activity expressed in this verse. In other words, we will need this power in order to witness on the level and in the manner in which Jesus describes here.

I get the two concepts. That's easy for me. The thing that is mind-blowing to me is the kind of power that Jesus promises. In this verse, he references what the Greeks call "dynamis" power, which literally means might, strength, force, and miraculous power. This is where we get our English root for the word "dynamite," so when Luke chooses this word, he's telling us something very important. Look at the folks he's telling us will be our target population for witnessing. He's saying they'll be people like us, but many of them will not be like us. He's saying that we will be reaching other races and nationalities. We will cross every kind of human boundary. Wow! That's awesome to me, but it still blows my mind how He says it's going to happen.

Again, let's look at what Paul is saying here. He's saying we are going to be phenomenal witnesses, but it will take a power like dynamite to get it done. Really? Dynamite just to witness? Well, if dynamite power is going to be used, where is it needed? Dynamite is explosive, right? So what needs to be blown up? This is the part that troubles me. Is there something in me or in you that needs to be blown up?

I submit to you today that the dynamite power Jesus refers to in this verse is needed to remove the walls in our hearts that hinder our reaching out to others as we should. When we talk about the internal work of the Holy Spirit, we are talking about the work that God does in the human heart. We're talking about how He transforms us into new creatures.

Folks, I've got to tell you something. Some of the work that must be done in us requires an explosion. This is where the dynamis or dynamite is needed. More than a shifting or rearranging of thoughts or ideas is required here. There must be a total and complete demolition of walls and ways of thinking. There must be destruction before there can be reconstruction—our old way of thinking must be torn down and destroyed before God can give us his way of thinking. When it comes to racism and prejudice, you can't talk to the head. You can't reason with it. You must destroy that mindset and establish a new way of thinking. Otherwise, we will just find a subtler, more crafty way of doing what we've always done. We must have a change of heart.

Let me tell you why we need a dynamite explosion in our hearts. First, we need an explosion because racism is grievous behavior. When we consider how we talk to and about different races or cultures—racial slurs and stereotyping—these are behaviors that are not pleasing to God. In fact, they grieve him. In Ephesians 4:29–32, the Apostle Paul indicates how the way we talk to and about each other, and how the way we treat each other, can be a source of grief for the Spirit:

> Do not let any unwholesome talk come out of your mouths, but only what is helpful for building others up according to their needs, that it may benefit those who listen. And do not grieve the Holy Spirit of God, with whom you were sealed for the day of redemption. Get rid of all bitterness, rage and anger, brawling and slander, along with every form of malice. Be kind and compassionate to one another, forgiving each other, just as in Christ God forgave you. (NIV)

We need an explosion because these behaviors come so naturally to us. It's too easy to talk about and even to people in ways that are racially offensive. It'll take an explosion to get rid of that kind of thinking and behavior. We need a change of heart.

Second, we need a dynamite explosion in the heart because racism is a growing problem. Racism is like a bad seed that sprouts and continues growing until it has taken over our lives. We see this as we look at what America is facing with the recent cases of police brutality and racial profiling. We see it in the disproportionate number of African Americans who are incarcerated and in the marginalization of Black boys in the educational system. I could go on and on talking about how racism is taking over our nation in subtler ways and how we tend to respond with more racism, as if that's the solution to the problem. We need an explosion in our hearts. Some of you feel you have been hurt by White people and have written off the whole race because of what one person or a few people have done, but I say to you today, the problem was not that they were White—it was the condition of the heart. They needed an explosion in the heart—the same kind you need today so that you will open your heart to them. Keep in mind that there are Black people who have hurt you too. It's not the color that makes people hurt people; it's a change of heart that is needed.

Finally, we need a dynamite explosion in our hearts because racism is a generational issue. Our tolerance for racism is because it has been passed down through generations. We breed and perpetuate racism in our families, churches, and other organizations. There is no reason why our children can't play together; no reason our families can't live together in unity; and no reason why our churches cannot worship and minister together. We are separate because that's all we know. It's the way we've always done it and it's the only model we have. Racism and division are what each generation teaches the next, either directly or indirectly. We can overcome this but only with a change of heart. We need an explosion.

I believe God is calling for a paradigm shift in our hearts and our churches today. Are there walls that have kept you from reaching out to others? Do you find yourself judging people based on their race rather than getting to know them? Do you reject people because of race or refuse to meet the needs of people who need you because they are different from you? If you know you are guilty of this, then you need an explosion in your heart. You need to receive the power of the Holy Spirit because when you receive his power every wall against others will come down. Those walls will only be reconstructed if you want to rebuild them or if you allow the enemy to rebuild them in you. It's your decision. I believe God wants us to have a change of heart today. Peter received it and you can too. Will you receive this dynamis power today? Let us pray.

Father, we come before You today thanking you for being our God. We thank you for the work that You have already done in our hearts, but we sense You knocking on the door of our hearts once again desiring to work in us once more. We release You to explode in our hearts today, destroying every wall and every negative thought against other people and other races. We want to see people as You see them and love them as You love them. As you remove every wall and every barrier, we experience a change of heart and receive the love that the Holy Spirit floods our hearts with for others. We thank you now for the work that You are doing in us and the work that You will be able to do through us from this moment forth, in the name of Jesus the living Christ, Amen, and so it is!

PART III—

HISTORICAL REFLECTIONS

17

Historical Eavesdropping:
A White Baptist Perspective

Andrew M. Manis

Although I am neither a musician nor the son of a musician, I did manage to teach in New Orleans at Xavier University, the only predominantly Black Catholic university in America. I would have had to be culturally deaf to live and work for three years in those two contexts and not come away with a least a rudimentary understanding of jazz. Hearing Wynton Marsalis in concert, riffing on a dozen musical themes in one song, even a novice cannot miss the improvisational quality of that distinctive genre. This chapter is an experimental attempt to mimic that effort to riff on the themes sounded in the sermons you have just read.

Picking up where I left off in my earlier efforts both to explain and break the sound of silence, perhaps we ought to begin with the theme of American exceptionalism. Imam Adam Fofana's variation on that theme almost shocks the reader with a radically different sort of exceptionalism. By Fofana's lights, America is unique among nations in its ability to "learn from its mistakes and emerge a better nation." For a people so often accused of being "ugly Americans" with a brand of patriotism boorish and boastful enough to brook no criticism of their country, such a claim to greatness is a bit of a surprise. "This nation," Fofana boldly asserts, "is more willing to make changes for the betterment of the future than any other." To think of the United States as uniquely self-critical and self-correcting is surprising enough, but to read the claim from the pen of a leader of American Muslims is almost shocking.

After all, the Imam's community of faith, Arab Americans and American Muslims, have been increasingly victimized by hate crime incidents since 2001 and the 9/11 attacks—and such attacks on Muslims increased in 2017 by 17 percent in comparison to 2016, the year Donald Trump was elected president of the United States.[132] In light of the president's efforts toward a national Muslim ban, it was an act of sheer and utter grace for Fofana to view the nation so charitably. Yet despite hailing the US as exceptional enough to learn from its historic mistakes, he does point America toward the biblical Joseph narratives as a place where Islamic concepts of reconciliation may be discovered. The chief roadblock for moving along these steps is our continued unwillingness to acknowledge the wrongdoing, admit the offense, and apologize for the continuing racial injustice. Specifically, Fofana points out that a string of police killings of young Black males demands acknowledgment." Sadly, he notes that our national unwillingness to acknowledge our errors in the past continues to block the way to racial reconciliation in America.

Father Allan McDonald also gives his variation of the theme of American exceptionalism from within Catholicism. He describes his congregation at Macon's St. Joseph's Parish fully accepting the civil religious concept of America as a nation chosen and set apart to promulgate freedom and justice in the world. His sermon describes President Barack Obama as called by Americans "through the election process and by God to the vocation of being a world leader" who would "draw the nations, religions, and races of the world together under the umbrella of respect for one another." Here McDonald delivers a Catholic version of the American Civil Religion that closely resembles a nineteenth century Black Protestant version of America as an experimental Eden where the nations might learn how to survive in a pluralistic world. If America could learn to survive its own cultural and religious differences, the rest of the world would follow America's example and learn to live with its diversity.[133]

These African American or Catholic understandings of the American purpose were safely hidden behind W.E.B. DuBois's metaphorical veil created by the color line. This concept of American destiny was both unheard by and inaccessible to White Christian ears in the nineteenth century. Sadly, it is hardly any more audible in the twenty-first. To hear it, most White Christians will be forced to eavesdrop.

This collection of sermonic reflections on reconciliation, while emphasizing eavesdropping across racial lines, also forces us to transcend the Christian traditions to listen in on sensitive interpreters in the other Abrahamic traditions. Imam Fofana's sermon gave us a fruitful beginning. The Conservative Jewish tradition has graciously shared with our larger religious community one of its treasures, Congregation Sha'arey Israel's Rabbi Aaron Rubinstein.

Rabbi Rubinstein's sermon reflects on what it means to bring a Jewish perspective on race in a city dominated by Black and White Christians. One thing it means is that as a Jew, the rabbi has felt the sting of prejudice with African Americans while also enjoying privilege with White people. Teasing out some of the existential questions that Yahweh asks in the book of Genesis, and answering such questions with racial reconciliation in mind, leads him to some powerful insights. "Where are you?" asks the One who already knows where we are in a physical sense. So where are we spiritually with regard to the ever-present problem of race? We are in Macon, Georgia, which like most cities across the country has had more than its share of racial episodes. At the time of this writing, a mayoral race looms ahead with a long list of candidates, both White and Black. Where will we be when the political rhetoric begins to fly in all directions? "What are you doing?" is the second question. Borrowing the words of the patriarch Joseph, Rubinstein's reply answers both questions: "I seek my brothers." In both Macon, Georgia, and more broadly in the hostile political atmosphere of the United States, can we find ways to seek our brothers and sisters across the color line? Across the aisle?

One thing is certain. It is impossible to make decisions about politics in America without broaching the subject of race. Ignoring this elephant in the room cannot be done. Nor can communities of faith enter the fray in Macon without being sensitive to racial tensions that periodically arise. Yet people of faith must not only hear the prophetic voice but also become prophetic themselves. Anti-Apartheid activist and minister Allan Boesak and Curtiss Paul DeYoung have issued a clarion call:

> The church and other religious institutions need prophets to warn when faith moves toward individualism, self-serving spiritual formulas, prosperity focus, and quietism. Reconciliation advocates need prophets because reconciliation often does not go deep enough or far enough. Prophets challenge reconciliation activists to not stop short of the full process of reconciliation.[134]

On matters relating to race, the current era could hardly be more needful of prophetic voices. A culture that rebounded from the eight-year Obama era by electing the possibly the most overtly racist person ever to walk through the White House doors is in need of prophets. Tallahassee, Florida, mayor Andrew Gillum, who just missed becoming the first Black governor of Florida in 2018, perhaps put it most pointedly regarding his opponent: "I'm not calling Mr. DeSantis a racist. I'm just saying the racists think he's a racist."[135] Ditto for the Republican standard bearer who won the presidency with by far the most blatantly racist and xenophobic campaign in American political history. For his demeaning efforts, Trump managed to win 81 percent of Evangelical Christian votes and presumably close to 100 percent of the White Nationalist, neo-Nazi, and neo-Klan votes.

Timothy Bagwell's sermon was coincidentally named "A Fire No Water Can Put Out." I would call the choice of title "providential," but I am not sure how fitting it is to describe as a providential sermon when it was preached by a Wesleyan-Arminian Methodist. But unbeknownst to the preacher, my book on the Reverend Fred Shuttlesworth, central figure of civil rights agitation in Birmingham, Alabama, bore the title *A Fire You Can't Put Out.* Since that title was used as a metaphor not only for Shuttlesworth but also for the Civil Rights Movement itself, Bagwell's version appropriately fits that theme. Bagwell notes similarities between the competing ethnic groups in Jesus' day with those of the groups in modern Macon, Georgia. Both Macon and first century Judea were divided by ethnic competition and outright religious-racial prejudice. The preacher's reference to actual racial incidents that have divided Black from White in Macon in recent years provides a straight-shooting critique of city residents. He holds out hope, however, that common people can overcome their common prejudices through Christian worship and meditation on alternative values similar to those of Jesus in his Sermon on the Mount.

Of course, clergy in all the religious traditions represented in this book are called to function as both prophet and priest, both to challenge the complacency of the people and to help heal their wounds. An impressive example of this balance is Ike Edwin Mack's sermon, "A Response to Injustice." He begins with the prophetic description of the murder of Trayvon Martin and the acquittal of his killer, George Zimmerman. The description is full of pathos with an incisive critique of a society that continues to allow similar such incidents—injustices so destructive of interracial community, so often repeated with the same results that one major response to *this category* of injustice is the Black Lives Matter movement.

But Mack deftly moves into his pastoral role, expounding advice from the book of Hebrews on how African American Christians might respond to such suffering and injustice, continuing to love each other within the Christian community. With all the current talk in the news regarding a wall on America's Southern border, Mack detects a proper response in the text's admonition to welcome the stranger. Applying that principle to Black-White relationships, he asserts that the Hebrews text compels us to be careful how we respond to strangers who are different from us. We cannot assume that every White man is a Klansman, or that every Democrat is good and that all Republicans are evil. We should never assume anything about anyone, but we are to keep a watchful eye of spiritual discernment in regards to others, their actions, and their behavior.

Mack's second response to injustice opens a central debate in America regarding the proper treatment of foreigners, immigrants, and refugees. American law and practice have both vacillated between welcome and nativist restriction. Still problematic is the frequency of people of faith who use the Bible as the arbiter of ethical behavior but who often "major on minors" and "minor on majors." For example, Evangelical Christians have based all their arguments against same-sex marriage on some eight biblical passages.[136] By contrast, one almost never hears Bible-believing Christians arguing for the humanitarian treatment of immigrants, aliens, and refugees. This in spite of the fact that *Strong's Concordance* of the Bible lists 124 mentions of the stranger, 178 mentions of the sojourner, and 343 mentions of aliens—a total of 645 biblical references, most of which admonish the welcome of such people.

Eddie Smith's sermon, "We Have Been There," was preached in commemoration of Black History Month to celebrate the presence and persistence of African American Christians in America's religious debates about slavery and Jim Crow. He finds in the book of Jeremiah a minor character named Ebed-Melek (literally, "servant of the king"), a Cushite with a "burnt face," and therefore a "Negro" or Black man. According to Smith, this otherwise obscure figure was placed by Providence in the right place at the right time, to rescue the prophet Jeremiah when the king had imprisoned him in a cistern. People of African descent likewise have always been there to embody God's concern and presence to the world. Smith asserts, "The Black race has come through the storm and rain; but through it all we have tried to keep our faith in God, to live peacefully with all humankind, and to share those gifts and talents that God has given us."

Both Eddie Smith and Billy Graham McFadden agree that the world has needed and benefitted from the faithfulness of African-derived peoples. That has been especially true of Christianity in the United States. Above all, the hyper-spiritual and otherworldly versions of Christian faith that have dominated White churches throughout most of the history of Christianity on the North American continent have desperately needed the corrective of the Black church. All three of the major evangelical denominations in the American South—Baptists, Methodists, and Presbyterians—have adhered to some version of the "spirituality of the church" conception of Presbyterian theologian James Henley Thornwell. All three denominations in turn defended the institution of slavery because of their mutual conviction that the church's theology pertained only to one's spiritual condition and not to the earthly conditions in which they lived.

By contrast, African American Christianity has always sought to affect both the soul and the body. Two factors have worked together historically to create this holistic understanding of the faith. First was the bedrock traditions of African Traditional Religions, which made no distinction between body and soul, primarily deriving from the African worldview of the universe as a sacred whole. In such a perspective all things have religious meaning and nothing is profane. Thus, White theologians and ministers argued that Christian conversion and baptism affected only the soul, which belonged to God, but not the slave's body, which belonged to his or her master. The second distinguishing factor in African American Christianity was its social context of being developed in a situation of oppression. This combination thus produced a version of the faith that cared about the slaves' earthly lives while also seeking to save his soul. Out of this dual context, Martin Luther King Jr. could later affirm:

> ...the Christian gospel is a two-way road. One the one hand it seeks to change the souls of men, and thereby unite them with God; on the other hand it seeks to change the environmental conditions of men so that the soul will have a chance after it is changed. Any religion that professes to be concerned with the souls of men and is not concerned with the slums that damn them, the economic conditions that strangle them, and the social conditions that cripple them is a dry-as-dust religion.[137]

Bereft of these lessons from Black Christianity, the truncated White version of the faith had and still has much to learn from our Black brothers and sisters. McFadden's repeated assertion that "we need each other" should elicit louder and more fervent amens from White Christians in the audience.

Happily, the gender line is transcended by this collection. Julie Whidden Long's sermon raises the hopeful possibility of God's dream coming true. That dream, hers as well as God's, is even more radical than the dream of colorblindness, which yearns for a church full of Christians who don't notice the color of their fellow Christians or fellow Americans. Long perceptively pushes past colorblindness to God's dream that God's people will still notice racial and other cultural differences but are "much too smart to let our colors tear us apart." Unfortunately, however, contemporary efforts to "make America great again" seem to be turning God's dream into a pipe dream. Even those "high-IQ individuals" who are "much too smart" to be overtly racist don't know what they don't know. James Baldwin pointed it out so straightforwardly that we hardly even need to eavesdrop. "Whatever whites don't know about Negroes," he wrote, "reveals what they don't know about themselves."[138] What White people don't know about themselves appears to be the fictive aspect of racial difference, a socially constructed myth. Or we don't know that our American addiction to individualism keeps us ignorant of the systemic nature of racism. Or we don't know how ignorant of American history, particularly African American history, we are. Or we are ignorant of the length and breadth and depth of America's devotion to White supremacy.

Another reality that many, perhaps most White Americans, cannot seem to fathom is what the Baptist biblical scholar Frank Stagg called the "polarities of human existence." Subject to several such polarities, all human beings are, Stagg argues, "individual, yet corporate"—they are singular, yet also simultaneously part of a group, indeed, part of many groups.[139] Baldwin's critique of White Americans is on point. Because of their African heritage and their shared experience of discrimination, African Americans readily recognize and experience racism toward them both as individuals and as a group. Most White Americans, so steeped in a mindset of rugged individualism, can only see racism in acts of prejudice by individual people. By contrast, Whites are inclined to deny that racism can be embedded in society itself.

As I wrote this reflection, my students were finishing a semester in my Multicultural America course with an assignment to write a review of the 2004 film, *Crash*. Winner of the 2004 Oscar for Best Picture, the film is a devastatingly hard look at the interconnectedness of various form of racism in Los Angeles. One of my more perceptive students offered this commentary: "Not one of these characters seems aware of the vicious circle of hate and racial discrimination that they seem to be caught in." Besides ending her sentence with a preposition, her observation might have been perfect had she substituted the word "system" for the word "circle." It is tempting to interpret *Crash* as simply the story of a succession of individuals who have been mistreated by someone of another race or culture and who then "pay it forward" to the next "alien" who angers them. We see the individual acts of racism but not the "unconscious racism" infecting the entire social system. We are blind to the unconscious racism built into a deliberately constructed and zealously maintained system of advantage rigged in favor of White people. This unconscious racism is the "wall of separation" that most Christian preachers in America have failed to address, despite the biblical assertion that this "wall of partition" has been destroyed by the cross of Jesus (Ephesians 2:11–14). Clerical pronouncements have failed adequately to address racism if they only critique the acts of individuals but cannot even recognize the system that creates and constrains these individuals.

More specifically, we White American Christians seem oblivious to the Scylla and Charybdis of White privilege and White supremacy. The former is a sociological concept applying to a taken-for-granted system of advantage for Whites that "cannot be similarly enjoyed by people of color." The anti-racist writer Robin DiAngelo has described White privilege as a social reality that "elevates white people as a group." She bolsters her argument with a list of who controls American institutions:

- Ten richest Americans: 100 percent white

- US Congress: 78 percent white (as of the 2018 midterm elections)

- US governors: 96 percent white

- Top military advisors: 100 percent white
- TV network executives: 93 percent white
- Teachers: 82 percent white
- College professors: 84 percent white[140]

The other dangerous twin, White supremacy, is the idea that creates a social structure designed and determined to give advantages to the superior group and exclude other groups from similar advantages. All of American history has been embedded within White supremacy. White supremacy was the ideology that justified European imperialism and colonialism. It colored colonial law in America virtually from the beginning. It shaped the US Constitution, which in turn was used to protect it. The entire economic system of the Antebellum period was shaped by it, in the North as well as the South. Our bloodiest war was fought over it and the system of slavery and social control it produced. Although finally outlawed *de jure* by Congress's response to the Civil Rights Movement and the federal legislation that movement stimulated, White supremacy has shaped our immigration and naturalization policy since 1790. Hence, for most of our history our government has allowed only "free white persons" to become American citizens. White supremacy has survived and even been reinvigorated by the election of Barack Obama. The nation's first Black president has been succeeded by a renegade Republican who has based both his election campaign and his presidency on a promise to build a wall on our Southern border. Such a wall, according to Evangelical writer Jim Wallis, is designed to protect White Americans from Brown people and, as such, would be a 2,200-mile monument to White supremacy.[141] And most Americans remain oblivious to this collective form of racism. We still don't know what we don't know.

One of the sermons in this collection, however, addresses not only our inability to detect systemic racism but also our impotence in overcoming it. In his sermon, "Making Bitter Water Sweet," Jeff Morris describes the relational fallout of historic Black-White tensions in the city of Macon. He also provides commonsense wisdom for reconciliation at the level of individual relationships: Stop being part of the problem. Recognize racism as a spiritual problem that cannot be solved by economics, education, or politics. Then Morris zeroes in on the culprit: "Satan is the problem." Morris asserts that *Satan* causes African Americans to blame the race problem on Whites. Satan makes Whites shift the blame upon Blacks who seem unable to "get over it."

The wisdom of this prescription soon emerged in my mind, although I believe it requires a bit of de-mythologizing. Even if one still believes in a personal being known as Satan, Lucifer, the Devil, Beelzebub, or the Prince of Darkness, our preaching cannot exonerate human beings for our part in creating the evils of racism. But by referencing Paul's image of wrestling "against principalities, against powers, against the rulers of darkness of this world, against spiritual wickedness in high places (Eph 6:12)," Morris opens the door to a theological explanation of racism as the demonic.

Both the exorcisms of Jesus in the Gospels and Paul's concept of the principalities and powers describe the power of the demonic over people who do not even recognize that they are being controlled. In perhaps the most thorough theological treatment of the power of the demonic over human beings of the twentieth century, biblical scholar Walter Wink found reason to move beyond the possession of individuals to the concept of "collective possession," the possession of groups or even nations by a "demon capable of bending them as one into the service of death." This could be a powerful description of White supremacy's stranglehold on American culture since at least 1619. Wink then argues that the church's task in the face of collective possession is to raise consciousness about the unconscious demonic power of America's system of racism. The church does this by formulating acts of exorcism, which reveal how much we Whites benefit from White privilege rooted in White supremacy. Wink writes, "To a much greater extent than we are aware, we are possessed by the values and powers of an unjust order. It is not enough to simply repent of the ways we have chosen to collude with evil, we must be freed from our unconscious enthrallment as well."[142]

In December 1862, a president of the United States, wrestling with the American carnage that his election had set loose on his country, struggled with both his soul and his political opponents over how to win the war to preserve the union. He had read the signs of the times from the battlefields and privately informed his cabinet of his decision to transform the war into a war of liberation. Having announced the preliminary Emancipation Proclamation in September, he penned a soaring concluding appeal for support for Emancipation just one month away added to an otherwise pedestrian Second Message to Congress. Had President Abraham Lincoln delivered it as a speech, it would have been among his most celebrated utterances: "The dogmas of the quiet past are inadequate to the stormy present. The occasion is piled high with difficulty, and we must rise with the occasion. As our case is new, so we must think anew, and act anew. We must disenthrall ourselves, and then we shall save our country."

White reaction to the Obama years has lurched further to the political and cultural right than perhaps ever before. Never before in American history has a major party candidate campaigned for the presidency on overt efforts to divide Americans on racial grounds, as has Donald Trump. Our contemporary occasion is piled with difficulty almost as high as a nation literally fighting a civil war. Again, "we must disenthrall ourselves" and commit to saying NO to building Trump's literal wall, but even more to demolishing the "walls of partition" known as White privilege and White supremacy. Many in this assembly of prophetic voices have sounded the appeal to "the better angels of our nature," to use Lincoln's powerful words. This new fiery trial through which America is passing will indeed "light us all, in honor or in dishonor, to the latest generation." We do hold the power and we do bear the responsibility.

Cassandra Howe's sermon addresses the actions of "taking up" and "laying down" that make up part of the process of repentance so central to one's personal involvement in anti-racism. Drawing from the lyrics of the Black spiritual "Down by the Riverside," she underscores attitudes that must be rejected or "laid down," especially one's "sword and shield." Looking beyond color and culture of the "aliens" from whom our president wants to protect us, we find ourselves called to dispense with our fear and defensiveness as a first step. Laying down our fear starts us off on our efforts to "receive the fugitive," as Thomas Paine exhorted the readers of *Common Sense*, "and in time create an asylum for mankind."

Indeed, some elements of our experience must be recognized as detrimental to a lifestyle of racial peacemaking. Howe addresses expressions of White privilege that remain mostly unrecognized by Whites in America. Included in this would be a worldview that sees the White perspective as the normal human response to racial stimuli. Among these, Howe's background research brought into focus social forces like common real estate practices (e.g., redlining, block busting) designed to disadvantage families of color. Her strategy is helping her hearers recognize the extent to which American society provides tangible, measurable advantage to White people. Going confessional in this sermon, she struggles with how to "lay down" at least some of her advantages for at least part of the time. She also comments on our ongoing controversies related to the Confederate battle flag: "Those who want to keep the flag up in public places say it is about preserving our history. I wonder, though, if it is less about preserving our history and more about protecting the American idea of innocence."

If these sermons share any fundamental weaknesses, the most significant is a failure to speak to specific areas of concern that have created specific racial tensions in a specific time and place. To their credit, the sermons do move beyond thinking of racism as individual expressions of prejudice, but the preachers also address specific ways White privilege is closely aligned with White supremacy. In this context, many of the contributors recognize what one minister sees as "the greatest obstacle to racial reconciliation" in America today. Noel Schoonmaker, pastor of the First Baptist Church of Murfreesboro, Tennessee, has noted that "openly racist hostility or blatantly racist policies such as slavery or segregation" have faded as the focus of anti-racist activism. Rather, he views "unconscious racism that upholds white privilege" as the current heart of the matter. He thus admonishes clergy to take the initiative in the effort to demolish "the wall of racist privilege." As Whites either deliberately or unconsciously built this wall, so Whites are ethically responsible to "tear down this wall," as President Ronald Reagan once admonished Soviet leader Mikhail Gorbachev. Schoonmaker calls on White clergy to challenge the "racism-based privileges" of White American Christians.[143]

Howe's theme of laying down old perspectives and taking up new ones is illustrated by the sermons of Gail Smith and Jason McClendon, who chose to preach on the same biblical passage— Paul's vision at the home of Simon the Tanner in Acts 10. The events depicted in this chapter mark a major turning point in the story of the church in Luke-Acts, namely the sign that Gentiles were eligible to "receive power from on high" (Luke 24:49), receive the Holy Spirit, be baptized, and become part of the church. Smith drills deeply into the passage, focusing on the meaning of the Greek word for power, *dynamis*. From this word, she notes, the English word "dynamite" is derived. We remain on familiar territory here, as many pulpiteers have made this connection. But Smith creatively applies the dynamite theme by asking, "Is there something in you and me that needs to be blown up?" The racism that still divides both church and community in America needs to be blown up and demolished, leading to an explosive "change of heart." Here is a "laying down" where racism and the attitudes of the heart that nurture it are not only laid down but blown up. Such an inward explosion is necessary to dislodge racist attitudes from the human heart.

But the more radical "laying down" needed in our day requires more than laying aside feelings of enmity or prejudice that occur, at least from time to time, in the hearts of most Americans. Such feelings typically come to mind unbidden and are often regretted by the people to whom they occur. But if these very real, very tangible racist thoughts are in truth laid aside by White American Christians, they are rarely followed by specific acts of commission to actively help bring down the tangible wall of White privilege that still separates White Americans from people of color.

Jason McClendon's variation on the "lay down, take up" theme leans more heavily on taking up, in particular communicating the need to recognize scriptural elements for building Christian community along racial lines. Aspirations to desegregate America's most segregated hour of the week need not, however, necessitate the merging of predominantly Black and White congregations. We are wise to remember the conditions that resulted in the rise of African American churches. Before the Civil War there were but a handful of African American congregations in the South. Most Christian slaves in the South attended services with their master's family, although they worshipped in secret services in the brush arbors and cane breaks, separate from White supervision. Typically after the war, but sometimes before, the biracial (and unequal) churches of the South fairly rapidly separated along racial lines. At times, the impetus for separation came from White members who blamed Blacks for the war, viewed the freedpeople as ungrateful, and resented their presence in their churches. At other times, Black members themselves needed no push from their White coreligionists, but they did not want Whites to call the shots in terms of who determined what happened in a worship service. At still other times, a push from the Whites combined with Blacks' intentions to pull out into separate congregations where they would serve as their own leadership.

With these issues impinging on the desire for interracial unity, the vast majority of White Christians in America are still far from ready to share congregational decision-making with African American members. Until White American Christians not only accept or tolerate Blacks in leadership positions but actively *insist* on Black leadership equality, White and Black congregations should retain their autonomy, while both being committed to active engagement with the other in areas of periodic, regular joint worship, joint religious education, shared mission projects in their communities, joint fellowship experiences, and joint musical performances. Until White congregations insist on the above-mentioned characteristics of church life, McClendon's sermon advises both individuals and congregations to examine their self-concepts, pay attention to the historic racial barriers in their communities, and have a session or two of intentional and self-conscious efforts to learn the cultures of other ethnic groups the congregation hopes to bring into the fellowship.

With a perspective similar to that of Cassandra Howe, the sermon delivered by C. Jarred Hammet uses the New Testament metaphor of "putting on Christ" in a creative, even novel way. He speaks eloquently of taking off the filthy rags of racism, taking off our tribal uniforms, and changing our clothing—all of us changing into the uniform of Christ. For Americans who are already on Christ's team, already part of the Christian community, the metaphor works. And if all Americans who are already on Christ's team could find a way to wear the same uniform, use the same playbook, cheer the same cheers, aspire to the same American mission of providing "liberty and justice for all," America could take some giant steps toward becoming the Beloved Community. But ultimately America still cannot cross that goal line. We are much too diverse—and always have been—to convince *all* our citizens to put on the uniform of Christ. If the collective voice of Christ's team becomes a harmonized voice of *inclusion*, instead of a collection of Christian communities each singing separately but in unison, with some singing *exclusion* and others not, then America can become a kinder, gentler, more Jesus-like "nation of behavers" who will "preserve, protect, and defend" the American core values of "liberty and justice for all" regardless of race, creed, or ethnicity.[144]

As always, the initiative of making a first step toward reconciliation with African Americans belongs with White Americans. Although we Whites may not have directly created the fault lines between Whites and Blacks in America, we continue to benefit from the built-in advantages of the current situation. Historically, White people—our people—created the current status quo in matters of race in Macon and throughout the nation. Marvin McMickle has posed a key prophetic question to White America, upon whom the responsibility to begin the process of reconciliation rests: "Can we decide whether we want to be Christian more than we want to be Americans?" Or to phrase it differently, Can we decide that our lives as Americans will be lived inside the value system of God's reign? Until we can so live, racial reconciliation in Macon or in America will remain a goal beyond our reach.

18

Historical Eavesdropping: A Black Baptist Perspective

Sandy Dwayne Martin

This chapter is a response to the sermons printed in this volume and devotes some attention to related issues and concerns. The chapter touches on a number of points: acknowledgment regarding the central and vital role that religious leaders play and the challenges they face regarding efforts to lead their congregations and other people of faith into a more authentic Jewish, Christian, and Islamic understanding of the importance of faith and race, particularly here in the United States; some words about the special character of sermons and in general religious ministry; reviews and brief comments regarding main points and some key contributions of the Macon sermons; and some thoughts on racial integration, nationalism, pluralism, and the issue of reparations. Let me draw attention to the word "response" in the first sentence of this paragraph. For reasons I will discuss below, this chapter does not attempt critiques of the sermons herein but is *an academic and faith response.*

RELIGIOUS LEADERSHIP, THE SERMON,
AND COMMUNITY MINISTRY

We congratulate and express deep appreciation for the men and women of various faiths and backgrounds for contributing sermons on race, for what they have done is very important and calls for emulation in Macon, Georgia, and elsewhere. They have brought a discussion of race into the pulpit. That appeal to bring such a message into the pulpit flows from the recognition of the vital and sometimes central role that religious leaders play in the lives of their congregants and the wider community. The rabbi, pastor, and imam are not only preachers and teachers of doctrine and religious practice but also, in some senses and in large measure, marriage counselors and advisors, psychologists and psychiatrists, lawyers, employment agents, educators, and community leaders. They are faithful servants laboring to assist people in some of the most intimate areas and in some of the most vulnerable circumstances of their lives. For that reason, people of faith and many others in both the religious community and general society still accord religious leaders great respect and trust. This special role of and esteem for the clergy present an opportunity and a challenge when it comes to issues of race. The opportunity is employing the goodwill and trust of the people to lead them toward greater interracial brotherhood and sisterhood. The challenge or danger is that many people do not want to venture along such a path and, therefore, might withdraw their goodwill and alter their stance toward clergy from a sense of trust to a perception of betrayal. Once again, the clergy sermonizers in this volume deserve our appreciation for accepting this opportunity and challenge.

To reiterate, this chapter is an academic and faith response to the sermons and not a critique. I take seriously the Jewish, Christian, and Islamic goal of proclaiming God's will for God's people and the larger world. The one proclaiming has the duty and privilege of speaking to the needs and concerns of a particular people in specific circumstances. One might examine a sermon devoted to a given topic and conclude that the clergyperson addressed only one of five important points. But given our limited human ability to receive and act upon information, one point might be more than sufficient for that assembly and that occasion. Do not misunderstand the following comments because all of these sermons are well organized and well done. But imagine a situation where we in a church, synagogue/temple, or mosque heard a sermon filled with repetitions, grammatical errors, and disorganization according to the canons of standard English writing and speaking. While such a sermon might in some measure bother grammarians, it might be the perfect format and content in that particular moment. And there is much to be valued in receptivity to the variety of sermonic style, both in terms of content and presentation. In other words, I consider the sermon a special activity by which the Divine conveys a message to the people. Therefore, with each of these sermons we are looking for a word or message that moves us closer to the goals of racial equity, justice, and interracial fellowship.

BRIEF SUMMARIES OF THE SERMONS IN THIS VOLUME

Let us then briefly review the sermons appearing in this volume. Some summaries are more brief than others, but the length or brevity of a sermon review neither intends nor implies any statement regarding its value. To begin with, the Reverend Dr. Tim Bagwell, Pastor of Centenary United Methodist Church, preached a sermon titled "A Fire No Water Can Put Out," in which he challenged the faithful to stand with their religious conviction rather than adhering to the norms of racist culture. His exhortation reminds us of H. Richard Niebuhr's classic text *Christ and Culture*.[145] Christians must not conform to culture but must struggle to overcome the detrimental things in culture—specifically for this occasion, racism—and indeed work to transform culture. Some might take issue with Pastor Bagwell's description of the culture of Jesus' day being one of *racism* in the sense that we usually apply the term for interactions among people for the past three hundred years or so. Such commentators might feel more comfortable with designating that culture *ethnocentric*. But the pastor's point would still be just as valid. Christ lived and ministered in a world where people's beliefs and actions toward other folks required changing. I am particularly appreciative of how Dr. Bagwell took the historical contexts of Christ and the early church and related them to our own contemporary contexts (or vice versa). Diversity of many kinds, inclusive of the variety of races, is still a part of our world and a fact that Christians cannot ignore. Pastor Bagwell's observation is a powerful one: "When you are standing close to the heart of God, there is no room for racism!" There must be a commitment to justice that matches the Birmingham struggle for equity in the 1960s, when the world witnessed that water hoses unleashed on men, women, and children striving for freedom in the streets of the city could not smother the fire of freedom in them.

The Reverend Scott Dickison of the First Baptist Church of Christ based his sermon, "Doing Something in the Present," on verses in 1 Corinthians, chapters 1 and 3 (found below in Part IV of this book). Pastor Dickison is pained by the fact that two congregations of believers in Christ, one principally White and the other mainly Black and in proximity to each other, have a history of division between them occasioned by racial differences and that it should be regarded as noteworthy the simple fact that two families of Christ's followers have assembled for joint worship. While the Bible calls Christians to unity, we must honestly confess that the church is divided. And the great tragedy of that division is not what has transpired in the past but that Christians are doing so little "in the present...to heal these divisions." The good news, Pastor Dickison reminds us with a reference to a traditional Black spiritual, is that in Christ there is a "balm," a medicine that heals these divisions.

While apparently preaching at the same program as Reverend Dickison, the Reverend James Goolsby, pastor of First Baptist Church on New Street, scripturally based his sermon (also found in Part IV below) on Acts 2:1–4, in which the followers of Jesus Christ were on Pentecost gathered together in the same place and on "one accord." The lesson for the contemporary churches is that, being in the same place on one accord, they will be able to receive power from God and that churches should with consistency act "under the power we have received." Though the pastor does not specifically reference race, such application seems appropriate since Reverend Goolsby is preaching in a context where two churches, one mainly White and the other mainly Black, hold fellowship with each other.

Imam Adam Fofana of the Islamic Center of Middle Georgia delivered a message titled "Reconciliation: An Islamic Perspective." Imam Fofana notes an Islamic theological conviction shared by Jews and Christians that human sin caused estrangement between God and people and among people themselves. But it is possible for humans to learn from their failures or mistakes and find reconciliation with God. Human beings, however, must acknowledge their failures, learn from them, and find reconciliation with each other. Imam Fofana helpfully outlines a process and principles by which true reconciliation becomes possible: (a) a willingness to admit wrong and express sorrow; (b) a willingness of the wronged party to forgive, even if he or she does not forget; and (c) the willingness of both parties to begin a new relationship. This pattern must continue if we are to have true racial reconciliation in our society. I found particularly interesting Imam Fofana's rather positive interpretation of American history with its record of racial discord and struggle. Rather than focusing on the negative aspect of this history and emphasizing the deficiencies of the US, the Imam has a more positive take. He says the nation through generations has made some serious mistakes; but once those mistakes became manifest, corrections have been made. Of additional interest is the Imam's reference to Martin Luther King Jr.'s words regarding the need for reconciliation with the offender, not his or her humiliation—a rejection of bitterness and a pursuit of reconciliation, redemption, and the beloved community.

The sermon "Can We Talk?" by the Reverend Jarred Hammet, senior pastor of Northminster Presbyterian Church, is based on Romans 13:8–14, a passage in which the Apostle Paul outlines some basic moral norms for Christians and calls on the believers to live accordingly, wearing "the armor of light," being clothed "with the Lord Jesus Christ." The sermon title is the use of a trademark saying of the late comedian Joan Rivers, who employed this phrase when preparing to make a serious critique of someone's clothing. The sermon asks if we can have a serious and perhaps uncomfortable talk about the spiritual clothes we are wearing, whether they are really the garments of righteousness of Christ that the Apostle Paul spoke about in the biblical text. "Paul says, 'Make no provision for the flesh.' Your attire is to be based on the one who claimed you in those baptismal waters." If we are changed people having been baptized into the way of Christ, then the old rags of racism and prejudice should be discarded.

The Reverend Cassandra Howe, pastor of High Street Unitarian-Universalist Church, preached about "Laying Down, Taking Up," basing her sermon on the traditional Black hymn, "Gonna Lay Down My Sword and Shield." Pastor Howe states how meaningful this spiritual has been relative to the quest for world peace: how we need to lay down the implements of war and take up the pursuit of peace. Yet, argues the Reverend Howe, this song also has deep meaning for the struggle for freedom, as a knowledge of its original setting among enslaved yearning for liberty reveals. The sermon challenges Whites to engage in a costly endeavor: surrendering many things most dear to them, collectively known as white privilege, in order to recognize and practice true human sibling-hood. Even the most common, everyday enjoyments, such as a be-loved set of novels, can be expressions of racial privilege or the communicators of racism. In a metaphorical story told toward the conclusion of her sermon, Pastor Howe illustrates the importance of sharing resources as a key to the overall happiness of everyone.

The Reverend Julie Whidden Long, the former Minister of Children and Families at First Baptist Church of Christ, bases her message on Galatians 3:26–29 in her sermon titled "We're Much Too Smart." Reflecting her specific ministry in a local congrega-tion, Reverend Long utilizes a children's book by John Reitano, *What If Zebras Lost Their Stripes?* The book asks whether all the zebras could still get along and be friends if one set of them be-came one color and the other set another color. Surely, the now two new types of zebras would continue in harmony because they would not allow their color differences to separate them. Focusing on the Bible's statements in Galatians, Minister Long says that while oneness in Christ supersedes and nullifies the possible dis-harmonies arising from differences in ethnicity, class or caste back-ground, and gender, that does not mean that people do not see dif-ferences. These are simply no longer the first things people observe about others. The Reverend Long shows by a number of concrete examples that anyone and everyone can contribute to breaking down the walls of racial division among us, regardless of their soci-oeconomic status or their political affiliation. She suggests simple but powerful things such as inviting someone of another race to one's home for dinner and sharing stories; voting for someone of a different racial background; and writing one's representative legis-lature regarding some measure that threatens the justice status of a certain set of people. The Reverend Long says we are different, but certainly we are too smart to let our differences be a cause for division and rancor rather than a source of harmony and understanding.

"A Response to Injustice" is the sermon by the Reverend Dr. Ike Edwin Mack, pastor of Unionville Baptist Church. Basing his sermon on Hebrews 13:1–3, Dr. Mack notes how the presence of injustice disturbs us, as it disturbed the Lord Jesus during his earthly ministry. Pastor Mack reminds us, however, that there must be a righteous response to injustice, not hateful, vengeful, bitter, and divisive ones. Reading these verses from the book of Hebrews, the Reverend Mack offers three ways of responding positively and meaningfully to the challenges of injustice, including racism: (a) continue to love everyone and not succumb to hatred and resentment; (b) be careful in our treatment of "strangers," making sure that we do not caricature, objectify, or treat them as enemies; and (c) empathize with those who suffer. Accepting God as our model for proper behavior, we must allow love, says Dr. Mack, to triumph over meanness, vice, and other forms of sin.

Dr. Andrew M. Manis, professor of history at Middle Georgia State University, presents a sermon demonstrating that his interest in effecting racial reconciliation is more than academic. It is clear that while he does not currently hold a pastoral charge, he still has a pastor's commitment to seeing that God's broken people are made whole. Basing his sermon, "Wrestling and Reconciling with Race," on Psalm 133:1; Genesis 32:22–30; and Genesis 33:1–20, Dr. Manis calls our attention to the importance of unity and uses the Old Testament account of the brothers Jacob and Esau to illustrate the pain of human division and the means by which reconciliation is possible. Of course, Professor Manis applies the lessons from these scriptural passages to the racial divide between Blacks and Whites in the United States. Being the historian that he is, Dr. Manis not only reviews the biblical accounts of the two siblings but also relates them to the long, painful history of race in the US. At one point in his sermon Dr. Manis notes that more than a century after the conclusion of the Civil War, all of us are still wrestling with the issue of race that perdures in dividing Blacks and Whites. And, whether we are Black or White, whether we are racial justice workers or White supremacists, we have to deal with the legacy of racism that "is within us, lurking and looking for those knee-jerk situations" in which it can make its destructive appearance. In addition to analyzing the nature and impact of racial prejudice, Dr. Manis offers some concrete suggestions on how the nation might erase the presence, and repair the damage of, societal racism. He calls society to remember the wrongs and to repent from them. He notes efforts of the Southern Baptist Convention in these directions. A more complete repentance, Manis says, would go further than the nation's and churches' actions hitherto and entail monetary contributions to the aggrieved community that would undo some of the damage caused. He issues a call for Christian churches to take the lead in raising and—in some constructive, meaningful way—distributing those funds. In a word, he is calling for some type of reparations to the Black community.

In his sermon, "Carrying Your Corner of the Blanket," Pastor Jason McClendon of the Community Church of God addresses the question of whether saved or Christian people can also be prejudiced, basing his sermon on the text of Acts 10:1–48, wherein Peter is directed to preach to the household of Cornelius, a Gentile in Caesarea. Pastor McClendon proceeds to analyze the nature of prejudice and its inconsistency with the Christian manner of life. Noting that there has been a strong reappearance of racial prejudice, the pastor notes that both the differences among and mistreatment of people contribute to the existence of prejudice. Like the early Christians of Jewish background, contemporary Christians must rise above their differences and mistreatment and embrace others, resisting the efforts of the world to separate people. Painfully pointing to his own religious denominational family that since the 1920s allowed racial differences to divide them, Pastor

McClendon challenges Christians to break down the barriers of racial prejudice and to engage in fellowship across racial lines, understanding the vital necessity of maintaining a genuine prayer life. It is possible to achieve true interracial fellowship if everyone resolves to hold their "corner of the blanket."

Father Allan J. McDonald of the St. Joseph Catholic Church bases his sermon, "On Religion, Race, and Reconciliation," on 1 Corinthians 6:13–20 and John 1:35–42. Father McDonald makes two important connections in his sermon. The first association is between the Reverend Dr. Martin Luther King Jr., and President Barack H. Obama. He notes that the day after King Holiday in January 2009, President Obama assumed his office with the hopes of many that he would lead the nation forward to the fruition of the goals of the Civil Rights Movement. Unfortunately, too many people continued to cling to prejudice, resisting the will of God to love God genuinely and their neighbors as themselves. Father McDonald also draws a connection between the efforts to achieve racial equity and justice with the need to cherish and sustain the lives of unborn children, which is truly a civil rights issue in itself. The morally just connection between the two struggles is the common respect for human life and dignity. There needs to be a recommitment of God's people to securing the will of God for both racial justice and preborn human life.

The Reverend Billy Graham McFadden, then pastor of Greater Allen African Methodist Episcopal (AME) Church, who later assumed pastoral leadership of St. Paul AME Church in Valdosta, Georgia, based his sermon, "We Need Each Other," on 1 Corinthians 12:14–26. In this scriptural passage the Apostle Paul likens the community of believers to the human body in which every member is important and the various members must work in harmony. Pastor McFadden applies that apostolic teaching to the church today and to the relationship between Whites and Blacks. He makes three profound points: (a) each one of us is significant, yet that importance should not be a self-importance but grounded in being part of a larger community; (b) we are unique, both similar and different from others; and (c) "we belong to each other." Our somebodyness, if correctly understood, cannot come at the expense of others. Each of us has a unique contribution to make that no other human being can make. We cannot live meaningfully apart from each other, for we require mutual support.

The Reverend Jeff Morris, pastor of First Assembly of God Church, preached on the subject "Making Bitter Water Sweet," based on 2 Kings 2:19–22. In this passage the prophet Elisha, acting according to the will of God, casts salt on water that was bad in a land that was unproductive. With this prophetic action, the Lord declares that he healed the water that will then cause the land to be productive. Pastor Morris, the leader of a church that is intentionally interracial in membership, relates this biblical account to the racial situation in the city of Macon, Georgia. His first point is that "racism causes bitterness," which can be countered by people refusing to be involved in maintaining the problem; by people understanding that the basic nature of the problem is not people themselves but is a spiritual problem requiring spiritual answers beyond mere politics, economics, or education however helpful they can be; and the need to believe in God first of all and to believe in the city of Macon. Second, the pastor notes that Elisha used a new bowl and that even a small church can be the new bowl that God uses to effect the healing of the racial divide. Third, Reverend Morris points out that the prophet cast *salt* into the bitter water, which lets us know that God used even something that physically speaking was counterproductive to bring healing. With the same faith as Elisha, involving both believing and acting on that belief, the city of Macon too could be redeemed from racial injustice and prejudice.

Rabbi Aaron Rubinstein of the Congregation of Sha'arey Israel bases his sermon, "Where Are We and What Are We Looking

For?" on Genesis 3:6–13, 16–19, but he also draws significantly from Genesis 37. The passages from the third chapter of Genesis deal with the interaction between the couple Adam and Eve and God. Having disobeyed, that is, failed the Lord, the couple is presented with the question, Where are you? Genesis 37 deals with the issue of one of the younger brothers, Joseph, in search of brothers with whom there is estrangement. Joseph is faced with the query, What are you looking for? Each of those questions— Where are you? and What are you looking for?—has not only an immediate meaning but a deeper spiritual one. The rabbi asks that those questions be applied to the problem of race and social justice in this country. Do we know where we are and for what we are looking when it comes to the matter of justice and equity? Perhaps we cannot solve the political, social, and economic problems surrounding those questions, but we are obligated to do our part.

Focusing on the scripture Jeremiah 38:1–13, the Reverend Eddie Smith, pastor of Macedonia Baptist Church, preaches in a sermon titled "We Have Been There" about the vital role that African Americans have played and must continue to play in the history of the nation. This biblical passage speaks of Ebedmelek, a Cushite, a Black African, who rescued the prophet Jeremiah from a slow death in a cistern after he was cast there when he dared to speak the word of the Lord in a situation that many people, including some powerful individuals, in that time understood to be treason. The pastor connects the experience of Jeremiah and the actions of Ebedmelek to the African American experience. Noting the great amount of suffering and oppression Blacks have endured in the US, Pastor Smith points also to the great contributions Blacks have made to world civilization with special focus on the US and provides a list of notable men and women, such as Mary McLeod Bethune, Charles R. Drew, Phyllis Wheatley, and William H. Hastie. According to the Reverend Smith, God has a providential plan for Blacks, not only for attaining their freedom but also for contributing to justice for everyone.

The Reverend Gail Smith, pastor of the Universal Light Christian Center, preaches about "A Change of Heart," based on Acts 10:9–48; 1:8; and Ephesians 4:29–32. Continuing her congregation's study of the book of Acts, Reverend Smith focuses on the change of heart that happened to the Apostle Peter as God led him to change his whole paradigm of how he thought about and interacted with others. The Lord Jesus had told his disciples that they would receive power with the coming of the Holy Spirit. Reverend Smith points out that the Greek word translated power is also at the root of the word "dynamite." The power that Christians have to conduct missions is a dynamic power, a dynamite power, a power that causes explosions. Such an explosive power is needed in the battle against racism because racism "is a grievous behavior," "a growing problem," and "a generational issue." Peter had a paradigm shift in which he moved completely from regarding Gentiles or non-Jews as an unworthy people to an understanding that God did not favor races or ethnicities of people. Likewise, modern Christians, White and Black, need an explosion in their hearts to move them to a new model of love and justice.

RESPONSES TO THE SERMONS IN THIS VOLUME

This collection of sermons represents an impressive variety along a number of fronts. First, Dr. Manis has assembled a truly diverse set of religious leaders that includes Christians, both Protestants and Catholics; Muslims; Jews; men and women; and Blacks and Whites. Furthermore, these clergy apparently lead varied types of congregations: small and large; those with long institutional histories reaching as far back as the Antebellum period as well as others emerging since the advent of the Civil Rights Movement; congregations with Black, White, and mixed memberships; churches that share common organizational histories with others as well as those that do not; and congregants of diverse socioeconomic status and levels of formal education.

Second, the reader will observe the wide use of the Bible in the preparation of these sermons. Clergy of the Jewish and Christian traditions have based their messages on selected passages from a wide range of books in both the Old Testament/Jewish Bible and New Testament: Genesis, the Prophets, the Gospels, Acts, and other books of the New Testament. While most practitioners in Judaism, Christianity, and Islam prefer a scriptural foundation for sermons, one clergyperson's use of a spiritual or sacred song from the enslaved Black Christian tradition is noteworthy in speaking of the rich sacred heritage of African Americans, surely an observation that has some relevance for our search to extol human sibling-hood rather than racial dominance. This extensive use of biblical texts demonstrates that the Jewish and Christian teachings regard-ing the unity of humanity as brothers and sisters under the parenthood of one God has strong and consistent basis in the scriptures of those two traditions. In other words, the affirmation of human siblinghood or the rejection of racial supremacy does not have its foundation on selective proof texting but is rather a central theme throughout these scriptural texts.

Equally so, Islam's scripture, the Qur'an, makes it abundantly clear that God's salvific concern includes the entire human race. As examples, we observe God's universal concern for humanity in one of the central doctrines of Islam that says that, over the centuries, God sent prophets to proclaim God's will to various peoples and in the Qur'anic statement that God has made humanity of different "peoples and tribes" so that they could recognize one another. This] verse, from the Qur'an 49:13, says that differences are not for hating and despising others.[146] Therefore, all three religions hold that a great sin of humanity is that they have used the blessing of God's diversity in human creation as a basis to dominate, mar-ginalize, and act unjustly toward other created children of God.

And this brings us to another point about these sermons. All of the imams, rabbis, and ministers clearly define racism and racial prejudice as sinful and adverse to God's will. These leaders also illustrate various approaches to combat the sin of racism, some of them quite concrete and accessible to everyone regardless of their socioeconomic status.

INDIVIDUAL VERSUS SOCIAL APPROACH

A fourth feature of these sermons is the different focus on (a) the personal and interpersonal dimension; (b) a more societal and systematic emphasis; and (c) some combination of the two. In other words, how do we go about solving the problem of racial separation and discrimination? One approach is to focus on changing the hearts of individuals with the belief that true and sincere racial change in the land will come when people on a personal and individual level rise above their prejudices, hatreds, and resentments and sincerely and genuinely accept people of the other race as equal human beings who are equally deserving of our love and respect. Some Americans argue that the eradication of racism cannot succeed by political pressure or governmental laws, that you can neither politically pressure people nor legislate and use government power to attain true brotherhood and sisterhood. A number of our sermons make the point that the hearts of people need changing and that people with faith in God must be at the forefront of any lasting change for the better.

On the other hand, some Americans contend with equal vigor that the urgent necessity is for governmental and other societal, systematic change to erase the stain of racism. People in our society who hold this view would argue that the magnitude of the task of eliminating racism requires the resources of our entire society. Achieving understanding between and among individuals is good and healthy, but the great racial pains and oppression in our society extend well beyond the prejudice or even hatred of individuals.

There is a system of oppression that often enlists the willing and unwitting service of even those who on an individual, personal level have denounced racism. Another way of expressing this position is to say that racism is not just about personal acceptance; it also involves societal justice. It is not simply that individual schoolteachers might be prejudiced against Black children. It is the whole apparatus of racist, social, generational thinking that impinges upon their thinking and inhibits those teachers' ability to be equitable to Black children. And even when White teachers rise above their own racial prejudices, the ravages of societal factors—such as the over policing of Black communities, excessive incarceration and criminalization of Black people, lack of access to well-paying jobs, and schools with inadequate educational resources—greatly hamper the work of even the most unbiased and dedicated teachers, Black or White, in providing the education that all children so desperately need.

This issue of the personal/individual versus the social/societal is reflective of an overall conservative/liberal, evangelical/social gospel debate or disagreement that has been present in American religion for at least the last century. To be sure, that divide between a personal and a social focus among religious people has not always been as prominent a point of contention as it is today. During the Antebellum period and for a couple of decades following the Civil War, some of the strongest advocates for societal and governmental actions to correct injustice and inequity were evangelical Christians with very traditional/conservative approaches to the Bible. We can see that evangelically based social activism in the struggles to overthrow racial slavery, to establish an alcohol prohibitive society, and to provide education to Blacks and other educationally marginalized or disadvantaged groups.

In the late 1800s Washington Gladden, Walter Rauschenbusch, George Washington Woodbey, and others fashioned and/or advocated a more intentionally social approach to dealing with societal ills, sometimes called Practical Christianity or Social Christianity but soon and now known best as the Social Gospel. The goal of the Social Gospel thinkers was to state much more emphatically the need for a social interpretation of scripture and theology as inherent in the basic meaning of Christianity itself.[147] But also developing during this Social Gospel era, ca. 1870–1920, was a deepening divide between religious liberalism and religious conservatism, between religious modernism and religious fundamentalism. What occurred often was a growing identification of religious conservatism/fundamentalism with a personal/charity/ humanitarian approach to dealing with social ills. Likewise, there was a growing identification of religious liberalism/modernism with the more pointed expression of social activism as represented in the Social Gospel movement. Hence, for many Christians as the decades passed, to be an evangelical/conservative/fundamentalist was not to be an advocate of the Social Gospel; and for many liberal/modernist Christians, to be an advocate for the Social Gospel was not to be evangelical or religiously conservative.[148]

To be sure, there are avenues other than the liberal/social versus the conservative/humanitarian approaches. Some evangelical Christians continued to pursue more socially systemic solutions to social ills, and some politically progressive Christians continued to be evangelical or conservative in their religious beliefs. And, of course, some Christians followed a middle ground between conservative and liberal and/or between the individual and the social approach to solving these problems. Two concrete examples since World War II illustrate some rupture in this chasm of conservative/liberal and individual/social approaches to issues of social justice. The modern Civil Rights Movement, especially as led by Martin Luther King Jr., and the Religious Right Movement, e.g., represented by Jerry Falwell Sr. and Jerry Falwell Jr., demonstrate in significant ways that a more orthodox and conservative approach to religion does not automatically exclude a social approach to what is perceived as a social ill. While advocating for social reform, King made it abundantly clear that he had a personal relationship with God and that his personal faith was the foundation of his social activism. Falwell opposed King during the height of the Civil Rights Movement, saying that the minister's duty was to preach the gospel and care for the church and emphasizing the personal dimension of Christianity as a foundation to change society for the better. But by the late 1970s Falwell also saw the need for people of faith to be engaged in social activism, though his choice was politically and economically more conservative than King's.[149] But it is also true that for many religious and/or community and civic leaders, being liberal politically is matched with being liberal religiously; and being conservatively politically is matched with being conservative religiously.

Many if not all of these sermons seem to avoid this type of either-or approach, reflecting that the answer to the original question is that we need both the personal and the social approaches to solve this massive problem. Those clergy emphasizing the need for change on the personal level realize that solutions to some problems lie beyond the resources of individual people. I believe that those clergy stressing institutional and societal changes likewise understand that unless people on a personal, individual level commit themselves genuinely to caring for all people, then societal remedies are unlikely to secure funding; and even if resources are provided, they ultimately will prove hollow without that personal commitment to racial justice. Therefore, as we read these sermons, the issue is not that one approach—the individual or the social—is effective and the other is not; rather, we need to hear both voices. We need to hear sermons challenging us to look into our hearts to seek right motivations and then follow up with right actions. Likewise, we require sermons that point out the enormous nature of this problem that cannot be definitively resolved until Americans collectively do the right thing.

THE ROLES OF BLACKS AND WHITES

Just as the sermons indicate the need for both a personal/individual as well as a social/societal approach to the solution of the problem of American racial prejudice, they also point to the fact that both Black and White populations must commit themselves to achieve social justice and interracial harmony. Of course, the overall, predominant picture of what has occurred in the United States is that people of European descent have enslaved and segregated people of African descent. To this day, including during the time the nation was under the presidency of its first Black president, the overwhelming political and economic power has been in the hands of Whites, who continue to enjoy influence and privilege far in excess of Blacks or any other racial/ethnic/cultural group. Therefore, it makes sense that discussions of racial liberation and interracial reconciliation focus a good deal on the necessity of Whites to confront racism among themselves—religiously, economically, and politically. Nevertheless, the sermons in this book also point to the reality that this Black-White problem requires some Black-White dialogue, cooperation, and activities. Blacks must respond ethically and meaningfully to sincere efforts of Whites to bridge the relational chasms and to obliterate injustices. In the paragraphs below I wish to focus attention on various models for Blacks to pursue that would grasp opportunities for our liberation while responding to the possibilities for interracial cooperation and reconciliation. Black America is not a monolith, and, hence, it would be beneficial for all of us, Black and non-Black, to understand the various theologies, philosophies, and theoretical approaches within the Black community so that our interactions might be more understandable and fruitful.

INTEGRATION, NATIONALISM, AND PLURALISM: RACIAL JUSTICE AND RECONCILIATION

We might say that overall there have been three main historical and current approaches within the Black community regarding liberation from oppression and injustice and achieving reconciliation with whites: Black nationalism, integration, and pluralism. At this point I should note that this section of the chapter is built very much on the outline of Peter Paris's book, *Black Religious Leaders: Conflict in Unity*, in which the author examines and compares the thinking of four leaders: Martin Luther King Jr., Malcolm X, Joseph H. Jackson, and Adam Clayton Powell Jr. For this chapter, particular attention falls on the first three as representative of integration, nationalism, and pluralism.[150] Furthermore, it is important to note that I am addressing ideologies and approaches that in the lives of particular individuals and communities are not always mutually exclusive. Sometimes people over a course of a lifetime change from one approach to another. Also, I am saying that we should expect many people not to fit neatly and exclusively into any one category. Occasionally the categories of integration and nationalism are fluid; for example, an individual or group might overall be integrationist while demonstrating some strong elements of nationalism. But these terms, used cautiously, are helpful in understanding the main parts of Black thought and strategies, historically and presently.

Let us begin with Black nationalism, not necessarily the predominant approach historically or even now but still a very important part of the Black experience.[151] Black nationalism emphasizes race solidarity; knowledge and pride of one's racial/ethnic culture; and control of those institutions and functions that impact the Black community or at least control of them to the extent that they impact Black people, e.g., schools, banks, newspapers, and law enforcement. Black nationalism implies, when it does not outrightly call for, some degree of racial separation. This is not to be confused with racial segregation, which is a legal enforcement whereby Blacks and Whites have been kept separate from each other to a considerable extent, especially in social and intimate ways that would recognize or suggest the equality of Blacks with Whites. Therefore, the point of racial segregation was not merely or even principally to keep the races apart but to separate them in such a manner as to ensure the supremacy and "purity" of the White race. Whereas segregation is a legally mandatory system, racial separation as a component of Black nationalism is a racially voluntary choice to treasure and advance the Black community.

Historically, Black nationalism in the US has taken different forms. Sometimes its advocates, such as Paul Cuffee and Lott Carey, have called for and sought to effect literal separation of the races as in emigration from the United States to other lands, such as the Caribbean area, Canada, or Western Africa. The last major "back to Africa movement" was that of Marcus Garvey, which reached its peak in the 1910s and 1920s.[152] People calling for emigration to foreign lands have generally held the following views: (a) Blacks and Whites cannot live peaceably and equitably together in the US. Emigration advocates often see a future of racial conflict, violent and otherwise, if Blacks remain in America. (b) African Americans need to reside in places controlled by people of African descent so that they can most fully develop their "Manhood" or human potentials, something that the restrictive laws and customs of Whites in the US will never allow. (c) Blacks have a providential destiny or God-ordained purpose in the world, that is, there are contributions Blacks as a race of people need to make to the world; and, in light of (a) and (b) above, they can only fully fulfill that divine destiny outside the United States.

Many advocates of emigration, however, called for relocation within the United States or its territories.[153] Often this domestic emigration was not necessarily predicated upon the idea of Black nationalism as such. Blacks, for example, in the first half of the 1900s left rural areas and smaller towns to live in larger cities in both the South and outside the South in a major relocation extending over decades that bears the name the Great Migration. Sometimes that move to a Northern or non-Southern area was because of a greater promise (often unrealized in many ways) of freer living in more racially inclusive and tolerant places than what was possible, say, in Mississippi or Georgia. But there were instances in which domestic emigration or relocation did involve the search for a great "Black space," such as founding all-Black towns like Mound Bayou, Mississippi, or journeying in the late 1800s to areas in Oklahoma and Kansas.

Yet even for those who never relocated abroad or to another American city, region, or state, the reality of Black life in America in many or even most places, whether by law or simple reality of American life, involved some type of racial separation. Gains from the modern Civil Rights Movement include a significant reduction in racial segregation legally, but there still remains a significant degree of racial separation (and sometimes segregation) in sectors such as housing and schools. Nonetheless, the idea of emigrating to an all-Black or mainly Black state, region, or country just about reached its end point in practicality and any important level of popularity among Blacks by the 1950s. To be sure, African American leaders, spokespeople, and just plain people refused to accept or endorse segregation for practical, legal, and ethical reasons. Those with Black nationalist leanings, however, had the remaining option and the historical practice to call upon fellow Blacks to build their own communities, businesses, media, etc., to benefit the race. In other words, people such as Malcolm X and Stokely Carmichael (later Kwame Ture) in the 1960s endorsed Black nationalism.[154] Yet the Black American community does not appear to accept a comprehensive policy of Black nationalism as a workable method or even express the desirability of adhering to it. While one could argue that African Americans have of necessity practiced some aspects of Black nationalism, it does not appear to be the predominant and preferred choice of the masses of Black people in the US.

No, a more popular choice of African Americans from colonial times to the present has been racial integration as an overall strategy to achieve full constitutional rights and economic justice. People advocating emigration outside or to other destinations within the US have met opposition from those who prefer residing in the US despite enslavement, racial segregation, disfranchisement, racial terror, and various forms of discrimination. Roughly contemporaries during the 1810s and 1820s, Lott Carey and Richard Allen differed in that the former was a Baptist minister and the latter was a Methodist minister and bishop. But a more relevant distinction for this chapter is that the former argued that Blacks should emigrate to Liberia where they could more fully exercise their humanity and help fulfill God's destiny for the Black race. Richard Allen, equally committed to people of African descent, refused to leave his homeland in America, choosing to struggle to make this a racially inclusive nation.[155] Frederick Douglass, the great abolitionist, said many critical things about racial injustice and the hypocrisy and callousness of White Christians during the Antebellum period.[156] But though he seemed at points to lean somewhat in the direction of emigration, he died an American in 1895, still fighting for the inclusion of African Americans into the basic economic and political fabric of the nation. The Jamaican immigrant Marcus Garvey especially during the second and third decades of the twentieth century sought to persuade Black Americans (and Blacks in other lands) that at least a significant number of Blacks in the Western Hemisphere should relocate to Africa and there build a strong African Republic dedicated to achieving Black freedom and progress. Yet more Black Americans agreed with the viewpoints of W. E. B. DuBois that he held at that point in his life. DuBois believed in unity, cooperation, and the same ultimate destiny of all people of African descent (Pan-Africanism), but he rebelled against the suggestion that Black Americans should renounce their citizenship; and, as one of the founders and early officers of the National Association for the Advancement of Colored People (NAACP), he labored for an America that would transcend racial segregation and injustice and become a truly interracial democracy.[157] Martin Luther King Jr. and other leaders often differed on specific strategies, but the basic philosophy/theology outlined in his famous "I Have a Dream" speech essentially captures the predominant thought of most African Americans, past and present. The basic goal of King, shared in great part by most other mainstream civil rights leaders and spokespeople, was an interracial democracy whose people rose above the ills of racism, poverty, and violence.[158]

This brings us to the third major option or method among African Americans regarding liberation of Blacks and interaction with Whites—the position of racial pluralism.[159] Whereas King represented African Americans' search for the inclusion into mainstream society—economically and politically—there were those who stood back from his move toward integration in the sense of racial assimilation. One of those dissenting was the Reverend Dr. Joseph H. Jackson, the president of the National Baptist Convention, USA, Incorporated (NBC), the largest Black religious body in the US at the time of his tenure in office (1953–1982). King looked forward to the day when not only public sectors would be integrated, with no Black or White schools, but also private sectors would be interracial. During the period of desegregation, as segregation is overturned and society marches toward full integration or assimilation, there is a need for race-specific churches, clubs, and other organizations, King believed. But true integration would be a society free of all racially distinct organizations. It is not that those holding pluralist views rejected the desirability or moral correctness of racial assimilation. But some may have questioned if such would ever be possible among sinful and flawed people; and some insisted that integration should truly be a two-way street and not a one-way avenue wherein Blacks surrendered their customs and organizations and embraced those of Whites.

We can see that the pluralist approach is a combination somewhat of the nationalist and the integrationist approaches. Like the integrationist, the pluralist desires a racially inclusive America where race and color are cast aside, where Blacks become a part of mainstream America both politically and economically. Pluralists do not see the practicality or the morality of a nationalism that would enshrine racial separation or suggest a difference in races that would open the door to either Black or White racism. Like the nationalist, however, the pluralist makes a greater appeal to the value and distinctiveness of Black culture, customs, and institutions. Here we see W. E. B. DuBois, during the early days of the integrationist NAACP, authoring "The Conservation of the Races," wherein he argues for distinctiveness of Black culture and the specific and unique contributions that the Black race should make to the world. In order to make those contributions, Blacks require their own race institutions.[160]

Closer to our time, Joseph H. Jackson during the middle 1960s foresaw the end of legal segregation but asked what would become of the cohesion of the Black community.[161] He queried if some people, in their eager quest for integration, were in part seeking to get away from their own people. The NBC president drew a distinction between "racial preference" and "racial prejudice." He did not consider it immoral that members of a race might prefer associating with their own. Sin enters the picture when that preference becomes prejudice, when people discriminate against others because they are different. We might paraphrase Dr. Jackson by saying that a Black church composed of mainly or solely Black people in a Black section of town did not morally bother him. He would, however, consider it sinful if that congregation refused fellowship and membership to people because of the color of their skin. The Reverend Jackson sounded very much like Malcolm X in a less racially charged manner when he called for economic development in the Black community. Jackson said that Blacks must become economically self-sufficient and productive, that they must move from "protest to production." No people can be truly free if they are a race of consumers and not producers.

In practical terms, pluralism is the reality of race relations in the US. Most Blacks, I would contend, do wish to retain Black culture, customs, and institutions, and perhaps expand them, just as Whites wish to keep theirs. One could argue that a strong system of genuine racial integration (and not merely desegregation) is when individuals and groups can traverse back and forth among a multiple number of racial and ethnic cultures, customs, and institutions. Some would insist that a quest for racial assimilation accompanied by the elimination of Black institutions and cultural identity would be very problematic. One pointed example of the shortcomings of integration or at least desegregation would be the desegregation of our public schools. Under the system of legalized segregation, Black schools in terms of material resources were generally less equipped than White schools. Some Blacks and Whites have argued over the years that Black children under segregation received inferior education. Indeed, a central argument in the *Brown versus Board of Education* (Topeka, KS) case—resulting in the 1954 US Supreme Court decision to outlaw segregation in public schools—was that racial segregation instilled a sense of inferiority in Black children. One proposed solution to closing the current achievement gaps between Black and White children is removing the de facto racial separation in schools generally occasioned by racial patterns in housing. If we could just get more economically disadvantaged Black children into the same schools as more economically advantaged White children, they would enjoy the same resources and thereby the achievement gap between the race would disappear, according to this argument.

Yet there have always been some Blacks who have seen some serious benefits for African American children in attending predominantly Black schools and some grave drawbacks for them being pupils in mainly White schools. Across the South, including in Georgia, "complete" school desegregation in the late 1960s and the 1970s resulted in the abandonment of Black educational institutions, even their physical destruction and the literal trashing of cherished artifacts, papers, and awards that documented the historical accomplishments and creativity of students, staff, and faculty. A disproportionate number of Black teachers were fired and principals and other officials demoted. Black children were thrust into an educational system created by and for White children, where often Black pupils were considered a nuisance. White prejudice in some instances declined when people came face to face with each other in ways they had not done so previously. But in some instances prejudice remained, was reinforced, and was passed on by White principals and school officials. Some Black students were greatly helped academically by desegregation and received opportunities they would not have otherwise known. Nonetheless, some Black students were severely hurt. In the face of cultural changes detrimental to family stability, school desegregation erased in many instances one vital institution that could have been a bulwark for family and individual esteem. White children have been hurt also by these cultural changes. But given the greater levels of poverty and the overall existence of prejudice in society, Black children in the absence of historic Black schools have suffered more than White children because the former no longer have an educational apparatus to support them.

And this is where advantages of pluralism enter the picture. Pluralists, like other Blacks, do not want to retreat to segregated schools. But they do not want to lose the distinctive strengths that come with Black educational autonomy. Pluralism rejects segregation and its codification of racial injustice; yet pluralists wish to retain racial avenues beneficial to self and race esteem as well as tools to effect change. I think racial pluralism, some combination of integration and Black nationalism, is where most Black people and progressive Whites are. We aim for a society that is eventually and truly colorblind or inclusive, where our differences act to unify us rather than divide us. Yet we realize that the continuing reality of human sin in all its complexity and the varied histories and customs of respective races indicate that there will continue to be some navigation between interracial and specifically racial contexts for the foreseeable future.

REFLECTIONS ON REPARATIONS

Another feature emerging from these sermons is the understanding that liberation from racism for both Blacks and Whites and reconciliation between the two groups means that there must be some recognition of the history and impact of injustice and mistreatment on Blacks and indeed in some ways on the nation as a whole. There is also the understanding that we must do some concrete things to bridge the chasm between the races and produce a more just social order. These actions can be as simple—yet also profound and impactful—as holding interracial and interreligious fellowships, opening ourselves to friendships with people of other races, or making a point of having lunch or dinner with someone or some family different from us. But there have also been suggestions in these sermons and in the religious, political, and economic sectors of our wider society that there should be more systemic and wide-ranging efforts to fix the inequality and discord affecting our entire nation. One of those suggestions is reparations.

Reparations may be understood as efforts involving significant amounts of monetary investments that are extended to the subjects of direct or historical racial injustice and oppression.[162] Reparations

234

are regarded as a just payment for uncompensated labor but also as an adjustment for and termination of the continuing damage of oppression done in the past and the present. They are seen as the ethical course of action because it is just to repay that which has been taken from others. But reparations also serve as a corrective series of actions that places the unjustly treated in the position they would have been had there been no oppression in the first place. Therefore, when we think of the institution of racial, chattel slavery reserved for the most part only for Black people; the unjust trading of peoples between European and African nations; the horrors of the Middle Passage (or transport of Africans under horrible conditions from the home continent to the Western Hemisphere and beyond); the multiple generational practice of racial segregation, disfranchisement, racial terror, and other forms of racial discrimination, we can make a strong moral case for the necessity of reparations to compensate for the past and address contemporary ills. And the idea of reparations is not a far-fetched idea without historical precedents. Some survivors of the Holocaust have received reparations by European governments as have Japanese-American victims of the World War II era internment or concentration camps by the US.

Ethically and for political and economic reasons, Black Americans should receive the justification or application of reparations. Even those who consider slavery a far too distant occurrence, the racial segregation era alone is an even more credible argument for reparations. Jim Crow segregation, redlining, and unfair employment and compensation practices have occurred since the passage of the 13th Amendment abolishing slavery, the 14th Amendment clearly defining American citizenship as being inclusive of Black people, and the 15th Amendment (as amplified by the 19th Amendment) constitutionally guaranteeing the right to vote regardless of race or color, and the segregation era and its continuing effects that have transpired and are transpiring within the lifetimes of everyone reading these words. Yes, a very strong case can be made for reparations for Black Americans.

Of course, we cannot expect any one sermon or group of sermons to address all possible concerns raised about the justification or application of reparations. It is sufficient that the moral case be made and that some specific ideas about the form of reparations be made clear. Yet if the strongest possible case for reparations is to be made, then we should point out that certain practical questions and issues will require addressing. First, we must be clear in defining the nature and scope of reparations. As has been done in this volume, we must point out the particularly strong claims of African Americans, the nature and intensity of their particular oppression and exclusion in American life. In other words, I argue, reparations must be singularly focused on the issue(s) of slavery and/or racial segregation. Or, if not, if we wish to apply it to a broader category of people, then perhaps we should employ another term so that we do not run the risk of providing many answers and slighting the main question.

Second, there is the issue of the practical administration of this program. If we target African American descendants of the enslaved and/or subjects of racial segregation as the sole worthy recipients, how much proof do we require for people to qualify on the basis of their enslaved ancestry? It might sound obvious that Black Americans are descendants of enslaved people, and we might think that demonstrating such is quite simple and easy. But many people often find it difficult to prove what is an obvious commonsense reality. For example, some individuals seeking to show their qualification to vote under laws passed in some Republican-controlled states, especially the elderly from more rural and small-town contexts, find retrieving a birth certificate a challenging and sometimes impossible feat. Likewise, if information passed down in one's family tradition is ruled as insufficient evidence, proving that one is in fact the descendant of slaves whose names one might not know could be extremely difficult or impossible for many, especially if the judges of that evidence are government officials who might be hostile to racial equality and even more adverse to reparations.

A third issue to bear in mind is the possibility of unforeseen and undesirable consequences. For example, many whites and other non-Blacks might interpret reparation payments to be a tacit agreement that all future discussions regarding racial injustice are unnecessary, that reparation payments will end the whole issue of racism—just as some Whites and some Blacks initially saw the election in 2008 of a Black person, Barack Obama, as president to be a signal of a post-racial America. Finally, and related to the above points, we all must be aware that reparations would not be a panacea to all problems of racial injustice. If everyone in the United States of America had equal sums of money tomorrow, there would still be racial prejudice and tensions the day after tomorrow. For one thing, we know the persistence of racial prejudice from history; second, we know the power of sin from the teachings of our respective religious traditions and our own experiences.

CONCLUSION

This chapter has attempted a personal and academic response to the fine sermons in this volume from a Black Baptist perspective. In so doing, there was an elaboration on issues and concerns regarding racial justice and interracial interactions. One book of sermons—or even many of them—will not resolve all the issues of racial prejudice. Indeed, this book may raise new questions. But the clergy making contributions to this present work have offered all of us important foundations for discussing means toward more concrete brotherhood and sisterhood. They, therefore, deserve our great appreciation for allowing us to "eavesdrop" as they brought the issue of race into the pulpit.

PART IV

A COVENANT OF RECONCILIATION: NARRATIVE, LITURGY AND PROCLAMATION

19

Macon's Two First Baptist Churches:
Narrative, Liturgy, and Proclamation

The Spirit of the Lord is upon us! We covenant before God and with each other to proclaim the year of the Lord's favor in Macon by being a witness to the body of Christ through our developing relationship, recognizing our shared history. We covenant, therefore, to worship, fellowship, and serve our community together by establishing tutoring and mentoring programs in our public schools.

On Sunday afternoon, May 24, 2015, the leadership of Macon's two First Baptist Churches publicly signed an oversize copy of the above covenant agreement in a joint service of commitment. One hundred ninety-four years ago, the African American First Baptist Church on New Street and the predominantly White First Baptist Church of Christ constituted one biracial congregation. In 1845, the same year that Baptists in the South broke ties with their co-religionists in the North and formed the Southern Baptist Convention, and by which time Black members outnumbered Whites in the original congregation, the White and Black factions at FBC Macon mutually agreed to become separate congregations. In 1887, the Black First Baptist Church began worshipping in a sanctuary on New Street, just around the corner from the White First Baptist Church of Christ. Relations between the two congregations were distant but cordial until the early twenty-first century when the Reverend Scott Dickison became pastor of the High Place congregation in 2012.

Within two years, Dickison invited the Reverend James W. Goolsby, pastor of FBC New Street, to lunch. The two ministers hit it off and began developing a strong friendship. Additional conversations turned to what both congregations might do to develop the relationship between them. At that point the two pastors met with Hannah McMahan, then the executive director of the New Baptist Covenant, a young organization founded by former President Jimmy Carter, to discuss ways that group might help the two First Baptists develop their relationship further. Those conversations precipitated a formal covenant service in which both congregations would participate and formalize a covenant between them.

Since that covenant service in 2015, a self-selected group of members of both congregations has met regularly for a variety of occasions. Thanksgiving potluck dinners and joint worship services have been held now for two years running. Two years also of joint Easter egg hunts have taken place in a nearby park. Youth groups from both churches made an autumn outing to Disney World in Orlando, Florida. James W. Goolsby has preached at FBCX's Founders' Day/Baptist Heritage Sunday, while Scott Dickison was invited to be the guest preacher at Goolsby's fifteenth anniversary as pastor of FBC New Street. The two congregations met for solemn discussion of race in America in the weeks after the June 17, 2015 mass shooting at Mother Emmanuel African Methodist Episcopal Church in Charleston, South Carolina. In the fall of 2018, a contingent of the two churches chartered a bus and traveled together to Montgomery, Alabama, to tour the Dexter Avenue Baptist Church, the church pastored by Martin Luther King Jr. during the 1955 Montgomery bus boycott, as well as the Legacy Museum and the National Memorial for Peace and Justice.

The two congregations are growing closer and their pastors have created a modern model for what used to be called a sister church relationship. This sort of arrangement has been encouraged by Christians concerned about racial reconciliation for some time. Everyone involved in the publication of this book now points to the example of Macon's First Baptist Church on New Street and the First Baptist Church of Christ and says to White and Black pastors and congregations across America, "Go now and do likewise." We are convinced that deep commitments and careful efforts along these lines will do more to heal racial wounds in America than anything that has been tried up to this very day.

For this reason we include in this volume a liturgical look at the service of worship that publicly launched the covenant relationship between the two First Baptist Churches of Macon. We include Scott Dickison's and James Goolsby's sermons from that service, held at First Baptist Church on New Street on May 24, 2015.

20

A Service of Worship and a Covenant of Racial Reconciliation

First Baptist Church on New Street and First Baptist Church of Christ, held at First Baptist Church on New Street, Sunday, May 24, 2015

The Worship of God

Prelude

Welcome/The Occasion   Rev. Scott Dickison

Choir Special: "Revive Us Again"   Joint Choirs

The Reading of Scripture   1 Corinthians 1:10–13; 3:21–23

(1:10) I appeal to you, brothers and sisters, in the name of our Lord Jesus Christ, that all of you agree with one another in what you say and that there be no divisions among you, but that you be perfectly united in mind and thought. (11) My brothers and sisters, some from Chloe's household have informed me that there are quarrels among you. (12) What I mean is this: One of you says, "I follow Paul"; another, "I follow Apollos"; another, "I follow Cephas (That is, Peter)"; still another, "I follow Christ." (13) Is Christ divided? Was Paul crucified for you? Were you baptized in the name of Paul?...(3:21) So then, no more boasting about human leaders!

All things are yours, (22) whether Paul or Apollos or Cephas (That is, Peter) or the world or life or death or the present or the future—all are yours, (23) and you are of Christ, and Christ is of God.

Sermon:

"DOING SOMETHING IN THE PRESENT"

Rev. Scott Dickison

It's a great day for our two churches. It's a great day, I think, for the city of Macon. But most importantly, this is a great day for the Body of Christ; for our two churches to gather under one roof— one beautiful roof, I'll add—to worship together, sing together, pray together, covenant together, and serve the Lord's Supper together—a great day, and a *newsworthy day.* I hope everyone saw the write-up in yesterday's *Telegraph* about this gathering and our partnership. There was even video of the choirs. And a photo gallery. It was listed as one of the most popular phone galleries on their website, right under pictures from all the high school graduations and pictures of adoptable pets—which seems about right. And James and I actually had our photo shoot right over there. They only published one of the pictures, but I hear a calendar is in the works. And all of this is a good thing, a great thing, and a story that needs to be told. And yet, as I told my folks this morning, there's a part of me that grieves the fact that what we're doing here this afternoon and what we plan to do in the future should be deemed "newsworthy."

There's a part of me that wonders what Christ would say if he came back today and read the newspaper and saw that the idea of two churches coming to worship together is newsworthy—even worthy of the front page!

There's a part of me that wonders what Christ would say if he came back and saw that the thought of two churches covenanting to hang out more and get to know each other a little better is newsworthy.

That the thought of two churches partnering in missions endeavors together, volunteering in the public schools together was newsworthy—I wonder what Christ would say about that?

There's part of me that wonders what Christ would say when he learned that these two churches who have come together to worship, and covenanted to get to know one another and work together, are right around the corner from each other and have a shared history together—albeit a complicated one—and only now, after 189 years, are coming together to partner in this way. And I wonder what Christ would say if he found out that these two churches even have almost the exact same name, and the only difference between the two are the words "of Christ" at the end of one—what would Christ say about that?

All of this makes our gathering, for me, just a touch bittersweet. But what's just plain sweet is that in God's strange providence and divine sense of humor, in the end, these two words separating us in name, "of Christ," are the very two words that have brought us together in this moment.

Now, as we've said, the story of our two churches in many ways is unique—especially the part of our story that has yet to be written. But there's a reason that our story and what we're doing together this afternoon and beyond has garnered interest, because sadly, these things don't happen every day. The body of Christ, sadly, is fractured—we must confess this—and these types of gatherings and covenants are too rare.

But in another important way, our story up to this point is not at all unique. To begin with, there are other cities and towns scattered across the South that share the same scar of having two "First Baptist Churches." It's appropriate this Memorial Day weekend that we acknowledge that the church in America holds our country's wounds like no other institution. In a much wider sense, we are just two of hundreds of thousands of churches in this country and around the world. Each with different names, denominations, creeds, worship styles, even calendars—and all of these divisions are very confusing for people outside the church, and difficult to explain, but it's a testament to how deeply rooted church division is that within the church we rarely even think about all the ways we're divided, and actually think in the end it's probably better that way.

We joke in the Baptist tradition that church splits are as much a part of being a Baptist as baptism by immersion and congregation governance, but the truth is that divisions in the church are as old as the church is—we can see that in Scripture.

"Has Christ been divided?" Paul writes. "Each of you says, 'I belong to Paul,' or 'I belong to Apollos,' or 'I belong to Cephas.' Was Paul crucified for you? Were you baptized in the name of Paul? In the name of Christ, be in agreement with each other—be united in the same mind of Christ and under the same purpose."

The church was still in its first generation, and already there were arguments about who's in and who's not—who's got it right and who's varying degrees of wrong. Who's a student of this teacher and of that teacher—today we might say this denomination or that denomination. This tradition or that tradition. Who lives in this neighborhood or that neighborhood, who's this color or that color. The names by which we divide ourselves have changed—Paul and Apollos are gone—but each generation makes new names. The body of Christ is still divided; this must be our confession.

And yet.

And yet I read this past week something that's stayed with me, that I shared with James, and that in truth, he has been saying throughout these last few months. I read somewhere that "the real sin of disunity in the church does not lie in what has happened in the past. It lies in what is *not* happening in the *present*, in our failure to heal these divisions."[163] The real sin of disunity in the church does not lie in what has happened in the past. It lies in what is *not* happening in the *present*, in our failure to heal these divisions. I think that's true, and friends, that's why I'm happy to say that we today are doing something in the present.

Today we're doing something in the present to heal the divisions of the past that sadly are still so much in the present, trusting that what we're doing today and what we will continue to do together will be a part of God's future. We're healing the body of Christ. You've heard the old gospel hymn, "There Is a Balm in Gilead." Well, this afternoon we know there is a balm in *Macon, Georgia*, too. There's balm enough "to make the wounded whole / there's power enough in heaven, to cure a sin-sick soul." There's a balm and there's power enough to heal even a city. Power enough to heal even the church. There's no limit to what we can do together, or better, what God can do through us—or as Paul puts it to the Corinthians, "all things are yours." "All things are yours," he tells them.

"All things are yours" was Paul's word to the church in Corinth, and it's God's word for this afternoon to the First Baptist Churches of Macon, Georgia: "all things are yours."

All things are yours, church! All things are ours. So let no one boast about human leaders, human affiliations, human divisions—for all things are already yours! All things are yours—whether Paul or Apollos or Cephas or the world or life or death or the present or the future; or Poplar Street or New Street or Cotton Avenue; or this sanctuary or the one on the hill; or Missionary Baptist or National Baptist or Cooperative Baptist; or Black or White—all belongs to you, and you belong to Christ, and Christ belongs to God. All things are yours.

Despite what division our city has known, what divisions our churches have known—what divisions the body of Christ has known—all things already belong to us because we belong to

Christ and Christ belongs to God, and God holds the past, God holds the present, and God holds our future.

What does the future hold for our churches and this partnership we're forming? Who can say? But as long as we remain in Christ and Christ remains in God, all things are possible. As Paul says elsewhere, it will be immeasurably more than we ask or imagine. And that, my friends, is truly newsworthy. Not what's being done in the present, but what God will do through us in the future. That is newsworthy. Good-newsworthy, you could say. And it's a story that, with God's help, we'll tell together. Amen.

Congregational Hymn: "Amazing Grace"

Choir Special: "Blessed Assurance"Joint Choirs

Sermon:

"IN COVENANT AND WITH ONE ACCORD"
Rev. James W. Goolsby

(1) And when the day of Pentecost was fully come, they were all with one accord in one place. (2) And suddenly there came a sound from heaven as of a rushing mighty wind, and it filled all the house where they were sitting. (3) And there appeared unto them cloven tongues like as of fire, and it sat upon each of them. (4) And they were all filled with the Holy Ghost, and began to speak with other tongues, as the Spirit gave them utterance. (Acts 1:2–4, KJV)

Scott said that the reason that we're here, the reason why we celebrate, the reason why we worship God together is that we were both excited about the opportunity and anticipated just what God would do. Of course, with Scott preaching before me, you'll hear a couple of things that you've already heard—thank you, Scott.

[Scott Dickison calls out, "You're the one who asked me to go first," with the congregation laughing in response.]

But it is exciting to see what God is doing. It *is* God and it is *his* doing. When Hannah McMahan, executive director of the New Baptist Covenant, commented that she was following along and building on the hard work that Scott and I have been doing, I could hardly contain my laughter. Hard work? We've just been following the vision that God has given us. We've been blessed to have so many people within our congregations who have taken hold of that and are doing the work. And for that we are grateful.

There might be some things that you may not notice, even today. I have thoroughly been enjoying seeing Stanley Roberts direct the choir. And we always enjoy James McCrary anytime he plays [the piano]. And our two drummers, one is James Keys and the other is my son, C.J. I often say they are the best paid drummers in the city of Macon. They get all of our love and no money.

As we look at where we are at this point in time, and we look at where the scripture we have read is taking us, the central message is found in Acts 1:8: "But you shall receive power when the Holy Spirit is come upon you. And you shall be witnesses unto me in all Judaea, to Samaria, and to the end of the earth." The problem with the church is that we have not consistently acted under the power we have received.

But perhaps today we should look not just at the power we have received but also at the position of the church at the time she received that power. Where was she? What was unique about that Pentecost Day? What was unique about the church at that time? The trouble with the church is that she has seldom remained in the position she was in on the day of Pentecost. The scripture says they were in the same place, in one accord. In the same place in one accord. They had assembled together with the expectation that God would do an awesome thing if they were in the same place. Regardless of their social status or political preference, race or gender, they were in the same place. Not divided by walls or circumstance or birth, but they were in the same place with the expectation that God would show up. And if he showed up, he would show out.

Not only were they in the same place; they also were with one accord. But as Scott emphasized in his sermon, it's not so much where we've been or where we are, but where we are going. My mother used to tell me all the time that there are certain people in your life who will cause you some heartaches, will cause you some difficulties. But you have to learn to get past that in your life. And the way you get past it is through your relationship with Jesus Christ. The way to get past that place of pain, that place of suffering, that place of injustice, if you can learn to get past that place, you will learn that the people who gave you the pain in the past will give you the biggest blessing in your present or in your future. But if you hold on to your pain from the past, you don't allow God to minister and bless you in your days to come. I say that because I have been the recipient of help from folk who I thought would never be a help to me but turned out to be a great blessing to me. This can happen if you allow yourself to be in the same place, but also with one accord, having the same agenda. These disciples, they had the same mind, they had the same desires, they had the same affection. There were no personal agendas.

The reason why Scott and I get along so well is that we don't have much in the nature of egos. At least he hasn't shown me that yet. But we seem not to have any personal agendas. We ask what can we do for the call of Christ in what God has placed before us in this time and this season. And how powerful would the body of Christ be if everyone had that mindset? No personal agendas— they were in the same place with one accord.

And something else struck me. They had the same prayer. Same prayer, same request: for grace, to have life in your own soul, to be established in the truth. The same prayer for the ascension of the kingdom of Christ in the salvation of men. They had the same request of God. When we mature as children of God, when we truly understand what it means to be part of the body of Christ, when we understand with certainty that we are many members but one body, then we understand that when God blesses the First Baptist Church of Christ it's a homerun for First Baptist Church on New Street. When we learn that when God elevates a child of God anywhere, it is a blessing to a child of God everywhere, that my blessing is not hindered by your blessing, then that puts us in a place where God is able to use us in a way that pleases Jehovah God.

I'm grateful today that not only are we in the same place, with one accord, praying the same prayer, but what brings us here today is that we have the same doctrine.

We were able to share the good news of Jesus Christ not in our own strength, not on the basis of our education—and there are some educated people in this place today. Between these two churches there are so many degrees...say Amen—now that's what we do in New Street, say "Amen." One doctrine, one faith, one baptism. We looked beyond all the differences between us. They're not big. We have love for our families. We have love for our brothers and sisters in Christ. We have concerns for the future. We have concerns for our well-being. There's nothing that is a concern on New Street that is not a concern on Poplar Street. We're the same, we're all the same, and we are all a part of the body of Jesus Christ. When we live in that, we can receive the power of the Holy Spirit. And with that power we can do all things through Christ who gives us strength. Yes, we can show by our relationship what it means to be a child of God. Yes, we can show in how we handle one another—not just in the church but outside of the church—what it means to be a child of God.

I'm excited about what God has in store. I'm excited about what we anticipate God will do through our working and our witnessing for the cause of Christ. I'm excited about the partnership that we are getting ready to sign in terms of the covenant agreement, that promise to God of what we will do as churches for the cause of Christ.

To God be the glory! Not only for the things he has done but what for what we believe that he's getting ready to do through the unity of these two churches. C'mon, and give God the praise right now.

Choir Special: "Total Praise" Joint Choirs

Invitation

Signing of the Covenant of Action

The Bread and the Cup

Benediction

Doxology: "Praise God from whom All Blessings Flow"

Postlude

Afterword: Christ, the Bible, and the Heresy of Racial Division

Andrew M. Manis

By the time readers have made it this far, they have encountered sixteen sermons and five essays analyzing the challenge of putting out a performative word of God that might strike a blow to begin tearing down "the middle wall of partition" that still separates us by race in church and American society (Ephesians 2:14). What is there left to say on the subject? Not much, both author and reader may say, and rightly so. This afterword will not take much more of the readers' time. Here I will simply emphasize one of the most crucial truths encountered in some forty years of studying racism in America. "The most important issue in understanding racism," suggested another analyst, "is not what it does to *hurt* people of color, but what it does to *help* white people."[164]

Speaking as a White American Christian, I think the overarching reason that Christian churches in the United States are more part of the problem than the solution is our customary, working definition of racism. We are so accustomed to seeing racism as overt individual acts of mean-spirited bigotry that we cannot see ourselves in that description. Indeed, Whites have defined racism so narrowly that it is all but impossible to see such nice, well-scrubbed, moral people like us as implicated in it. Hence, millions of White American Christians angrily resist preaching and preachers who dare to identify us as racists. We then have often concluded that Sunday morning worship is not the place to consider such a divisive topic.

Closer to the central issue of this book, we are also prone to view race as a social or political concern rather than a profoundly spiritual issue. Churchly things like sermons, many continue to insist, should be concerned with getting American churchgoers into heaven, instead of recruiting for any sort of this-worldly do-goodism.

A serious reading of the Bible—in both Testaments—will discover much in the biblical tradition that combats the ancient tendency to divide people according to race. In both early and late writings, the Hebrew Scriptures fight bigotry in the community of faith. One strand of the Genesis tradition announces that Abraham's calling had a universal theme of the patriarch's offspring becoming a blessing to all peoples (Genesis 12:1–3). The book of Ruth tells the story of a Gentile foremother of Jesus who proclaims that her mother-in-law Naomi's people would be her people, and her God would be her God. The prophets often called on the Israelites to care for the stranger, while one of them who resisted taking Yahweh's message to the Gentile Ninevites finds a divine punishment in the belly of a whale (see the entire book of Jonah).

In the New Testament the story is much the same. While the religious intelligentsia of first century Judaism displayed an eager separation from Gentiles, how different were the life and teachings of a first century Galilean prophet named Jesus? The Jesus tradition in the Gospels depicts a prophet willing to extend radical acceptance to all manner of sinners, whether Jewish or Gentile. One of his most famous parables spoke of a Good Samaritan who crossed both religious *and* racial boundaries to become the neighbor of a Jewish traveler and victim of a violent crime (Luke 10:25–37). When religious professionals find ways to avoid having to minister to such riff-raff, the Samaritan—deemed by most Jews to be both religiously *and* racially inferior—becomes the man's compassionate caretaker.

Many similar examples from the Gospels might be cited. Jesus healed the son of a Roman centurion (Matthew 8:5–13; Luke 7:1–10). Against Jewish custom, he engaged a Samaritan woman in conversation in public in broad daylight (John 4:1–26, 38–42). Moreover, his life was ended by a crucifixion calculated to punish his nonnegotiable love for, acceptance of, and identification with sinners, Gentile as well as Jewish. Those who engineered his demise argued that he deserved divine punishment because he "ate with publicans and sinners." So while prejudice in first century Palestine was mostly of a religious nature, a racial component also intruded into the drama unfolding between Jesus and the "teachers of the Law." Thus the most important voice in the New Testament witness drives us to but one conclusion: that Jesus of Nazareth lost his battle with the religious authorities of the day because of his willingness to blur the lines that separated first century Palestinian Jews from their religiously and racially "unclean" neighbors.

Another central voice in the Christian Bible echoes similar themes. On the road to Damascus, Saul the Pharisaic persecutor of Christian believers is converted into Paul the Apostle to the Gentiles. He dedicated his life to evangelizing the Graeco-Roman world, enlisting Gentile converts to become leaders of Christian congregations in almost every important city of the ancient Near East. His message to the Christians in Galatia was that in Christ there is neither Jew nor Gentile, male nor female, or slave or free (Galatians 3:28). To the Ephesians, either he or one of his disciples wrote that earthly divisions of Jew and Gentile had been united by grace into one New Man, as the death of Jesus destroyed the "middle wall of partition" in the Jerusalem temple, which separated the Jewish from the Gentile children of God (Ephesians 2:11–22). Christian supporters of Mr. Trump's wall, take heed!

Paul did not always intuit the full extent of a truly Christian ethic, as when he did not take the opportunity to send word to slave-owning Philemon to set his slave Onesimus fully free. But he did consistently coach his converts on how Christian Jews ought to relate to Christian Gentiles and vice versa. And through it all, in every letter to his predominantly Gentile congregations, he reminded them of his collection of financial aid for the impoverished Jewish Christians in Jerusalem. He even suspended plans to make a missionary voyage beyond Rome to Spain, in order to cement together the Jewish and Christian factions in the Jerusalem congregation.

Two other New Testament witnesses continue these unmistakable themes. The author of Luke-Acts writes about not only how Jesus took his gospel of God's grace to Gentiles in Judea and Galilee but also how that word of grace continued to break through humanly constructed racial and religious boundaries in the Gentile world, until an "unhindered" gospel of Christ moved by the Spirit from Jerusalem to Samaria and to "the uttermost part of the world" (Acts 1–28). Even further out into the Gentile world, the Beloved Disciple taught his communities of faith to prove they loved God by loving their brothers and sisters.

Looking closely at the Bible and the life of Christ, any perceptive reader of scripture and close observer of Jesus' life and teachings can easily detect an obligatory and radical ethical center. We live in a time when some of Christ's most fervent followers gaze so intently at the issues of same-sex marriage and homosexuality that they have reduced Christian ethics to these two controversies. They give so much attention to defending a president who appoints conservative justices to the Supreme Court that they have become oblivious to the prophet Micah's list of what God requires of us human beings. "To do justice, love mercy, and walk humbly with one's God" has become nothing but a saying on a plaque in a novelty shop.

Robin Meyers, a United Church of Christ pastor in Oklahoma City, concluded his 2013 Lyman Beecher Lectures by noting the changes that developed in the church between the times of the

Sermon on the Mount and the Apostles' Creed. In Jesus' sermon, Meyers observes, the focus is on what a Christian should be and do. By contrast, the creed emphasizes what a Christian should believe.[165] By ignoring or minimizing the ethical values of Jesus, Paul, Luke, and John while emphasizing the theological beliefs enumerated in the creeds, we fall victim to the heresy of White supremacy and continued racial division.

The fifteen preachers whose words are enshrined in this book have courageously challenged racial division and sought to convert their congregations from mere collections of believers to brothers and sisters who embody and reenact Jesus' radical ethic of grace. This volume goes out with a prayer that preachers throughout our city, state, and country will join the Macon Fifteen in a ministry of racial reconciliation and spiritual defiance.

Notes

[1] Martin Heidegger, *Being and Time* (San Francisco: Harper Perennial Modern Classics; reprint edition, 2008), 132.

[2] Andrew Michael Manis, *Southern Civil Religions in Conflict: Black and White Baptists and Civil Rights, 1947–1957* (Athens: University of Georgia Press, 1987).

[3] See Andrew M. Manis, *Macon Black and White: An Unutterable Separation in the American Century* (Macon, GA: Mercer University Press and the Tubman African American Museum, 2004).

[4] The statement appears in several places in King's writings, but he seems to have first used it in the sermon, "Communism's Challenge to Christianity," preached on 9 August 1953. He apparently borrowed the statement from Helen Kenyon's speech to the Women's Society of New York's Riverside Church, published in the *New York Times*, 4 November 1952 (cited in Clayborne Carson, ed., *The Papers of Martin Luther King Jr., Volume VI: Advocate of the Social Gospel, September 1948-March 1963* [Berkeley: University of California Press, 2007], 149). The statement is also found four times in James Melvin Washington's collection of King's most important writings, *A Testament of Hope: The Essential Writings of Martin Luther King Jr.* (New York: Harper & Row, 1986): King's 19 July 1962 "Address to the National Press Club" (p. 101); his 1962 writing, "The Case Against Tokenism" (p. 108); his 31 March 1968 address at the National Cathedral in Washington, DC, "Remaining Awake through a Great Revolution" (p. 270); and his *Stride Toward Freedom: The Montgomery Story* (p. 479). King's earliest mention of the "most segregated hour" in print appears to be in the 1958 publication of *Stride Toward Freedom: The Montgomery Story* (New York: Harper & Row). As King was famously inattentive to proper attribution, whether the statement was borrowed from someone else or originated with him is unknown.

[5] Three local ministers—two White, one African American—declined the invitation to take part in this project. One of the White ministers replied that he needed to pray over the matter (before he eventually said no), while the other said he was not qualified to comment on matters of race. Both of

these would have been the most conservative ministers represented in our lineup, and both *do* feel qualified to provide traditional ethical guidance to their congregations on other matters. The African American minister quickly said "thanks but no thanks," adding frankly that after two decades in the racial reconciliation trenches, he was simply tired of talking to White people about this subject. I later asked him a second time and his answer was the same.

[6] See the organization's website at www.NewBaptistCovenant.org.

[7] Interview with Lawrence Leamer, "The Lynching," *Progressive Spirit* podcast, 10 July 2016, https://www.podomatic.com/podcasts/progressivespirit/episodes/2016-07-10T08_04_02-07_00.

[8] *Miami Herald*, 7 November 2016.

[9] Robin R. Meyers, "Faith as Resistance to Empire," 2013 Beecher Lecture, Yale University Divinity School, published in *Spiritual Defiance: Building a Beloved Community of Resistance* (New Haven: Yale University Press, 2015), 116–17.

[10] Quoted in Juan Williams, *Thurgood Marshall: American Revolutionary* (New York: Random House, 1998), 199.

[11] Ronald W. Walters, *The Price of Racial Reconciliation* (Ann Arbor: University of Michigan Press, 2008), 80.

[12] Richard Lischer, "Preaching about Race Relations—The Hope of Reconciliation," in Thomas G. Long and Neely D. McCarter, eds., *Preaching In and Out of Season* (Louisville: Westminster/John Knox Press, 1990), 19.

[13] Gerald L. Keown, "A Word About...Racism and the Church," *Review and Expositor* 108 (Fall 2011): 501.

[14] Ida B. Wells-Barnett, *The Red Record*, 1895, https://www.gutenberg.org/files/14977/14977-h/14977-h.htm.

[15] Ida B. Wells-Barnett, "Lynching: A National Crime," April 1909, https://patriotpost.us/documents/213.

[16] Quoted in Edward J. Blum, "'O God of a Godless Land': North African American Challenges to White Christian Nationhood, 1865–1906," in *Vale of Tears: New Essays on Religion and Reconstruction*, ed. Edward J. Blum and W. Scott Poole (Macon, GA: Mercer University Press, 2005), 100–101.

[17] Ibid.

[18] Alfreda M. Duster, ed., *Crusade for Justice: The Autobiography of Ida B. Wells-Barnett* (Chicago: University of Chicago Press, 1970), 151–52.

[19] Ibid., 154–55.

[20] Marvin A. Mcmickle, *Where Have All the Prophets Gone? Reclaiming Prophetic Preaching in America* (Cleveland: Pilgrim Press, 2006).
[21] National Public Radio/Kaiser Family Foundation/Harvard University Kennedy School of Government Poll on Poverty in America, 2001, https://kaiserfamilyfoundation.files.wordpress.com/2001/04/3118-f-poverty-in-america-survey.pdf. (The file is only accessible to members of the blog.)
[22] Bill Schneider, "Polling the Poor and Non-Poor on Poverty: 1986 and 2016," August 2016. See http://www.aei.org/wp-content/uploads/2016/08/Polling-the-poor-and-non-poor-on-poverty.pdf.
[23] See "Christians Are More than Twice as Likely to Blame a Person's Poverty on Lack of Effort," *Washington Post*, https://www.washingtonpost.com/news/acts-of-faith/wp/2017/08/03/christians-are-more-than-twice-as-likely-to-blame-a-persons-poverty-on-lack-of-effort/?noredirect=on&utm_term=.fae4b7c78db3. The article cites a *Washington Post*/Kaiser Family Foundation poll, conducted 15 April–1 May 2017.
[24] Geoffrey Noel Schoonmaker, "Preaching about Race: A Homiletic for Racial Reconciliation" (PhD diss., Vanderbilt University, Nashville, TN, 2012), p. 31; Michael O. Emerson and Christian Smith, *Divided by Faith: Evangelical Religion and the Problem of Race in America* (New York: Oxford University Press, 2000), 117.
[25] Peter Callero, *The Myth of Individualism: How Social Forces Shape Our Lives* (Lanham, MD: Rowman & Littlefield, 2013), 9, 15.
[26] Leonora Tubbs Tisdale, *Prophetic Preaching: A Pastoral Approach* (Louisville: Westminster/John Knox Press, 2010), 11. By "prophetic" biblical texts, Tisdale does not have in mind futuristic predictive texts interpreted as giving "signs of the times" for the end of the world. Rather, with Walter Brueggemann, Tisdale focuses on biblical texts that convey "a future different from that envisioned by the ruling elite." The old saw still applies: the prophetic element in the Hebrew scriptures has more to do with forth-telling the "Thus says the Lord" than with "foretelling" the future end times. See Walter Brueggemann, *The Prophetic Imagination* (Philadelphia: Fortress Press, 1978), 30–31, 44.
[27] John Hayes, "Hard, Hard Religion: The Invisible Institution of the New South," *Journal of Southern Religion* 10 (2007): 6.
[28] Tisdale, *Prophetic Preaching*, 15.

[29] Otis Moss Jr., in Martha Simmons and Frank A. Thomas, eds., *Preaching with Sacred Fire: An Anthology of African-American Sermons, 1750 to the Present* (New York: W. W. Norton and Company), 779–80.

[30] Tisdale, *Prophetic Preaching*, 21.

[31] George Mason, "Gospel Politics in the Midst of Social Turmoil," *Baptist News Global*, 16 March 2018. See also *Washington Post*, 16 November 2016.

[32] Emerson and Smith, *Divided by Faith*, 188, 160; Eric Tranby and Douglas Hartmann, "Critical Whiteness Theories and the Evangelical 'Race Problem': Extending Emerson and Smith's *Divided by Faith*," *Journal for the Scientific Study of Religion* 47/3 (2008): 354.

[33] See Frank Stagg, *Polarities of Man's Existence in Biblical Perspective* (Philadelphia: Westminster Press, 1973), 75–87.

[34] Sidney E. Mead, *The Lively Experiment: The Shaping of Christianity in America* (1963; repr., Eugene, OR: Wipf & Stock Publishers; Reprint edition, 2007).

[35] John McKivigan, *The War against Proslavery Religion: Abolitionism and the Northern Churches, 1830–1865* (Chapel Hill: University of North Carolina, 1984), 26.

[36] McKivigan, *War against Proslavery Religion*, 7–8; 14–15; 21–22; 31; 41–42.

[37] Ibid., 90–92.

[38] Beth Barton Schweiger, "The Restructuring of Southern Religion: Slavery, Denominations, and the Clerical Profession in Virginia," in John R. McKivigan and Mitchell Snay, eds., *Religion and the Antebellum Debate over Slavery* (Athens: University of Georgia Press, 1998), 292, 299; Larry E. Tise, *Proslavery: A History of the Defense of Slavery in America, 1701-1840* (Athens: University of Georgia Press, 1987), 363–66.

[39] Schweiger, "Restructuring of Southern Religion," 301; Frederick Douglass, "Address in London" (1846), excerpt reprinted in James T. Baker, ed., *Religion in America: Primary Sources in U.S. History* (Belmont, CA: Wadsworth, 2006), 196.

[40] Schoonmaker, "Preaching about Race," 20–21; Soong-Chan Rah, *The Next Evangelicalism: Freeing the Church from Western Cultural Captivity* (Downers Grove, IL: Intervarsity Press, 2009), 35.

[41] "Polls: Is America Exceptional?" *CNN Politics Political Ticker*, 12 September 2013, http://politicalticker.blogs.cnn.com/2013/09/12/polls-is-america-exceptional/.

[42] Steve Wyche, "Colin Kaepernick Explains Why He Sat During National Anthem," *NFL News*, 27 August 2016, https://www.nfl.com/news/colin-kaepernick-explains-why-he-sat-during-national-anthem-0ap3000000691077.

[43] Jesse Kornbluth, "May 4, 1970: National Guardsmen Kill Four Students at Kent State, 'The Most Popular Murders Ever Committed in America,'" *Huffington Post*, 6 December 2017, https://www.huffingtonpost.com/jesse-kornbluth/may-4-1970-national-guard_b_1476017.html.

[44] Quoted in "Seven Americans on Patriotism, Protest, and the President," *Washington Post*, 4 July 2018, https://www.washingtonpost.com/politics/seven-americans-on-patriotism-protest-and-the-president/2018/07/03/6265c1d8-7df4-11e8-b0ef-fffcabeff946_story.html?utm_term=.708408c3c7d6.

[45] Theodore Roosevelt, "Lincoln and Free Speech," *Metropolitan Magazine* 47 (May 1918): 7.

[46] James Baldwin, *Notes of a Native Son* (Boston: Beacon Press, 1955), 9.

[47] Ibid., 162.

[48] Robert P. Jones, *The End of White Christian America* (New York: Simon and Shuster, 2017), 89.

[49] Ibid. 85-86.

[50] Perry Miller, "Errand into the Wilderness," *William and Mary Quarterly* 10 (January 1953): 3–32.

[51] John D. Wilsey, *American Exceptionalism and Civil Religion* (Downers Grove, IL: IVP Academic, 2015), 16–36.

[52] Ibid., 19. The classic bibliography on civil religion can only be sampled in this space. It begins with the following: Robert N. Bellah, "Civil Religion in America," *Daedalus* 96 (Winter 1967): 1–21; Bellah, *Beyond Belief: Essays on Religion in a Post-Traditionalist World* (New York: Harper & Row, 1970); Bellah, *The Broken Covenant: American Civil Religion in Time of Trial* (Chicago: University of Chicago Press, 1992 [1975]); Bellah and Phillip E. Hammond, *Varieties of Civil Religion* (New York: Harper & Row, 1980); Sidney E. Mead, *The Nation with the Soul of a Church* (New York: Harper & Row, 1975); Andrew M. Manis, *Southern Civil Religions in Conflict: Black and White Baptists and Civil Rights, 1947–1957* (Athens: University of Georgia Press, 1983); Manis, "Zivilreligionem und das Problem von 'Race' von der Bürgerrechtsbewegung bis zu den Kulturkriegen," in Heike Bungert and

Jana Weiss, eds., *"God Bless America": Zivilreligion in den USA im 20. Jahrhundert* (Frankfurt/New York: Campus Verlag), 353–84; and Manis, "Civil Religion and National Identity," in *The Columbia Guide to Religion in American History*, ed. Paul Harvey and Edward J. Blum (New York: Columbia University Press, 2012). More recent studies include Peter Gardella, *American Civil Religion: What Americans Hold Sacred* (New York: Oxford University Press, 2014); Philip Gorski, *American Covenant: A History of Civil Religion from the Puritans to the Present* (Princeton: Princeton University Press, 2017).

[53] Blum, "O God of a Godless Land," 95–96.

[54] Cornel West and Christa Buschendorf, *Black Prophetic Fire* (Boston: Beacon Press, 2014), 71.

[55] Quoted in Andrew M. Manis, *A Fire You Can't Put Out: The Civil Rights Life of Birmingham's Reverend Fred Shuttlesworth* (University of Alabama Press, 1999), 186.

[56] For discussion of the general nature of race, racism, and related matters, see Cornell West, *Race Matters* (Boston: Beacon Press, 1994, 2001, 2017); Andrew Hacker, *Two Nations: Black and White, Separate, Hostile, Unequal* (New York: Scribner, 2003); Beverly Daniel Tatum, *Why Are All the Black Kids Sitting Together in the Cafeteria? And Other Conversations about Race* (New York: Basic Books, 2017); and Mahzarin R. Banaji and Anthony G. Greenwald, *Blind Spot: Hidden Biases of Good People* (New York: Bantam Books, 2013).

[57] For a solid history of African Americans and the role that race has played in American history and culture, the following classic text is useful: John Hope Franklin and Evelyn Brooks Higginbotham, *From Slavery to Freedom: A History of African Americans*, 9th ed. (New York: McGraw-Hill, 2011).

[58] In addition to sources such as Franklin, *From Slavery to Freedom*, cited above, these works are excellent sources for the relationship among race, religion, and slavery: Albert J. Raboteau, *Slave Religion: The "Invisible Institution" in the Antebellum South*, Updated Edition (New York: Oxford University Press, 2004); and Donald G. Mathews, *Religion in the Old South* (Chicago: University of Chicago Press, 1977).

[59] James M. Washington, ed., *A Testament of Hope: The Essential Writings of Martin Luther King, Jr.* (New York: HarperCollins Publishers, 1986), 480–81. For the complete excerpt from *Stride toward Freedom*, see 417–90.

[60] King's letter in Washington, *Testament*, 289–302; see especially 294–95.

[61] Quoted in Lewis V. Baldwin, *The Voice of Conscience: The Church in the Mind of Martin Luther King, Jr.* (New York: Oxford University Press, 2010). For the discussion, see 136–37; partial and complete quotes on 137.

[62] James H. Cone, *Black Theology and Black Power* (1969; repr., Maryknoll, NY: Orbis Books, 1997).

[63] J. Deotis Roberts, *Liberation and Reconciliation: A Black Theology* (Philadelphia: Westminster Press, 1971). In James H. Cone, *My Soul Looks Back* (Maryknoll, NY: Orbis Books, 1986), an autobiography, Cone on pp. 41–63 deals with the advent of his first book and the responses/critiques he received from both Whites and Blacks, including those supportive of Black Theology. Also consult a text of wide-ranging sources and analyses on the emergence and impact of academic Black Theology: Gayraud S. Wilmore and James H. Cone, eds., *Black Theology: A Documentary History, 1976–1979* (Maryknoll, NY: Orbis Books, 1979).

[64] See the official website for the motto of the AME Church: https://www.ame-church.com/our-church/our-motto/.

[65] Two very good sources on the thought and life of Malcolm X are: Manning Marable, *Malcolm X: A Life of Reinvention* (New York: Viking, Published by the Penguin Group, 2011); and Malcolm X and Alex Haley, *The Autobiography of Malcolm X as Told to Alex Haley* (New York: The Ballantine Publishing Group, a Division of Random House, Inc., 1964).

[66] See "Christianity in the United States," *Wikipedia*, https://en.m.wikipedia.org/wiki/Christianity_in_the_United_States.

[67] For a focus on the role of religion in the Black American freedom struggle, consult Gayraud S. Wilmore, *Black Religion and Black Radicalism: An Interpretation of the Religious History of African Americans*, Third Edition (Maryknoll, NY: Orbis Books, 1998).

[68] For the complete report of Moynihan regarding the Black family in the 1960s, see *The Negro Family: The Case for National Action*, https://web.stanford.edu/~mrosenfe/Moynihan%27s%20The%20Negro%20Family.pdf. An overview of the Moynihan Report including critiques of it is located at "The Negro Family: The Case for National Action," *Wikipedia*, https://en.wikipedia.org/wiki/The_Negro_Family:_The_Case_For_National_Action.

[69] Gregory Acs, Kenneth Braswell, Elaine Sorensen, and Margery Austin Turner, *The Moynihan Report Revisited*, 13 June 2013, https://www.urban.org/research/publication/moynihan-report-revisited.

[70] Two websites might be of interest regarding Christianity and same-sex relationships: "Living Out," a website for Christians embracing same-sex relationships, at https://www.livingout.org; and Focus on the Family's "Biblical Perspective on Homosexuality and Same-Sex Marriage," the view of Christians opposing same-sex relationships, at https://www.focusonthefamily.com/family-qa/biblical-perspective-on-homosexuality-and-same-sex-marriage/.

[71] See Rosemary Skinner Keller and Rosemary Radford Ruether, eds., *In Our Own Voices: Four Centuries of American Women's Religious Writing* (New York: HarperSanFrancisco, 1995. This text covers a wide range of writings by women in the US, containing both editors' historical narratives as well as primary documents. See, e.g., ch. 4, "Black Women," by Emilie M. Townes, pp. 153–206; and ch. 7, "Women and Ordination," by Barbara Brown Zikmund, pp. 291–340. For an overview of attempts to emphasize masculinity in the practice of Christianity, see "Muscular Christianity," *Wikipedia*, https://en.wikipedia.org/wiki/Muscular_Christianity.

[72] Evelyn Brooks Higginbotham, *Righteous Discontent: The Women's Movement in the Black Baptist Church, 1880–1920* (Cambridge, MA: Harvard University Press, 1993). See chapter 7, "The Politics of Respectability," 185–229.

[73] One of the strongest critiques of the critics of respectability politics is Randall Kennedy's "Lifting as We Climb: Progressive Defense of Respectability Politics," in *Harper's Magazine*, October 2015, at https://harpers.org/archive/2015/10/lifting-as-we-climb/. Also see Rita Roberts, *Evangelicalism and the Politics of Reform in Northern Black Thought, 1776–1863* (Baton Rouge, LA: Louisiana State University Press, 2010). While she does not attack the arguments of "politics of respectability" critics, Roberts does point out in this excellent work that earlier moral endeavors and uplifts were consistent with, and indeed undergirded, "the politics of reform."

[74] When writing the name of God (Allah), Muslims often follow it with the abbreviation "SWT," which stands for the Arabic words "Subhanahu wa ta'ala." Muslims use these or similar words to glorify God when mentioning his name. The abbreviation in modern usage might appear as "SWT," "swt," or "SwT." In Arabic, "Subhanahu wa ta'ala" translates as

"Glory to Him, the Exalted" or "Glorious and Exalted Is He." In saying or reading the name of Allah, the shorthand of "SWT" indicates an act of reverence and devotion toward God.
[75] See the definition at https://www.merriam-webster.com/dictionary/reconciliation.
[76] Ibn Manzur, *Lisan al-Arab* [Arabic dictionary] (Beirut: Dar Sader, 2000), definition of the word SLH صلح.
[77] The abbreviation AS designates the status of prophet in Islam.
[78] Sirah Ibn Ishaq, *Life of Muhammad*, by Muhammad, son of Isaac. Ibn Ishaq (AD 704–768) was an Arab Muslim historian and biographer of the Prophet. The biography was based on oral traditions collected by Ibn Ishaq.
[79] Benjamin Mueller and Al Baker, "2 N.Y.P.D. Officers Killed in Brooklyn Ambush; Suspect Commits Suicide," *New York Times*, 20 December 2014, https://www.nytimes.com/2014/12/21/nyregion/two-police-officers-shot-in-their-patrol-car-in-brooklyn.html.
[80] Re Eric Garner, see Al Baker J. David Goodman, and Benjamin Mueller, "Beyond the Chokehold: The Path to Eric Garner's Death," *New York Times*, 13 June 2015; Joseph Goldstein and Marc Santora, "Staten Island Man Dies from Chokehold during Arrest, Autopsy Finds," *New York Times*, 1 August 2014. Re Michael Brown, see Monica Davey and Julie Bosman, "Protests Flare after Ferguson Police Officer Is Not Indicted," *New York Times*, 25 November 2014. Re Trayvon Martin, see Chris Francescani, "George Zimmerman: Prelude to a Shooting," Reuters, 25 April 2012.
[81] These extended quotations of Martin Luther King Jr. are accessed at www.wearethebelovedcommunity.org/bcquotes.html.
[82] These names have been changed.
[83] Lester Maddox was a famously segregationist governor of Georgia (1967–1971); Dylann Roof was the White supremacist perpetrator in the 2015 Emanuel African Methodist Episcopal Church shooting in Charleston, South Carolina; Malik el-Shabazz is the Muslim name of Malcolm X.
[84] Paired Clergy is a sister organization of Mercer University's annual Building the Beloved Community Symposium. Another event sponsored by the Paired Clergy is the twice-annual Unity Service.
[85] Reverend Howe is currently a stay-at-home mom in Asheville, North Carolina.

[86] Daniel Katz, *Why Freedom Matters: The Spirit of the Declaration of Independence in Prose, Poetry, and Song* (New York: Workman Publishers, 2003), 155.

[87] James H. Cone, *The Spirituals and the Blues: An Interpretation* (Maryknoll, NY: Orbis Books, 1991), 15.

[88] Ibid.

[89] Desmond Tutu, *Hope and Suffering* (Grand Rapids, MI: William B. Eerdmans Publishing Company, 1983), 52.

[90] Marjorie Bowens-Wheatley and Nancy Palmer Jones, eds., *Soul Work: Anti-Racist Theologies in Dialogue* (Boston: Skinner House Books, 2003), 172.

[91] Reverend Long served the First Baptist Church of Christ, Macon, Georgia, from 2004 to 2018 as Minister of Children and Families. She is currently a member of the same congregation and serves as an Empowerment Coach.

[92] John Reitano, *What If the Zebras Lost Their Stripes?* (New York: Paulist Press, 1998).

[93] Ibid.

[94] Ibid.

[95] Archbishop Desmond Tutu and Douglas Carlton Abrams, *God's Dream* (Sommerville, MA: Candlewick Press, 2008).

[96] Ibid.

[97] Reitano, *What If the Zebras Lost Their Stripes?*

[98] Alexander H. Stephens, "The Cornerstone Address, delivered in Savannah, Georgia, on March 21, 1861." See text in Thomas A. Scott, *Cornerstones of Georgia History: Documents that Formed the State* (Athens: University of Georgia Press, 1995), 85.

[99] Quoted in Gene Roberts and Hank Klibanoff, *The Race Beat: The Press, the Civil Rights Struggle, and the Awakening of a Nation* (New York: Alfred A. Knopf, 2006), 71.

[100] Told by Archbishop Desmond Tutu to Krista Tippett, "On Being," American Public Media, 16 February 2012. See http://www.onbeing.org/programs/desmond-tutu-a-god-of-surprises/#transcript.

[101] "Strange Fruit," lyrics by Abel Meeropol, recorded by Billie Holiday on 20 April 1939.

[102] See Larry E. Tise, *Proslavery: A History of the Defense of Slavery in America, 1701–1840* (Athens: University of Georgia Press, 1987), "Appendix

1: Proslavery Clergymen," 363–66; John Patrick Daly, *When Slavery Was Called Freedom: Evangelicalism, Proslavery, and the Causes of the Civil War* (Lexington: The University Press of Kentucky, 2002), 3. See also Douglas Ambrose, "Of Stations and Relations: Proslavery Christianity in Early National Virginia," *Religion and the Antebellum Debate over Slavery*, ed. John R. McKivigan and Mitchell Snay (Athens: The University of Georgia Press, 1998), 35–67; Drew Gilpin Faust, ed., *The Ideology of Slavery: Proslavery Thought in the Antebellum South, 1830–1860* (Baton Rouge: LSU Press, 1981), 136–67; Paul Finkelman, ed., *Defending Slavery: Proslavery Thought in the Old South: A Brief History with Documents* (Boston: Bedford/St.Martins, 2003), 136–37.

[103] Frederick Douglass, "Address in London" (1846), excerpt reprinted in James T. Baker, ed., *Religion in America: Primary Sources in U.S. History* (Belmont, CA: Wadsworth, 2006), 196.

[104] 2014 figures: https://www.cdc.gov/nchs/products/databriefs/db244.htm#summary.

[105] 2017 figures: National Center for Education Statistics, https://nces.ed.gov/fastfacts/display.asp?id=61.

[106] Dina Gerdeman, "Minorities who 'Whiten' Job Resumes Get More Interviews," *Working Knowledge* (a publication of Harvard Business School), 17 May 2017, p. 205.

[107] News Release, Bureau of Labor Statistics, 7 August 2020, p. 2.

[108] See "Real Median Household Income by Race and Hispanic Origin: 1967 to 2018," https://www.census.gov/content/dam/Census/library/visualizations/2019/demo/p60-266/figure2.pdf.

[109] Kriston McIntosh, Emily Moss et al., "Up Front: Examining the Black-White Wealth Gap," *Brookings Institution Updates*, 7 February 2020.

[110] Quoted in Gary Darrien, *Economy, Difference, Empire: Social Ethics for Social Justice* (New York: Columbia University Press, 2010), 404.

[111] Walter Brueggemann, *Genesis: Interpretation: A Commentary for Teaching and Preaching* (Louisville: Westminster/John Knox Press, 2010), 266.

[112] Robert Jensen, *The Heart of Whiteness: Confronting Race, Racism, & White Privilege* (San Francisco: City Lights Publishers, 2005), 6.

[113] J. Mills Thornton, *Dividing Lines: Municipal Politics and the Struggle for Civil Rights in Montgomery, Birmingham and Selma* (Tuscaloosa: University of Alabama Press, 2002), 582–83.

[114] Belden C. Lane, "Rabbinical Stories: A Primer on Theological Method," *Christian Century* 98 (16 December 1981): 1307–1308.

[115] Interpretation of "Amazing Grace" by the Rev. Wintley Phipps. See http://www.youtube.com/watch?v=qNuQbJst4Lk.

[116] Since delivering this sermon in Macon, Father McDonald has assumed new responsibility as pastor of the Saint Anne Church in Richmond Hill, Georgia.

[117] Since this sermon was delivered, Reverend McFadden has assumed a new place of service as pastor of the St. Paul AME Church in Valdosta, Georgia.

[118] Martin Luther King Jr., "When Peace Becomes Obnoxious," sermon delivered 18 March 1956 at Dexter Avenue Baptist church, in Clayborne Carson, Stewart Burns et al., eds., *The Papers of Martin Luther King, Jr., Volume III: Birth of a New Age, December 1955–December 1956* (Berkeley: University of California Press, 1997), 207.

[119] This sermon refers to Macon's annual community-wide breakfast honoring Martin Luther King Jr., held at Saint Peter Claver Catholic Church.

[120] Daybreak is a charity organization in Macon whose mission is providing care for the homeless.

[121] See Joel D. Gereboff, *Rabbi Tarfon, the Tradition, the Man, and Early Rabbinic Judaism* (Missoula, MT: Scholars Press, 1979).

[122] Jeremiah 1:1 (NIV).

[123] Jeremiah 1:5 (NIV).

[124] Genesis 50:19-20 (VOICE)

[125] Genesis 50:19-20 (VOICE)

[126] Jeremiah 38:4-6 (VOICE)

[127] Jeremiah 38:6 (VOICE).

[128] Psalm 34:19 (NLV).

[129] Jeremiah 38:6 (NIV).

[130] Jeremiah 38:7.

[131] Jeremiah 38:12–13.

[132] See Omar Baddar, "Hate Crimes Continue to Surge in America," https://thearabdailynews.com/2018/11/13/hate-crimes-continue-to-surge-in-america/. In addition, the FBI reported the first three-year annual increase since 2001 (consecutive increases of 6.8 percent in 2015, 4.6 in 2016, and 17 percent in 2017).

133 During the Civil War, the *Christian Recorder*, the official organ of the African Methodist Episcopal Church, conceived America's divine mission to be "the great field of training for…solving the great problem of a universal brotherhood, the unity of the race of mankind, and the eternal principles of intellectual, moral, and spiritual development" (*Christian Recorder*, 8 October 1864; 27 February 1864; 14 February 1863).

134 Curtiss Paul DeYoung and Allan Aubrey Boesak, *Radical Reconciliation: Beyond Political Pietism and Christian Quietism* (Maryknoll, NY: Orbis Press, 2012), 118.

135 German Lopez, " 'The racists believe he's a racist': Andrew Gillum calls out his opponent for Florida governor," *Vox*, 25 October 2018, https://www.vox.com/policy-and-politics/2018/10/25/18022094/gillum-desantis-florida-governor-debate-racists.

136 Jack Rogers, *Jesus, the Bible, and Homosexuality* (Louisville, KY: Westminster John Knox, 2006), 69–90.

137 Martin Luther King Jr., "Pilgrimage to Nonviolence," quoted in James Melvin Washington, ed., *A Testament of Hope: The Essential Writings of Martin Luther King, Jr.* (New York: Harper and Row, 1986), 37–38. The essay originally appeared as chapter 6 of King's *Stride Toward Freedom: The Montgomery Story* (New York: Harper and Row, 1958) and later appeared in the *Christian Century* 77 (13 April 1968): 439–41. The quotation comes from *Stride Toward Freedom*, 36.

138 James Baldwin, *The Fire Next Time* (New York: Vintage Press, 1962), 34.

139 Frank Stagg, *Polarities of Human Existence in Biblical Perspective* (Philadelphia: Westminster Press, 1973), 75ff.

140 Robin DiAngelo, *White Fragility: Why It's So Hard for White People to Talk about Racism* (Boston: Beacon Press, 2018), 31; Abigail Geiger, Kristen Bialik, and John Gramlich, "The Changing Face of Congress in 6 Charts," Pew Research Center Report, 15 February 2019, https://www.pewresearch.org/fact-tank/2019/02/15/the-changing-face-of-congress/.

141 Jim Wallis, "A Crisis of Trump's Own Making," *Sojourners*, 9 January 2019, https://sojo.net/articles/crisis-trumps-own-making.

142 Walter Wink, *Unmasking the Powers: The Invisible Forces That Determine Human Existence* (Philadelphia: Fortress Press, 1986), 43, 66–67.

[143] Geoffrey Noel Schoonmaker, *Preaching about Race: A Homiletic for Racial Reconciliation*, PhD dissertation, Vanderbilt University, Nashville, Tennessee, 2012, 92–93.

[144] The phrase "nation of behavers" is borrowed from Martin Marty's classic book. See Martin E. Marty, *A Nation of Behavers* (Chicago: University of Chicago Press, 1976).

[145] H. Richard Niebuhr, *Christ and Culture* (New York: Harper and Row, 1951). For an overview of Niebuhr and his contributions, see https://en.wikipedia.org/wiki/H._Richard_Niebuhr.

[146] For various English translations of this verse, see http://corpus.quran.com/translation.jsp?chapter=49&verse=13.

[147] For a fairly recent account of the Social Gospel Movement in the US, see Christopher H. Evans, *The Social Gospel in American Religion: A History* (New York: New York University, 2017). Also consult Walter Rauschenbusch, *A Theology of the Social Gospel* (New York: The MacMillan Company, 1917; reprinted in 2017 by CrossReach Publications); and Philip S. Foner, ed., *Black Socialist Preacher: The Teachings of Reverend George Washington Woodbey and His Disciple Reverend George W. Slater, Jr.* (San Francisco: Synthesis Publications, 1983).

[148] For an account of evangelicals' movement away from social activism in the early twentieth century, see David O. Moberg, *The Great Reversal: Reconciling Evangelism and Social Concern* (Eugene, OR: Wipf and Stock Publishers, 1977), especially 13–45.

[149] A fine source on the religious and political mind of King is Lewis V. Baldwin, *The Voice of Conscience: The Church in the Mind of Martin Luther King, Jr.* (New York: Oxford University Press, 2010). A comprehensive article treatment of Jerry Falwell Sr. is found at https://en.wikipedia.org/wiki/Jerry_Falwell.

[150] Peter J. Paris, *Black Religious Leaders: Conflict in Unity*, 2nd ed. (Louisville, KY: Westminster/John Knox Press, 1991); see especially chapters 2, 3, and 5.

[151] A very solid historical and comprehensive treatment of Black nationalist thought among Black Americans is Wilson Jeremiah Moses, *The Golden Age of Black Nationalism, 1850–1925* (New York: Oxford University Press, 1978).

[152] For an account of Lott Carey (note: the author spells the surname differently), see "Lott Cary (ca. 1780–1828)," *Encyclopedia Virginia*, Virginia Humanities, 13 April 2017, contributed by John Saillant and *Dictionary of*

Virginia Biography, https://www.encyclopediavirginia.org/Cary_Lott_ca_ 1780-1828#contrib. A treatment of Paul Cuffee is presented by Henry Louis Gates Jr. in "Who Led the First Back-to-Africa Effort," originally published in *The Root*, available at https://www.pbs.org/wnet/african-americans-many-rivers-to-cross/history/who-led-the-1st-back-to-africa-effort/. For a study on Marcus Garvey, see John Henrik Clarke, ed., *Marcus Garvey and the Vision of Africa* (New York: Random House, Vintage Books, 1973).

[153] For example, consult Nell Irvin Painter, *Exodusters: Black Migration to Kansas after Reconstruction* (New York: Knopf, 1977); and Milton C. Sernett, *Bound for the Promised Land: African American Religion and the Great Migration* (Durham, NC: Duke University Press, 1997).

[154] A solid treatment of Malcolm X is Manning Marable, *Malcolm X: A Life of Reinvention* (New York: Viking, The Penguin Group, 2011). The thought of Kwame Ture (previously Stokely Carmichael) is found in the book he co-authored with Charles V. Hamilton, *Black Power: The Politics of Liberation* (New York: Random House, 1967; Vintage Edition, 1992).

[155] These are fine sources for the life and work of Richard Allen: Carol V. R. George, *Segregated Sabbaths: Richard Allen and the Emergence of Independent Black Churches, 1760–1840* (New York: Oxford University Press, 1973); and Charles H. Wesley, *Richard Allen: Apostle of Freedom* (Washington, DC: Associated Publishers, 1935).

[156] See Moses, *Black Nationalism*, 38–40, 55, 65, and 87–88; and Douglass's "Slaveholding Religion and the Christianity of Christ," in Milton C. Sernett, *African American Religious History: Documentary Witness*, 2nd ed. (Durham, NC: Duke University Press, 1999), 102–11.

[157] See Moses, *Black Nationalism*, e.g., 9–11 and 134–36.

[158] James M. Washington, ed., *The Essential Writings and Speeches of Martin Luther King, Jr.* (New York: HarperOne/HarperCollins Publishers, 1986), especially 217–20.

[159] For a discussion of Jackson's pluralist approach, see Paris, *Black Leaders*, 64–97.

[160] Moses, *Black Nationalism*, discusses "The Conservation of Races," 11, 134–36, 177. The original text of the essay may be found at: http://www.webdubois.org/dbConsrvOfRaces.html.

[161] The following is a discussion of Jackson's article, "National Baptist Philosophy of Civil Rights," found in Sernett, *African American Religious History*, 511–18.

[162] A case for reparations by William Darity Jr. is found in a 9 September 2019 issue of *The Crisis*, an organ of the National Association for the Advancement of Colored People. See https://www.thecrisismagazine.com/single-post/2019/09/09/The-Case-For-Reparations.

[163] Herbert McCabe, "Christian Unity," in *God, Christ, and Us*, 159.

[164] Joseph Barndt, *Understanding and Dismantling Racism: The Twenty-First Century Challenge to White America* (Minneapolis: Fortress Press, 2007), 23.

[165] Robin Meyers, *Spiritual Defiance: Building a Beloved Community of Resistance* (New Haven: Yale University Press, 2015), 103–104.

Bibliography

BOOKS

Baker, James T, editor. *Religion in America: Primary Sources in U.S. History,* Wadsworth, 2006.

Baldwin, James. *The Fire Next Time.* New York: Vintage Press, 1962.

————. *Notes of a Native Son* Boston: Beacon Press, 1955.

Baldwin, Lewis V. *The Voice of Conscience: The Church in the Mind of Martin Luther King, Jr.* New York: Oxford University Press, 2010.

Bellah, Robert N. *Beyond Belief: Essays on Religion in a Post-Traditional World.* New York: Harper & Row, 1970.

————. *The Broken Covenant: American Civil Religion in Time of Trial.* Chicago: University of Chicago Press, 1992 [1975].

————, and Phillip E. Hammond, *Varieties of Civil Religion.* New York: Harper & Row, 1980.

Blum, Edward J., and W. Scott Poole, editors. *Vale of Tears: New Essays on Religion and Reconstruction.* Macon, GA: Mercer University Press, 2005.

Brueggemann, Walter. Genesis*: Interpretation: A Commentary for Teaching and Preaching* Louisville: Westminster/John Knox Press, 2010.

Callero, Peter. *The Myth of Individualism: How Social Forces Shape Our Lives.* Lanham, MD: Rowman & Littlefield, 2013.

Carmichael, Stokely [Kwame Ture], and Charles V. Hamilton. *Black Power: The Politics of Liberation.* New York: Random House, 1967; Vintage Edition, 1992.

Carson, Clayborne, editor. *The Papers of Martin Luther King Jr., Volume VI: Advocate of the Social Gospel, September 1948-March 1963.* Berkeley: University of California Press, 2007.

Clarke, John Henrik, editor. *Marcus Garvey and the Vision of Africa.* New York: Random House, Vintage Books, 1973.

Cone, James H. *The Spirituals and the Blues: An Interpretation.* Maryknoll, NY: Orbis Books, 1991.

Daly, John Patrick. *When Slavery Was Called Freedom: Evangelicalism, Proslavery, and the Causes of the Civil War.* Lexington: The University Press of Kentucky, 2002.

DiAngelo, Robin. *White Fragility: Why It's So Hard for White People to Talk about Racism.* Boston: Beacon Press, 2018.

Duster, Alfreda M., editor. *Crusade for Justice: The Autobiography of Ida B. Wells-Barnett.* Chicago: University of Chicago Press, 1970.

Emerson, Michael O., and Christian Smith. *Divided by Faith: Evangelical Religion and the Problem of Race in America.* New York: Oxford University Press, 2000.

Evans, Christopher H. *The Social Gospel in American Religion: A History.* York: New York University, 2017.

Faust, Drew Gilpin, editor. *The Ideology of Slavery: Proslavery Thought in the Antebellum South, 1830–1860.* Baton Rouge: LSU Press, 1981.

Finkelman, Paul, editor. *Defending Slavery: Proslavery Thought in the Old South: A Brief History with Documents.* Boston: Bedford/St. Martins, 2003.

Foner, Philip S., editor. *Black Socialist Preacher: The Teachings of Reverend George Washington Woodbey and His Disciple Reverend George W. Slater, Jr.* San Francisco: Synthesis Publications, 1983.

Gardella, Peter. *American Civil Religion: What Americans Hold Sacred.* New York: Oxford University Press, 2014.

George, Carol V. R. *Segregated Sabbaths: Richard Allen and the Emergence of Independent Black Churches, 1760–1840.* New York: Oxford University Press, 1973.

Gorski, Philip. *American Covenant: A History of Civil Religion from the Puritans to the Present.* Princeton: Princeton University Press, 2017.

Gereboff, Joel D. *Rabbi Tarfon, the Tradition, the Man, and Early Rabbinic Judaism.* Missoula, MT: Scholars Press, 1979.

Harvey, Paul, and Edward J. Blum, editors. *The Columbia Guide to Religion in American History.* New York: Columbia University Press, 2012.

Hatch, John B. *Race and Reconciliation: Redressing the Wounds of Injustice.* Lanham, MD: Rowan & Littlefield Publishers, Inc., 2009.

Heidegger, Martin. *Being and Time.* San Francisco: Harper Perennial Modern Classics; Reprint edition, 2008.

Higginbotham, Evelyn Brooks. *Righteous Discontent: The Women's Movement in the Black Baptist Church, 1880–1920.* Cambridge, MA: Harvard University Press, 1993.

Katz, Daniel. *Why Freedom Matters: The Spirit of the Declaration of Independence in Prose, Poetry, and Song.* New York: Workman Publishers, 2003.

Keller, Rosemary Skinner, and Rosemary Radford Ruether, editors. *In Our Own Voices: Four Centuries of American Women's Religious Writing.* New York: HarperSanFrancisco, A Division of HarperCollinsPublishers, 1995.

King, Martin Luther, Jr. *Stride Toward Freedom: The Montgomery Story.* New York: Harper & Row, 1958.

Lischer, Richard. "Preaching about Race Relations—The Hope of Reconciliation," in Thomas G. Long and Neely D. McCarter, editors, *Preaching In and Out of Season.* Louisville: Westminster/John Knox Press, 1990.

Manis, Andrew M. *The Columbia Guide to Religion in American History.* Edited by Paul Harvey and Edward J. Blum. New York: Columbia University Press, 2012.

——. *A Fire You Can't Put Out: The Civil Rights Life of Birmingham's Reverend Fred Shuttlesworth.* University of Alabama Press, 1999.

——. *Southern Civil Religions in Conflict: Black and White Baptists and Civil Rights, 1947–1957.* Athens: University of Georgia Press, 1987.

——. *Southern Civil Religions in Conflict: Civil Rights and the Culture Wars.* Macon, GA: Mercer University Press, 2002.

————. *Macon Black and White: An Unutterable Separation in the American Century.* Macon, GA: Mercer University Press and the Tubman African American Museum, 2004.

Marable, Manning. *Malcolm X: A Life of Reinvention.* New York: Viking, The Penguin Group, 2011.

McKivigan, John R. *The War against Proslavery Religion: Abolitionism and the Northern Churches, 1830–1865.* Chapel Hill: University of North Carolina, 1984.

McMickle, Marvin A. *Where Have All the Prophets Gone? Reclaiming Prophetic Preaching in America.* Cleveland: Pilgrim Press, 2006.

Mead, Sidney E. *The Lively Experiment: The Shaping of Christianity in America.* Wipf & Stock Publishers; Reprint edition, 2007.

————. *The Nation with the Soul of a Church.* New York: Harper & Row, 1975.

Meyers, Robin R. "Faith as Resistance to Empire." 2013 Beecher Lecture, Yale University Divinity School. Published in *Spiritual Defiance: Building a Beloved Community of Resistance.* New Haven: Yale University Press, 2015.

Moberg, David O. *The Great Reversal: Reconciling Evangelism and Social Concern.* Eugene, OR: Wipf and Stock Publishers, 1977.

Moses, Wilson Jeremiah. *The Golden Age of Black Nationalism, 1850–1925.* New York: Oxford University Press, 1978.

Niebuhr, H. Richard. *Christ and Culture.* New York: Harper and Row, 1951.

Painter, Nell Irvin. *Exodusters: Black Migration to Kansas after Reconstruction.* New York: Knopf, 1977.

Paris, Peter J. *Black Religious Leaders: Conflict in Unity.* Second edition. Louisville, KY: Westminster/John Knox Press, 1991.

Rah, Soong-Chan. *The Next Evangelicalism: Freeing the Church from Western Cultural Captivity.* Downers Grove, IL: Intervarsity Press, 2009.

Rauschenbusch, Walter. *A Theology of the Social Gospel.* New York: The MacMillan Company, 1917.

Reitano, John. *What if the Zebras Lost Their Stripes?* New York: Paulist Press, 1998.

Roberts, Gene, and Hank Klibanoff. *The Race Beat: The Press, the Civil Rights Struggle, and the Awakening of a Nation.* New York: Alfred A. Knopf, 2006.

Roberts, Rita. *Evangelicalism and the Politics of Reform in Northern Black Thought, 1776–1863.* Baton Rouge: Louisiana State University Press, 2010.

Simmons, Martha, and Frank A. Thomas, editors. *Preaching with Sacred Fire: An Anthology of African-American Sermons, 1750 to the Present.* New York: W. W. Norton and Company.

Sobel, Mechal. *The World They Made Together: Black and White Values in Eighteenth Century Virginia.* Princeton: Princeton University Press, 1989.

Sernett, Milton C. *Bound for the Promised Land: African American Religion and the Great Migration.* Durham, NC: Duke University Press, 1997.

Stagg, Frank. *Polarities of Man's Existence in Biblical Perspective.* Philadelphia: Westminster Press, 1973.

Stephens, Alexander H. "The Cornerstone Address." Delivered in Savannah, Georgia, on 21 March 1861. See text in Thomas A. Scott, *Cornerstones of Georgia History: Documents that Formed the State.* Athens: University of Georgia Press, 1995.

Thornton, J. Mills. *Dividing Lines: Municipal Politics and the Struggle for Civil Rights in Montgomery, Birmingham, and Selma.* Tuscaloosa: University of Alabama Press, 2002.

Tisdale, Leonora Tubbs. *Prophetic Preaching: A Pastoral Approach.* Louisville: Westminster/John Knox Press, 2010.

Tise, Larry E. *Proslavery: A History of the Defense of Slavery in America, 1701–1840.* Athens: University of Georgia Press, 1987.

Tutu, Desmond. *Hope and Suffering.* Grand Rapids, MI: William B. Eerdmans Publishing Company, 1983.

————, and Douglas Carlton Abrams. *God's Dream.* Sommerville, MA: Candlewick Press, 2008.

Walters, Ronald L. *The Price of Racial Reconciliation.* Ann Arbor: University of Michigan Press, 2008.

Washington, James Melvin, editor. *A Testament of Hope: The Essential Writings of Martin Luther King Jr.* San Francisco: Harper & Row, 1986.

Wells-Barnett, Ida B. *The Red Record.* https://www.gutenberg.org/files/14977/14977-/14977-h.htm.

Wesley, Charles H. *Richard Allen: Apostle of Freedom* Washington, DC: Associated Publishers, 1935.

West, Cornel, and Christa Buschendorf. *Black Prophetic Fire.* Boston: Beacon Press, 2014.

Williams, Juan. *Thurgood Marshall: American Revolutionary.* New York: Random House, 1998.

Willimon, Will H. *Who Lynched Willie Earle: Preaching to Confront Racism.* Nashville: Abingdon Press, 1999.

Wilmore, Gayraud. *Black Religion and Black Radicalism: An Interpretation of the Religious History.* Third edition. Maryknoll, NY: Orbis Books, 1998.

Wilsey, John D. *American Exceptionalism and Civil Religion.* Downers Grove, IL: Intervarsity Press Academic, 2015.

ARTICLES

Acs, Gregory, Kenneth Braswell, Elaine Sorensen, Margery Austin Turner. *The Moynihan Report Revisited.* 13 June 2013. https://www.urban.org/research/publication/moynihan-report-revisited.

Baddar, Omar. "Hate Crimes Continue to Surge in America." https://thearabdailynews.com/2018/11/13/hate-crimes-continue-to-surge-in-america/.

Bellah, Robert N. "Civil Religion in America." *Daedalus* 96 (Winter 1967): 1–21.

"Christians Are More than Twice as Likely to Blame a Person's Poverty on Lack of Effort." *Washington Post.* https://www.washingtonpost.com/news/acts-of-faith/wp/2017/08/03/christians-are-more-than-twice-as-likely-to-blame-a-persons-poverty-on-lack-of-effort/?noredirect=on&utm_term=.fae4b7c78db3.

Darity, William Jr. "The Case for Reparations." *The Crisis.* 9 September 2019. https://www.thecrisismagazine.com/single-post/2019/09/09/The-Case-For-Reparations.

Geiger, Abigail, Kristen Bialik, and John Gramlich. "The Changing Face of Congress in 6 Charts." Pew Research Center Report. 15 February 2019. https://www.pewresearch.org/fact-tank/2019/02/15/the-changing-face-of-congress/.

Kennedy, Randall. "Lifting as We Climb: Progressive Defense of Respectability Politics." *Harper's Magazine.* October 2015. https://harpers.org/archive/2015/10/lifting-as-we-climb/.

Keown, Gerald L. "A Word About...Racism and the Church." *Review and Expositor* 108 (Fall 2011): 501.

Kornbluth, Jesse. "May 4, 1970: National Guardsmen Kill Four Students At Kent State, 'The Most Popular Murders Ever Committed in America.'" *Huffington Post.* 6 December 2017. https://www.huffingtonpost.com/jesse-kornbluth/may-4-1970-national-guard_b_1476017.html.

Mason, George. "Gospel Politics in the Midst of Social Turmoil." *Baptist News Global.* 16 March 2018. See also *Washington Post,* 16 November 2016.

Lane, Belden C. "Rabbinical Stories: A Primer on Theological Method." *Christian Century* 98 (16 December 1981): 1307–308.

Manis, Andrew M. "Zivilreligionem und das Problem von 'Race' von der Bürgerrechtsbewegung bis zu den Kulturkriegen." In Heike Bungert and Jana Weiss, editors, *"God Bless America": Zivilreligion in den USA im 20. Jahrhundert* (Frankfurt/New York: Campus Verlag), 353–84.

National Public Radio/Kaiser Family Foundation/Harvard University Kennedy School of Government Poll on Poverty in America. 2001. https://kaiserfamilyfoundation.files.wordpress.com/2001/04/3118-f-poverty-in-america-survey.pdf on 19 September 2018.

Roosevelt, Theodore. "Lincoln and Free Speech." *Metropolitan Magazine* 47 (May 1918): 7.

Schneider, Bill. "Polling the Poor and Non-Poor on Poverty: 1986 and 2016." August 2016. See http://www.aei.org/wp-content/uploads/2016/08/Polling-the-poor-and-non-poor-on-poverty.pdf.

Schweiger, Beth Barton. "The Restructuring of Southern Religion: Slavery, Denominations, and the Clerical Profession in Virginia." In John R. McKivigan and Mitchell Snay, editors, *Religion and the Antebellum Debate over Slavery*. Athens: University of Georgia Press, 1998.

"Seven Americans on Patriotism, Protest, and the President." *Washington Post.* 4 July 2018. https://www.washingtonpost.com/politics/seven-americans-on-patriotism-protest-and-the-president/2018/07/03/6265c1d8-7df4-11e8-b0ef-fffcabeff946_story.html?utm_term=.708408c3c7d6.

Tranby, Eric, and Douglas Hartmann. "Critical Whiteness Theories and the Evangelical 'Race Problem': Extending Emerson and Smith's *Divided by Faith*." *Journal for the Scientific Study of Religion* 47/3 (2008): 341–59.

Wallis, Jim. "A Crisis of Trump's Own Making." *Sojourners.* 9 January 2019. https://sojo.net/articles/crisis-trumps-own-making.

PODCASTS

Leamer, Lawrence. "The Lynching." Interview. *Progressive Spirit* podcast. 10 July 2016. https://www.podomatic.com/podcasts/progressivespirit/episodes/2016-07-10T08_04_02-07_00.

Tutu, Desmond. Interview with Krista Tippett. "On Being." American
Public Media. 16 February 2012. See
http://www.onbeing.org/programs/desmond-tutu-a-god-of-
surprises/#transcript.

DISSERTATION

Schoonmaker, Geoffrey Noel. "Preaching about Race: A Homiletic for
Racial Reconciliation." PhD dissertation, Vanderbilt University,
Nashville, TN, 2012.

Contributors

THE REVEREND DR. TIMOTHY J. BAGWELL is senior pastor of the Centenary United Methodist Church in Macon. He holds an Associate of Arts degree from Oxford College of Emory University and a BA from American University in Washington, DC. His theological education (MDiv) is from Candler School of Theology, Emory University in Atlanta, and a Doctor of Ministry from Garrett-Evangelical Theological Seminary, Evanston, Illinois. He has served as pastor of several United Methodist congregations in Central Georgia, including twelve years as pastor of the Martha Bowman Church in Macon. Throughout his ministerial career, he has been a respected leader as a board member and in numerous trusteeships in the South Georgia Methodist Conference, where he is also Director of New and Revitalized Congregational Development. He received the Martin Luther King Jr. Award for Albany, Georgia, in 2001, has been a guest columnist in both the *Macon Telegraph* and the *Wesleyan Christian Advocate*, and is the author of *Preaching for Giving: Proclaiming Financial Stewardship with Holy Boldness* (Discipleship Resources, 1993).

THE REVEREND SCOTT H. DICKISON has been pastor of the First Baptist Church of Christ in Macon, Georgia, since 2012. A native of Charlotte, North Carolina, Scott holds degrees from Wake Forest University (BA) and Harvard Divinity School (MDiv). He completed a unit of Clinical Pastoral Education at the Brigham and Women's Hospital in Boston, Massachusetts. As an AmeriCorps volunteer, he worked for two years with the West Tallahatchie County (Mississippi) Habitat for Humanity. Prior to coming to

Macon, he served as a pastoral resident at Wilshire Baptist Church in Dallas, Texas.

IMAM ADAM FOFANA is the spiritual leader and a teacher at the Islamic Center of Middle Georgia. He was born into the religion of Islam in Guinea, where he attended primary, secondary, and high school. From 1994–1997, he attended the University of Madinah, Saudi Arabia, majoring in Qur'an and Religious Studies. He was appointed Imam of the University Mosque of Madinah. He earned a master's degree in Islamic Revealed Knowledge and Heritage from International Islamic University of Malaysia in 2002.

THE REVEREND JAMES W. GOOLSBY JR. is pastor of the First Baptist Church at New Street in Macon, where he has served since 2004. Before answering the call to the gospel ministry, for ten years he served as a deacon at the Beulah Baptist Church in Decatur, Georgia. Eventually he served as youth minister and later as minister of pastoral care for the same congregation.

THE REVEREND DR. C. JARRED HAMMET was pastor of the Northminster Presbyterian Church in Macon (2001–2016). He holds a BA (1980) from Wofford College, Spartanburg, South Carolina, and an MDiv (1985) and a DMin (2003) from Columbia Theological Seminary in Atlanta, Georgia. He now serves as pastor of the First Presbyterian Church of Tifton, Georgia.

THE REVEREND CASSANDRA HOWE is formerly the pastor of the High Street Unitarian-Universalist Church in Macon, Georgia. She holds a Master of Divinity from Starr King School for the Ministry in Berkeley, California, and her Bachelor of Arts from Western Washington University in Bellingham, Washington. She was born and raised in Seattle, Washington, where her parents and sister live. She has served as a hospital chaplain, a young adult coordinator, and as the vice president of the Heartland Unitarian Universalist Minister's Association. Her call to ministry came to her while she served as an AmeriCorps volunteer. Reverend Howe is currently a stay-at-home mom and community activist.

THE REVEREND JULIE WHIDDEN LONG served the First Baptist Church of Christ in Macon, Georgia, for nineteen years, first as minister of children and families and later as associate pastor. She is still a member of that congregation and serves as a private Empowerment Coach. She is a summa cum laude graduate of Mercer University and earned her Master of Divinity from Mercer University's McAfee School of Theology. She currently serves on Mercer's Board of Trustees. The author of *Portraits of Courage: Stories of Baptist Heroes*, Reverend Long has written chapters for several other books, including a sermon in *And Your Daughters Shall Prophesy: Sermons by Women in Baptist Life* (Mercer University Press, 2012).

THE REVEREND DR. I. EDWIN MACK has been the pastor of the Unionville Missionary Baptist Church in Macon since 1986. He has served as the president of the Sixth District of the General Missionary Baptist Convention, Inc. He is a native of Cochran, Georgia. He is married to the former Eloise Cliett of Byron, Georgia, and father to Brittany Mack. As a pastor, he is well known for his gifts as a mentor, preacher, teacher, and revivalist par excellence.

THE REVEREND DR. ANDREW M. MANIS is emeritus professor of history at Middle Georgia State University in Macon, Georgia. He earned a BA in history and religion at Samford University in Birmingham, Alabama, and an MDiv (1980) and a PhD (1984) in the History of Christianity at The Southern Baptist Theological Seminary in Louisville, Kentucky. In seminary he studied homiletics with both George Buttrick and his son, David Buttrick, and won the 1978 Clyde Francisco Award for preaching. He also studied at the University of Chicago Divinity School. He has served numerous churches as interim pastor in Alabama, Kentucky, Indiana, Virginia, and North Carolina. He has authored or edited four other books, including *A Fire You Can't Put Out: The Civil Rights Life of Birmingham's Reverend Fred Shuttlesworth*, winner of the 2000 Lillian Smith Book Award.

THE REVEREND DR. SANDY DWAYNE MARTIN is chair of the Department of Religion at the University of Georgia in Athens. He has earned a Bachelor of Arts degree from Tougaloo College in Jackson, Mississippi, an MA, MPhil, and the PhD (1981) from Columbia University and Union Theological Seminary in New York City. He has served on the faculty of the University of Georgia since fall 1988 and as chair of the Religion Department since 2005. He is the author of two books: *Black Baptists and African Missions: The Origins of a Movement* (Macon, GA: Mercer University Press, 1989/1988); and *For God and Race: The Religious and Political Leadership of AMEZ Bishop James Walker Hood* (Columbia, SC: The University of South Carolina Press, 1998). An ordained Baptist minister, he serves as associate pastor of the East Friendship Baptist Church in Athens, Georgia.

THE REVEREND JASON E. MCCLENDON is the senior pastor of Community Church of God in Macon, Georgia. He has served his denomination as the Urban Missions Director for the Southeastern Region of the US for the Global Church of God (Anderson, Indiana) and as the Credentials Chairman for the Georgia Fellowship of the Church of God. He has preached in Mexico, Kenya, Tanzania, Uganda, Honduras, England, United Arab Emirates, Canada, Cayman Islands, Puerto Rico, Jamaica, and the Bahamas.

THE REVEREND FR. ALLAN J. MCDONALD was the pastor of Saint Joseph's Catholic Church in Macon when he preached the sermon in this collection. Since then he has served as the pastor of Saint Anne Church in Richmond Hill, Georgia. He has recently become the vice-rector of Redemptoris Mater Seminary in Dallas, Texas.

THE REVEREND JEFF MORRIS is the pastor of First Assembly of God Church in Macon, a congregation that shares its pastor's vision that First Assembly of God might become a healthy, happy interracial church "that will help transform" the Macon community.

THE REVEREND BILLY GRAHAM MCFADDEN served in the United States Air Force for twenty-two years, after which he earned a BS in Social Work from the Fort Valley State University in Fort Valley, Georgia, and an MDiv from Turner Theological Seminary at the Interdenominational Theological Center (ITC) in Atlanta, Georgia. He served as pastor of the Greater Allen African Methodist Episcopal Church in Macon and now serves as senior minister of the Saint Paul AME Church in Valdosta, Georgia. He is a member of the Turner Seminary Hall of Fame.

RABBI AARON RUBINSTEIN is spiritual leader of Congregation Sha'arey Israel in Macon, Georgia. Rabbi Rubinstein earned his bachelor's degree from UCLA and a Master of Education from the University of Judaism (now called American Jewish University). He received his rabbinic ordination from Jewish Theological Seminary (JTS). He especially enjoys studying, singing, and teaching Torah with kids and adults. His local mitzvah work includes organizations such as Macon Outreach and Daybreak, and this is an important component of the rabbi's vision of spiritual leadership.

Contributors

THE REVEREND EDDIE D. SMITH SR. is a second-generation minister, born and reared in Macon. Holding Bachelor and Master of Science degrees from Fort Valley State University in Fort Valley, Georgia, he has served as pastor of the Macedonia (Baptist) Church since 1972. He has served on the Macon City Council, two terms on the Bibb County Board of Education, and on the boards of the United Way, American Cancer Society, Macon Ministerial Association, and the Macon Police and Firefighter Disciplinary Hearing Board. In 2015 he received the Gardner C. Taylor Preaching Award from the Morehouse College School of Religion at the Interdenominational Theological Center, Atlanta, Georgia.

THE REVEREND GAIL TOLBERT SMITH has been pastor of Macon's Universal Light Christian Center since 1989. She holds a BS in sociology from Georgia College and State University in Milledgeville, Georgia, an MS in Christian Counseling from Carolina University of Theology, and an MA in Christian Leadership from Liberty University in Lynchburg, Virginia. She is currently pursuing a PhD in Public Service Leadership from Capella University. In 1985 Gail made history as the first woman licensed to preach in the Black Baptist denomination in Macon, Georgia. She is recognized as one of Georgia's most accomplished female pastors, and she writes occasional columns for the *Macon Telegraph*.